More Than Allegory

On religious myth, truth and belief

More Than Allegory

On religious myth, truth and belief

Bernardo Kastrup

BOOKS

Winchester, UK
Washington, USA

First published by iff Books, 2016
iff Books is an imprint of John Hunt Publishing Ltd., No. 3 East St., Alresford,
Hampshire SO24 9EE, UK
office1@jhpbooks.net
www.johnhuntpublishing.com
www.iff-books.com

For distributor details and how to order please visit the 'Ordering' section on our website.

ISBN: 978 1 78535 287 4
Library of Congress Control Number: 2015953413

A CIP catalogue record for this book is available from the British Library.

Cover photo: ancient Karelian Onega petroglyphs depicting mythological, probably
religious symbols.

Design: Stuart Davies

UK: Printed and bound by CPI Group (UK) Ltd, Croydon, CR0 4YY
US: Printed and bound by Thomson Shore, 7300 West Joy Road, Dexter, MI 48130

We operate a distinctive and ethical publishing philosophy in all
areas of our business, from our global network of authors to
production and worldwide distribution.

CONTENTS

Other books by Bernardo Kastrup

Rationalist Spirituality:
An exploration of the meaning of life and existence informed by logic
and science

Dreamed up Reality:
Diving into mind to uncover the astonishing hidden tale of nature

Meaning in Absurdity:
What bizarre phenomena can tell us about the nature of reality

Why Materialism Is Baloney:
How true skeptics know there is no death and fathom answers to life,
the universe, and everything

Brief Peeks Beyond:
Critical essays on metaphysics, neuroscience, free will, skepticism
and culture

Coming March 2019
The Idea of the World:
A multi-disciplinary argument for the mental nature of reality

Acknowledgments

This book has evolved and taken shape slowly. I am indebted to those who graciously read and commented on its earlier drafts. Their contribution has been invaluable. At the risk of leaving out equally important names, I'd like to explicitly acknowledge Jeffrey Kripal, Saajan Patel, Rob van der Werf, Paul Stuyvenberg, Richard Stuart, Robert Perry, Peter Jones, Deepak Chopra and Rupert Spira. I am particularly indebted to Jeff for his encouragement and validation of my work, his valuable criticisms, as well as the wonderful introduction he wrote for this book. I am also particularly grateful to Paul and Rob, friends who were there with me that crucial evening, in that crucial restaurant.

I am thankful to my mother for having planted in me, at a very early age—before my intellectual development would have made it impossible—the seeds of religious transcendence. I would discern their meaning and value only much later in life, having denied them at first.

Finally, my girlfriend Claudia Damian has been the inspiration behind this work. Her spontaneous, genuine and intimate connection with religion rekindled in me a way of being I'd lost touch with. Her example gave me courage to acknowledge views and events I thought I'd never dare to acknowledge. This book exists largely thanks to her, though it is not meant for her: she doesn't need it.

Introduction by Jeffrey Kripal:

Reading Inside God's Brain

I was so delighted when I found Bernardo Kastrup's books. Actually, I didn't find them. A mutual colleague working in Paris on medieval Christianity, Troy Tice, read us both and encouraged me to read Bernardo. He thought our books somehow spoke to one another, and that I would appreciate Bernardo's books. Troy could not have been more right. I read all five of Bernardo's previous books within a few weeks. Just gobbled them up.

I have thought about why I did this. I seldom read this many books by a single author. Indeed, at mid-life, I barely have time or energy to read at all. But this was different. I just dropped everything and read, and read, and read. Why? What did this author's words awaken in me? What glowing ember did he spark back to life in this exhausted middle-aged professor?

Part of my enthusiasm was a double function of Bernardo's philosophical precision and contemporary relevance. Obviously, here was a man who could *think*, but who could also speak to the digital age on its own terms and against its own obsessions and naïve uses of computer metaphors for understanding consciousness (more on that in a moment). Part of my pleasure was also a function of the fact that the author is an unapologetic idealist, that is, someone who is convinced that mind or consciousness is the fundamental nature of reality. I was very familiar with this position, but I had never actually met an idealist. They are terribly rare these days, at least in the academic circles in which I move.

Oh, I had read plenty of idealists within my own historical area of research, and Bernardo sounds *a lot* like the comparative mystical literature to which I have given my life—except that, unlike my historical sources, he answers my e-mails. There is Meister Eckhart, the great Dominican professor and philosopher whose sermons on the always-happening incarnation of the Word in the individual soul and the Now of eternity read like medieval versions of the books of Bernardo Kastrup (or Eckhart Tolle). But Meister Eckhart died almost seven hundred years ago. There is Ramana Maharshi, the great South Indian Hindu mystic of the immortal Self, or what I like to call the Same in us all. But he left us over sixty years ago. Much closer culturally (and digitally), there is Philip K. Dick, the great American science fiction writer who realized through an encounter with the Logos or Cosmic Mind that "reality *is* a giant brain" that appears to work like a binary computer code network.[1] But he died over thirty years ago.

Dick is worth dwelling on for a moment here, as his weird thought eerily reflects the more precise and calmer books of Bernardo Kastrup. Both certainly share a digital or computer-based model of intellectual cognition. Both also understand that consciousness is not intellectual cognition. Here is a typical passage from Dick's *Exegesis*, the 8,000 page private journal that Dick scrawled in the last eight years of his life after getting energetically zapped in the winter of 1974 by a cosmic Mind that he came to call "VALIS," for Vast Active Living Intelligence System:

> All that I could fathom was that the conventional picture that we normally get—and seem to share—is not in fact what is there; what is there is not even in time or space, nor is causation involved. There seems to be a mind and we are in it .... "We are all but cells in a colossal mad brain that both makes and perceives reality"—something like that, the main thrust being that there is some relationship between the creating of reality and perceiving of it . . . the percipient is cosmogenitor [literally, "creator of the universe"], or

conversely, the cosmogenitor wound up as unwilling percipient of its own creation.[2]

You will see, in due time, just how close Dick's *Valis* is to the idealist vision worked out in the following pages. In Bernardo's system, the conventional picture of material reality that we assume to be the case is simply false. It's an extremely elaborate hoax. More accurately, this material world can be thought of as a kind of dream in which God incarnates through sexual reproduction and evolutionary biology in order to reflect back on itself and come to know itself inside the dream. We are all living in God's brain. More on that in a moment, too.

So there was Bernardo's philosophical precision and contemporary relevance, and there was the uncanny way that his words resonate with the comparative mystical literatures I know and love. But there was also something more that drew me to these books, and to this book in particular: the fact that Bernardo Kastrup emerged from the professional fields of physics, mathematics, and computer science and is a successful computer engineer in the corporate world. I confess that I was so pleased by this because I have long found the pretensions of the Artificial Intelligence world to be patently stupid. That's a bit inappropriate, and it is certainly crabby, but it is nonetheless honest and, I think, quite accurate.

Here is why. The AI community has long been laboring under what Bernardo calls the deprived myth of materialism. This very practical, very common consensual delusion states that mind or consciousness is an emergent product of material processes, and that, in the end, all there is is matter, that is, little tiny dead things bouncing or waving around in empty space in perfectly random and mechanical ways. If this base axiom were true, of course, one could well expect sufficiently sophisticated computer chips to become conscious. That makes perfect sense. The problem is that such a claim is not an established fact but a metaphysical interpretation of the scientific evidence. Moreover, and most importantly, the same materialistic model continues to fail us, and spectacularly so, when it comes to the "hard problem" of consciousness. This utter failure suggests that the materialist paradigm is not up to the task, is not sufficient to the question. We don't have the slightest bit of evidence that matter produces consciousness, nor do we even have a clue how this might work. Probably because it doesn't.

Indeed, if Bernardo Kastrup and the idealist mystical literatures of the world are pointing us in the right direction—and I think they are—the materialist hypothesis is the exact opposite of the truth. It is fantastically wrong. Mind does not emerge as a fragile and temporary product of matter. Matter emerges as a fragile and temporary product of what Aldous Huxley famously called "mind-at-large" and its own mathematical structures and symmetrical beauty. Or, if you prefer, what we so pathetically call "mind" and "matter" emerge from some deeper superstructure or symmetry that is at once mental and material, at once mind and math—a kind of Möbius strip of Material Mind or Mental Matter, then.

We do not need to get into the philosophical arguments here (Bernardo does this for us in his six books, including now this one). It is enough to point out that the AI scene is a perfect example of how materialist assumptions and the computer modeling of mind can lead us astray, and why philosophical training and a profound understanding of comparative mystical literature are both crucial to any real grasp of the nature of consciousness—scientific, philosophical, or otherwise. I will just say it: *any future, truly adequate philosophy of mind or science of consciousness will have to go through the study of religion, and in particular the comparative study of mystical literature.*

This, of course, is exactly what Bernardo is doing here. He is thinking comparatively through the idealisms and nondualisms of Advaita Vedanta, Mind-Only Buddhism, mystical forms of

Christianity, and a select number of creation myths, which he reads not as descriptions of some past creation event but as "icons of the now," that is, as scripts of consciousness itself. He understands perfectly well that as long as philosophers and scientists do not engage these literatures seriously and respectfully, as full and equal partners in the question, there will be no adequate understanding of mind, which is to say: there will be no adequate understanding of us *or* the universe in which we find ourselves as intimate and bizarrely successful knowing expressions. Why *do* we know so much? Why *does* math work so well? Because we participate in and are expressions of the deepest structures of reality. Because we *are* that universe and those mathematical structures.

Bernardo understands all of this. Accordingly, he treats the mystical literatures with a seriousness and a thoughtfulness that is extremely rare in the technological fields. He takes comparative mystical literature as seriously as mathematics. He does not confuse the two realms of human knowing. He does not turn to one to establish the other. But he puts them into deep conversation and emerges on the other side with a most extraordinary story or "myth" of who we are and why we are here.

This is where his idealist mysticism morphs into a contemporary or emergent mythology. This is where mind expresses itself, as in a dream, through a narrative or story. And this is where we, as a culture now, always stumble. Entranced by the technological successes of science and engineering, we have come to think of reality as composed of invisible numbers. Everything real is numerical. Anything worth knowing can be measured. Anything not worth knowing cannot be measured. The only real form of knowledge is mathematical or scientific knowledge. Such is the claim, anyway. It's more than a claim. As I write this, the education minister of Japan is issuing a decree to "abolish" all of the social science and humanities programs of the Japanese universities. Of the 60 national universities, 26 have agreed to do so in some measure.[3]

What Bernardo shows us, as a computer engineer no less, is that this materialist paradigm that wants to reduce everything to practical numbers is a half-truth and, if taken as the whole truth, a profound mistake with morally and existentially awful consequences. His message is not simply a negative or polemical one, though. He also has a powerfully positive message. He wants to show us that the fundamental nature of reality expresses itself not just through math but also through myth, which is to say: *through symbol and story.* Reality is not just made of numbers, it turns out. It is also made of words and narratives. We are not just living in a gigantic machine. We are also living in a whirl of stories and dreams.

It's not "just a story," either, as the story always tells us something about the story-teller, just as the dream always tells us something about the dreamer. The project then becomes not simply one of measurement, but also one of meaning. The question becomes not "How can we measure or prove the dream?" but "What is the dream trying to tell us?" We are not after explanation here. We are after understanding, wisdom, gnosis.

The same wisdom leads to another question. "Do we like the story we are dreaming in now? Does this dream lead to human flourishing and long-term sustainability? Or to yet more intercultural violence and existential depression? Why *are* we fighting over our dreams and myths? And why *do* we deny the dreamer?" These are difficult questions, but there is a shimmering silver lining here. After all, if we are dreaming our own stories, we can always dream others. We can tell new stories. We can develop new myths, perhaps even myths that point back to the mythmaker. We do not have to keep living in stories that have long ago spent their shelf lives. We do not have to be so naïve.

Toward such ends, Bernardo tells us a story. He weaves a

modern myth whose message goes something like this. We are embodied forms of cosmic mind, split off "alters" in some vast multiple-personality order. These alters have entered God's dream through sexual reproduction and evolutionary biology (note that eros becomes the energy and portal of divine incarnation here) in order to wake up within the dream, look around the physical universe as the interior of God's brain, and reflect on our own cosmic nature within this same neural galactic network. Here is how he summarizes it: "Put in another way, *the universe is the scan of God's brain*; except that you don't need the scanner: you're already inside God's brain so all you have to do is to look around. Your perceptions of the sun, rainbows, thunderstorms, etc., are as inaccessible to God as the patterns of firing neurons in your brain—with all their beauty and complexity—are inaccessible to you in any direct way."

We are the universe becoming self-aware. We know what God does not know. In the symbolic and mythical terms of Bernardo's Cologne Cathedral realization, we are all Christs, crucified on the cross of space and time: "we are all hanging from the self-conceptualized cross of space, time, confinement and impermanence. His divine nature is our true nature as timeless mind taking particular, seemingly limited perspectives within its own dream. That Christ is both God *and* the Son of God born into God's creation is a hardly disguised way to express this symbolically."

Obviously, the present book is not simply an idealist tract, an abstract philosophical exercise for the curious. It is a piece of profound story-telling based on the author's own scientific and technical training, his own mystical Aha!, and his own subsequent philosophical conclusions. It is an exploration of how cosmic consciousness projects itself into narrative forms, into story, or what we have come to call "myth," and then wakes up out of that same story or myth to know itself not as other but as Self.

Myth for Bernardo, of course, is not some falsehood or super-stitious embarrassment, something we can easily leave behind. But neither is it some literal truth or map of history. Rather, myth is "symbolic." It points. It evokes. It reminds and remembers. But it never quite speaks literally, and for a simple reason: that of which and from which it speaks cannot be captured in language, in number, or by any other act of intellectual cognition. It is simply beyond, or before, all of this. Symbols speak of and out of consciousness, but never literally. A myth here is a story that recalls a mystical experience of transcendence. At any point, it may shock, trip or "flip" the listener-reader into a similar awakening through an "involuntary shift in cognitive perspective." Here is Bernardo: "the full realization of transcen-dence is a kind of quantum leap: it happens spontaneously, suddenly, in one swift movement without any apparent cause. It's a kind of grace." As such, the myth teaches us nothing new. It simply causes us to remember who we really and already are.

Do not kid yourself. This is no ordinary book. It is a tangle or reflexive loop in the brain of God. To invoke an image from Bernardo's earlier book, *Why Materialism Is Baloney*, it is a whirlpool in the mercurial Ocean of Mind that, at any point, might suck itself into the same infinite and immortal waters. It is certainly not a book to provide your already overloaded life with yet more information or mere data. It is not about information at all. It is about the knower of any and all information. Read on, then, inside God's brain, but be careful. You just might wake up God.

Jeffrey J. Kripal
J. Newton Rayzor Professor of Religion
Rice University
Houston, Texas

Notes

1 Pamela Jackson and Jonathan Lethem, eds, *The Exegesis of Philip K. Dick*, Erik Davis, annotation editor (Boston: Houghton Mifflin Harcourt, 2011), 588.

2 Ibid., 717-8.

3 See: https://www.timeshighereducation.co.uk/news/social-sciences-and-humanities-faculties-close-japan-after-minis-terial-decree

Overview

This book is a three-part journey into the rabbit hole we call the nature of reality. Its ultimate destination is a plausible, living validation of transcendence. Each of its three parts is like a turn of a spiral, exploring recurring ideas through the prisms of religious myth, truth and belief, respectively. With each turn, the book seeks to convey a more nuanced and complete understanding of the many facets of transcendence.

Part I will resonate especially with those who yearn for the richness that religious myths can bring into life, yet cannot get around the fact that these myths aren't literally true. It tries to reach those whose souls are at war with their intellects. One of its goals is to restore the meaning of human life by helping the intellect give itself permission to accommodate the intuitions of the soul, without sacrificing reason or plausibility. Indeed, Part I puts forward the controversial notion that *many religious myths are actually true; and not just allegorically so.* It is the transcendent truth uniquely portrayed by these myths that our culture so desperately needs in order to understand the real. This transcendent truth, for not being amenable to words or equations, cannot be communicated through any other means— scientific or philosophical—but religious mythology. To make sense of all this, Part I attempts to articulate the nature of mythical truth in a manner that honors both religion and our skeptical rationality.

Part II pursues the next turn of the spiral by first taking a step back: while we all seek truth—be it through religion, science or philosophy—we very seldom inquire into the meaning of truth. What does it mean to say that something is true or false? What hidden assumptions do we make about the underlying nature of reality when we talk of truth? Tackling these questions is the journey of Part II. In its search for answers it leverages our direct experience of world and self to inquire into the nature of time and space, the framework where truth is supposedly to be found. It then concludes that *our own inner storytelling plays a surprising role in creating the seeming concreteness of things and the tangibility of history.* Finally, it points to clear echoes of its conclusions in many of the world's religious myths.

Part III, as the final turn of spiral, is the pinnacle of this work. It brings all of the book's core ideas together in the form of a modern, plausible religious myth. In laying out a complete cosmology for making sense of reality and restoring its transcendence, Part III highlights the critical role of belief in everything we take for granted. Indeed, it explains how *deeply ingrained belief systems create the world we live in.* Its narrative is based on the story of a modern explorer of consciousness who, during his participation in a secret scientific project, has a series of transcendent encounters. The metaphysics he brings back from these encounters integrates the themes of the book in one coherent framework. It also opens whole new horizons for the restoration of meaning and purpose to our daily lives.

Naturally, the optimal sequence to read this book is that in which it is presented: from Part I to Part III. Indeed, the ideas discussed in Parts I and II are meant to enrich the reading of Part III. That said, if one prefers to go straight to the heart of the matter and enjoy a gripping story without analytical preludes, it is entirely possible to jump directly to Part III and then return to Parts I and II afterwards.

In whichever order you choose to read it, you will notice that the three themes of this book—myth, truth and belief—flow into and interpenetrate each other at multiple levels and meta-levels throughout the text. Part I, for instance, examines mythology with a mindset characteristic of a quest for factual truth. Part II explores the nature of truth by appealing to our own felt intuitions, as we do when we pursue our beliefs. Finally, Part III elaborates upon the role of beliefs in the format of a myth. The goal is to illustrate, both explicitly and implicitly, through concepts and style, the intimate relationship that exists between myth, truth and belief.

The three parts of this book are meant to echo and reinforce each other content-wise as well. Its central ideas return in all three, being explored from a different angle each time. This allows me to convey—often indirectly and implicitly—many more nuances than otherwise possible. For instance, the nature and role of myth is explored in Part I, but the *contents* of certain myths come back in Parts II and III, where they echo what is discussed there about truth and belief.

The ebb and flow of the book's trinity of themes ultimately circles around one of them: *truth*, the central motif of this work. All three parts revolve around it: Part I by exploring how myths can deliver truth, Part II by unveiling the nature of truth through dispelling unexamined beliefs, and Part III by appealing to belief in a myth in order to hint at truth.

You will notice that what I mean by the words 'myth,' 'truth' and 'belief' is richer and more nuanced than the flattened denotations of everyday language. This may, and probably will, surprise you at first. Nonetheless, the attempt to push the boundaries of words and reveal a much bigger, deeper reality behind them is an essential aspect of this work. My intent is to help you see beyond the dull, superficial cultural dialogue reigning in society today.

I hope you find many new vistas and avenues of inquiry in this book. I've poured much of myself into it; more than I think most authors would consider prudent. Whatever else it may or may not be, this work is most certainly a sincere, openhearted account of my own way to relate to life, the universe, truth and transcendence.

PART I: Myth

The religious myth is one of man's greatest and most significant achievements, giving him the security and inner strength not to be crushed by the monstrousness of the universe.
Carl Jung

Chapter 1

The role and importance of myth

A myth is a story in terms of which one can relate to oneself and the world. The myth of the Holy Trinity, for instance, provides *context* to the lives of millions of Christians: God, as the Father, explains and justifies the creation of the world. As the Holy Spirit, He maintains the world's significance on an on-going basis by infusing it with an invisible divine essence. The myth also provides *perspective:* God, this time as the Son, offers a concrete example of how to live life in accordance with His grand plan and achieve salvation. The divinity's entrance into its own creation in forms both ethereal (the Holy Spirit) and concrete (the Son) provides a bridge between ordinary life and a transcendent order (the Father). This brings meaning into the world of many Christians, preventing ordinary life from being experienced as aimless and futile.

Myth has historically provided context and perspective to our presence in the world and has enriched the lives of human beings since the dawn of our species. In a culture obsessed with literal truth and pragmatism, such as our own, the impoverishment of myth is increasingly—if only instinctively—felt. Never before in history has a civilization been so desperately devoid of context and perspective. Who are we? Where do we come from? Where should we go? What's the point of it all? We feel lost because we are unable to take seriously the maps that could give us directions. We can no longer take myths seriously because, after all, they are *only* myths.

Historically speaking, the contemporary attitude toward myth is an aberration. The skewed assumptions that sustain this aberration and the reasons why they are mistaken will be addressed in the next chapters. For now, though, let us briefly review the role and importance of myth.

Myth and consensus reality

We can roughly divide the chain of subjective experiences we call life into two realms: an outer realm of perceptions and an inner realm of emotions and thoughts. Indeed, while identifying with our emotions and thoughts, we usually don't identify with experiences mediated by our five senses. In other words, we tend to think that our perceptions—despite still being subjective experiences—are outside us, while our emotions and thoughts are part of us. For reasons that will become apparent later, I will refer to the contents of perception—that is, everything we see, hear, smell, taste and feel through the skin—as *images and interactions*. For instance, a lion and a wildebeest are images, while a lion eating a wildebeest is an interaction between images. A rock and a hill are images, while a rock rolling down a hill is an interaction between images. And so on.

The sole *facts* of the outer realm are images and their respective interactions in space and time.[1] Everything else arises in the inner realm through an act of interpretation. After all, in and by themselves the images and interactions express no meaning or emotion. They are simply the movement of pixels in the canvas of a world outside the ego—outside the control of our personal volition—which *evokes* thoughts and feelings within us.

Let us belabor this a bit. What I am saying is that the potentials for emotion and meaning remain unexpressed in the outer realm, which our culture has come to call *consensus reality*. It is a domain of pure form. It's not sad or happy, pointless or purposeful, boring or exciting. In and by itself, consensus reality doesn't express any conclusion, emotional or intellectual. All we can consider to be its *facts* are the images and interactions themselves, not our interpretations of them. The horror or the natural beauty one sees in a wildebeest being devoured alive by a lion are evoked, *by interpretation*, entirely within one's inner realm. Then they are projected outward onto the world. 'We tell ourselves stories in order to live. ... We interpret what we see ... We live entirely ... by the imposition of a narrative line upon disparate images, by the "ideas" with which we have learned to freeze the shifting phantasmagoria which is our actual experience,'[2] observed Joan Didion.

The outer realm is shared across individuals. After all, we all seem to live in the same world. We all know what lions, wildebeests, rocks and hills are. We go to theaters, museums and parks to share perceptual experiences with others. But the meaning and emotion evoked by these perceptual experiences aren't necessarily shared: they arise in our private inner realm alone. Two people observing the exact same outer events may conclude different things from, and react emotionally in different ways to, the images. As such, meaning and emotion aren't part of the *consensus*. To convey meaning or emotion to another individual, we even have to first translate them into consensus images—such as gestures, facial expressions, spoken or written words, etc.—in the hope that these images will then evoke the same meaning and emotion in the inner realm of another. Meaning and emotion cannot be *directly* shared the way the images of consensus reality are.

In summary: *none of what we call consensus reality, or the 'real world out there,' expresses meaning or emotion directly.* Only in our inner realm do meaning and emotion arise. This may sound like a nod to existentialists like Jean-Paul Sartre, who considered the world senseless, as all meaning is admittedly projected onto it by us. But it is not what I mean to imply. The world is only senseless if one sees the outer realm as *fundamentally separate* from the inner realm, which is by no means an established fact. Indeed, insofar as we can know, *outer and inner realms are simply different modalities of subjective experience.* As discussed in my earlier books *Why Materialism Is Baloney* and *Brief Peeks Beyond*, they are two facets of the same coin. Whether meaning is anchored in the outer or inner realm is thus irrelevant: the world is meaningful in both cases for these realms are, at bottom, expressions of one and the same reality.

All this said, my argument holds whether one adopts Sartre's view or my own: the images and interactions of consensus reality evoke meaning and emotion in our inner realm. *As such, these outer images work as keys to unlock our affective and intellectual potentials.* Without them, our capacity for feeling and thinking wouldn't actualize. Just try to imagine how you could possibly feel romantic love or ponder about the nature of existence without consensus images, such as other sentient beings and the universe they occupy. You will quickly realize that you can't.

And here is the key point: *our mind needs a code to translate consensus images into thoughts and feelings.* Without it, there would be no bridge or commerce between outer and inner realms. The inputs of this translation code are the images and interactions of consensus reality, as perceived by our five senses. Its outputs are the corresponding thoughts and feelings evoked within. Now, because our self-reflective mind operates according to linguistic patterns (an assertion I will substantiate in Chapter 3), the translation code takes the form of a mental narrative we tell ourselves; a story that implies particular correspondences between outer images and inner feelings and ideas. *The translation code is thus a myth.*

Indeed, the English word 'myth' derives from the Ancient Greek μῦθος (*muthos*): something said in words, like a story, speech or report. That we think of reality according to myths is even suggested by the Common Slavic derivative of the original Greek: мысль (*mysl'*), which means 'thought' or 'idea.' Therefore, the word 'myth' originally meant a story that evokes thought; not necessarily an *untrue* story, as it is often understood today. Throughout this book, I use the word 'myth' in this broader, original sense: *myth is a story that implies a certain way of interpreting consensus reality so to derive meaning and affective charge from its images and interactions.* As such, it can take many forms:

fables, religions and folklore, but also formal philosophical systems and scientific theories. Clearly, a myth can be true or false without ceasing to be a myth.

Myth is the code that each one of us constantly uses, whether we are aware of it or not, to interpret life in the world. For instance, the ancient myth of astrology links daily events to celestial rhythms and cycles meant to explain the ups and downs of life.[3] Myth is the very thing that allows the events of consensus reality to mean anything to us. A hard-earned promotion at work only means a life well lived if one has adopted the myth that status, power and wealth accumulation are the purpose of life. If none of these things were assumed to be important, what could a promotion mean? Myth is also the very thing that allows the events of life to impact us emotionally. The death of a loved one is only a permanent loss under the myth of materialism. Our disgust toward acts of wickedness is entirely dependent on our respective myths of morality. And so on. Notice that I am not passing judgment on these myths. I am simply stating that they are a necessary condition for the images of the world to convey any meaning to us, intellectual or emotional. Without these myths, consensus images and their respective interactions would be just dancing pixels.

Without a code for *interpreting* the consensus images all around us, life in the world would evoke no thought, no emotion, no conclusion. It would consist of pure and neutral *observation*, without commentary.

> Consensus reality is a realm of pure form. It triggers our myth-making capacity so to evoke thought and emotion within. Our role is to interpret the pure forms by projecting a myth onto consensus reality. The myth implies a way to translate pure form into meaning.

A vacuum of myth?

It is nearly impossible to live life without a myth. A continuous and relentless effort at interpreting consensus reality is part-and-parcel of the human condition. And this on-going interpretation, as we've seen above, entails the code we call myth. It is already a huge challenge for most people to become lucid of the myth underlying the somewhat instinctive way in which they relate to the world. So to deliberately do away with all interpretations, and all codes, is at best a very tough call indeed.

Myth is disguised in subtle forms. Take, for instance, the notion that consensus reality exists outside mind: it's an inference, an *interpretation* of perceptions, since the perceptions themselves are always in mind. Or take today's materialist neo-Darwinian cosmology: its story suggests that the whole universe is a kind of machine and that its entire dynamics, including life, are driven by a combination of blind chance and some mechanical laws. One might think that such a cosmology dispenses with myth altogether, but nothing is farther from the truth. To say that nature is a mechanical apparatus without purpose or intentionality is itself an interpretation; a myth. The absence of myth would require a complete lack of interpretation or judgment of consensus reality. In the absence of myth, no analogies would be made between the cosmos and machines, and no judgments would be passed regarding whether existence has a purpose or not. One would simply witness images and notice the patterns and regularities of their interactions without commentary or conclusions.

A deprived myth is not the same as an absence of myth. A deprived myth is one that favors narrow and lame interpretations of consensus reality, interpretations that do not resonate with one's deepest intuitions. A deprived myth makes life in the world seem futile and claustrophobic. But it is a myth nonetheless, because it entails an interpretation. Today, we don't live in a mythless society. Our condition is much more tragic: we live in a society dominated by increasingly deprived myths.

The dominance of deprived myths is insidious and has severe consequences as far as one's psychic health and relationship with truth is concerned. Yet, these consequences are usually overlooked in the first half of life, because deprived myths have a strong *distractive* power in that period.[4] Young adults, in a natural attempt to self-affirm, are often distracted by the deprived myths of consumption, power and status. Many manage to continue distracting themselves almost all their lives and, in that sense, we live in an adolescent society. But once these deprived myths are seen for what they are, one needs a *richer* myth that does justice to the scope of life and imbues it with timeless meaning. Let us elaborate on these ideas a bit more.

> One always lives according to a myth, for a continuous interpretation of consensus reality is inherent to the human condition. The question is whether one's chosen myth resonates with one's deepest intuitions or runs counter to them.

The impetus of human life

Renowned psychologist James Hillman, in his 'acorn theory,' suggested that each person has a *call*: an often-obfuscated but passionate idea of what her life is meant to be, just like an acorn holds within itself a blueprint of the oak it's meant to become. A life lived so as to bring that idea into reality—thus turning the acorn into the oak—is a life of purpose and timeless meaning.[5] As such, 'the call offers *transcendence*, becoming as necessary to a person's life on Earth as performance to [Judy] Garland, battle to [George] Patton, painting to [Pablo] Picasso.'[6] It is this *transcendence* that imbues life with the eternal significance of destiny fulfillment, as opposed to the evanescence of a mere chain of chance events. 'To live on a day-to-day basis is insufficient for human beings; we need to transcend ... we need meaning ... we need to see over-all patterns in our lives. ... And we need freedom ... to get beyond ourselves ... to rise above our immediate surroundings,'[7] observed Oliver Sacks.

The whole impetus of life is to transcend: to get beyond the separateness, insignificance and transience of the ordinary human condition through association with something timeless and boundless.

Notice that true transcendence should not be confused with mere fame and influence: while it's true that Garland's performances enchanted millions, Patton's victories changed the course of history and Picasso's influence on the arts cannot be overestimated, are their fame and influence truly timeless and boundless? Our planet is like a spec of dust floating in the vastness of space. Are Garland, Patton and Picasso of any significance anywhere beyond this tiny spec? The Earth is about 4.5 billion years old. Will Earthlings even remember them a mere million years from now? How could mere fame and influence possibly embody the eternal significance of destiny fulfillment? Garland, Patton and Picasso transcended not because of their celebrity—transcendence is far subtler than that—but because, by 'following their bliss,'[8] they embodied 'a flowering of existence in a very creative and new way.'[9] I am going to elaborate more on this subtle notion of transcendence later.

Our innate drive to transcend is a natural and legitimate response to the existential despair that characterizes the ordinary human condition, as powerfully described by the existentialist philosophers. Deep inside, we feel small and powerless before the immensity and impersonal character of a seemingly absurd world. We know that 'everything changes and nothing remains still,'[10] so none of what we find important can last. Investing our identity in a fragile body confined in both space and time, we—uniquely among animals—also know that our own death is inevitable. Every thought, feeling, choice and action of our lives will—or so we fear—eventually be reduced to irrelevance. Aren't they all then, at bottom, *already* irrelevant? Aren't our lives meaningless, our suffering pointless and our dreams frivolous? These questions are the source of our existential despair. 'If you have lived in despair, then, regardless of whatever else you won or lost, everything is lost for you, eternity does not acknowledge you, it never knew you,'[11] wrote Kierkegaard. Our despair propels our soul—our deepest drives and intuitions—toward some form of transcendence. We long for a more-than-merely-human condition; a form of immortality and boundlessness that would allow us to observe the drama of our ephemeral lives from 'above,' as opposed to being engulfed and drowned by it.

But can we, in subtle and indirect ways as the case may be, somehow achieve a form of immortality or boundlessness? Is the drive to transcend grounded in valid intuitions or is it mere wish fulfillment? The predominant intellectual answer in our culture today is that transcendence is fundamentally impossible, for there is nothing to a human being but his biological body. *This, in itself, is a myth; an interpretation of images.* And although this myth is disputed on very solid logical and empirical grounds,[12] the main counterforce to it seems to be the *experiential* one: throughout history, countless people have had transcendent—spiritual, mystical—experiences.[13] They have felt and cognized directly that our true identities extend far beyond our bodies and that our lives in this world are pregnant with meaning.[14] One can make a very strong case for the validity of these transcendent experiences. The question of validity, however, isn't the problem.

The problem is this: although the personal and direct experience of a transcendent order leaves an indelible mark in the human mind, *the experience itself is almost never abiding.* Once it ends, one quickly falls victim again to the irresistible pull of ordinary life and its claustrophobic ethos. The issue is compounded by the impossibility to properly translate the experience into words and concepts, which makes recall very difficult. This way, the transcendent order quickly becomes a rather abstract and distant idea, as opposed to a present and felt reality. One is left with 'the agony of absence of the eternally further-beyond,'[15] in the words of Henry Corbin. At best, life becomes divided into the baseline dullness of ordinary existence and fleeting, occasional excursions into transcendence. *Either way, transcendence does not penetrate ordinary life.* A clear boundary persists between the two, like a dam that prevents the riches amassed on the other side from flowing down into the river of our everyday existence. The two worlds don't seem to overlap. Ordinary life remains, to a large extent, devoid of meaning.

> The impetus of human life is to transcend the limitations of the ordinary human condition and realize a form of eternal significance. Although transcendence can be experienced in mystical or spiritual states, the experience is almost never abiding and does not permeate one's daily life.

Religious myths and transcendence

Are we then condemned to a life wherein our deepest yearnings can never be realized? Not really, for *a special type of myth—a religious myth—can bring transcendence into everyday life, thereby saving the human animal from existential despair.* Indeed, we can even define a religious myth as a myth that imbues life with purposefulness, timelessness and boundlessness. In other words, a religious myth is a story capable of lifting the experience of being from the confines of time, space, randomness and blind automatism.

A religious myth infuses ordinary aspects of life with enchantment and significance: accidents and coincidences become invested with hidden purposes; our actions in the world acquire the importance of a cosmic mission; our suffering becomes the carrier of critical insights; even objects and people around us acquire a numinous aura. In the Talmudic myth of conception, *Lailah*—an angel of the night—touches the fetus on the upper lip immediately prior to birth, causing him to forget everything about the transcendent order of reality whence he originates. This angelic action is supposedly what creates the philtrum, that little groove between the nose and the upper lip that we all have. Every time a Rabbinic Jew looks at someone's face on the streets, he potentially sees the footprints of transcendence, the touch of Lailah. Through the religious myth, the 'otherworld' enters *this* world. The dam is broken and the river flows.

In a life informed by a religious myth, nothing is 'just so.' Everything has a reason for being and a purpose to fulfill. Everything belongs in a bigger and timeless context; the 'over-all pattern' mentioned by Sacks. Religious myths turn ordinary life into an abiding transcendent experience; a small but crucial segment of an epic cosmic drama. The boundaries between this world and a bigger world dissolve. There is no more 'here and there.' Instead, transcendence abides in the *here and now.* Religious myths provide the ground where the acorn can grow into the oak.

A religious myth can bring transcendence into daily life in an abiding manner. It can infuse ordinary aspects of life with enchantment and timeless significance, thereby saving the human animal from existential despair.

The lamentable state of religious myths today
Religious myths are much disregarded and belittled today. Not

that myth itself has disappeared: moral and ethical codes, ideologies of every kind and ontological interpretations of science—such as the metaphysics of materialism—are, quite literally, myths. They are stories that provide context and direction to our lives, be they lives of scientific pursuit or social activism. Undeniably, however, *religious* myths have been steadily losing their power. The hyping of religious fundamentalism by the mainstream media simply masks the faster-advancing loss of authentic religious vibrancy: a noisy minority makes the headlines while a majority falls into apathy and cynicism. The richness and variety of religious folklore is quickly being swallowed up by globalized, packaged, market-driven worldviews that impart no meaning to one's local community, geography, history or traditions. Perhaps as a desperate, instinctive effort to compensate for this unnatural state of affairs, scientific myth-making is on the rise, as the latest multiverse cosmologies illustrate.[16] But that's a lame form of mythologizing: science's blind devotion to the gods of chance and automatism condemns its myths to hollowness. 'Random events, nothing truly necessary. Science's cosmologies say nothing about the soul, and so they say nothing to the soul, about its reason for existence,'[17] said Hillman. The transcendence that only religious myths can bestow upon our lives is dissipating fast in a globalized, pragmatic, cynical and market-driven society.

This process unfolds along two apparently opposite avenues that, ultimately, lead to the same destination. On the one hand, the crucial usefulness of *skepticism* is degenerating into the narrow-mindedness of *cynicism*. The allegedly skeptical scientific myth that dominates contemporary culture is, in fact, based on a peculiarly biased value-system: an emotional and irrational need to deny all meaning and purpose in nature.[18] Alan Watts saw this as a reflection of the nineteenth century ethos under which the values of contemporary science congealed. He wrote:

The world-conquering West of the nineteenth century needed a philosophy of life in which *realpolitik*—victory for the tough people who face the bleak facts—was the guiding principle. Thus the bleaker the facts you face, the tougher you seem to be. So we vied with each other to make the Fully Automatic Model of the universe as bleak as possible.[19]

In other words, science, as the exclusive domain of men in the nineteenth century, incorporated in its very fabric the adolescent male's need to look tough. When listening to the spokespeople of science and neo-atheism today, one in fact wonders whether much has changed since then. Be it as it may, the result is that contemporary science cannot acknowledge even the possibility of meaning and purpose—let alone transcendence—for real men and tough chicks face bleak facts. This isn't skepticism but cynicism: an arbitrary commitment to the impossibility of something. It reflects an attitude as beset by blind belief as any religious dogma. Consequently, authentic religious myths are now allowed no role in the mainstream, academically-endorsed worldview of our culture. The natural and legitimate psychic impulse towards transcendence has become artificially associated with ignorance, stupidity and weakness. Such marginalization of religion has robbed us of context and perspective. We now find our gods not on the altar, but in the bottle of alcohol, the football match on television, the new pair of shoes and the arms of the casual lover.

On the other hand, the crucial usefulness of *faith*—a word whose meaning I am going to elaborate upon later—is degenerating into the narrow-mindedness of *fundamentalism*. So petrified are we at the specter of a meaningless life that we now cling rather desperately to a particular, narrow interpretation of our chosen religious myth. Like the fear that blinds a cornered animal, our insecurities cloud our view of subtlety and nuance. We squash the many facets of the myth—the multiple *entendres*, perspectives and contradictions necessary for conveying the deeper, intellect-transcending intuitions underlying the myth[20]—into a single facet. We see a square for the cube, a triangle for the diamond. We make the religious myth *small*, a flattened shadow of what it is truly meant to represent, so we can hold on to it more easily. As a result, we've succumbed to lives of uptightness, intolerance and even hatred.

Both cynicism and fundamentalism blind us to the full breadth and depth of religious myths. Consequently, we've lost our ability to experience the comprehensive way in which transcendence can envelop our entire existence. We now desperately lack context, perspective and purpose. Our lives have become uprooted, our journey lonely and scary, and our suffering pointless and nearly unbearable.

Because of the contemporary tendency toward cynicism and fundamentalism, we've marginalized our religious myths and made them small and flattened. Consequently, we've lost our connection with transcendence.

Chapter 2

The rich colors of mythical life

It hasn't always been like this. In fact, during the vast majority of history and pre-history things have been very different. But to reencounter the lush colors that religious myths could once bring into human life, we have to turn to those dwindling cultures that still manage to keep them partly alive, precariously as the case may be. We have to turn, for instance, to the *Arandan*, an aboriginal Australian people with an extraordinarily evocative account of the origins of their world.

The Arandan religious myth

The Arandan believe that *Karora*, the creator, dreamed the world up in his sleep.[21] As he lay in darkness on the ground, a kind of tree grew from his head all the way to the heavens, its roots planted on Karora's head. The thoughts, wishes and desires in his head then became real as Karora dreamed them: animals and men sprung from his navel and armpits.

Eventually, when the sun rose, Karora awoke. As he stood up, he left a hole on the ground in the place where he had lain asleep. This hole then became the Ilbalintja Soak, a sacred place for the Arandan, which connects their daily life with the transcendence of their deity. Now awake, Karora lost his magical powers and, to his own surprise, met the animals and men that he had dreamed into existence the previous night. He even cooked and ate some of the animals for, without his magical powers, he felt hungry. Over a series of subsequent nights, Karora again fell asleep and dreamed more creatures into existence, coming in contact with them upon awakening the next morning.

All of this supposedly took place around the Ilbalintja Soak, a location integral to Arandan life. The animals that sprouted from

Karora's dreaming body are animals the Arandan see every day. The myth thus endows their very environment and its inhabitants with transcendence. Their whole existence is colored by the myth. It gives their lives meaning.[22]

One way to look upon the Arandan myth is to take it literally and then proceed to dismiss it as absurd. Another way is to try and look *beyond* the words, taking the images of the myth as evocative *symbols* that point to deeper and ineffable intuitions. An extensive analysis of the Arandan myth is beyond the scope or purposes of this book, but it is useful to highlight a few salient aspects.

Clearly, the myth evokes the notion that the world is a *mental creation* of a deity who dreams it into existence while *lacking lucidity*. In the stupor of the dream, this deity has the magical power of bringing things forth into existence; the freedom unique to the *imagination* to concoct images without being bound by logic, resource constraints, ordinary causality or consistency. In other words, *during his dream the deity doesn't know what is supposed to be impossible and, therefore, nothing is impossible.* However, he can also *enter the dream*, as it were, by waking up in it. When this happens, the deity gains the ability to self-reflect but loses his magical powers, for he is now a participant in his own dream, subject to its constraints and internal logic like the rest of his creation. In other words, by waking up he becomes aware of, and subject to, what is supposedly impossible. Yet, it is this act of waking up *inside* the dream that gives his creation concreteness and solidity, for only now creation is experienced in the state of lucid self-reflection that fixes it in place, as opposed to the ever-flowing slumber of sleep.

The idea built into this religious myth is sophisticated and striking. Karora can find himself in two different mental states: one lacking lucidity, which is linked to the unconstrained freedom to imagine things into existence; and a self-reflective state linked to becoming subject to self-imposed constraints.

Upon waking up inside his own dream, Karora even has to find food, cook and eat! There seems to be a trade-off between lucidity and unconstrained creative freedom; they don't come together.

I will leave it to you to consult your own intuition and determine what—if any—ring of truth and significance this myth might have. Be it as it may, the Arandan are not alone in their sophisticated intuitions...

The Uitoto religious myth

On the other side of the planet, in the Amazon jungle, the *Uitoto* tribe has a mind-bending myth of their own.[23] According to it, a creator deity, *Nainema,* also created the world by imagining it while in a state of slumber. Initially, his imaginings were a tenuous and evanescent illusion, which could easily be lost and forgotten. However, Nainema held on to the illusion by the thread of a dream, not allowing it to escape him. He tied the thread with magical glue and then proceeded to stamp on the illusion until he could, as it were, *break into it,* so to sit down on the earth he was imagining. Now *inside* his own dream, he spat on the earth, thereby sprouting the jungle from his saliva. At last his original, tenuous illusion had become the actual, concrete world of the Uitoto.

The Hindu religious myth

There are many other examples of similar myths. The Hindu tradition in India, for instance, is particularly rich.

According to a foundational Hindu myth, the primary formative principle behind everything is called *Brahman.* Brahman *thought* primordial 'waters' into existence, forming the basic scaffolding of the world to come. Brahman's seed in the primordial waters then became a *cosmic egg*—a universal motif across the world's religious myths[24]—from which Brahman Itself was born. Having achieved *self-generation* by being born inside the basic scaffolding of Its own creation, Brahman gave it content:

through further acts of thought, It created Heaven, Earth and all the concrete elements of the world.[25] In some versions of the myth, the utterance of a sound, or 'the Word,' is what fills the world in with content.[26]

What richness of color and transcendence the Arandan, Uitoto and Hindu myths must bestow on the lives of the people who live by them.

> Traditional religious myths flood a community's very environment and its inhabitants with transcendence. The temporal and eternal worlds become linked. Mere trees, animals and holes on the ground take on the significance of divine footprints.

The common motifs behind the world's religious myths

Alert readers will have noticed conspicuous and even striking similarities across the myths discussed. In all cases, the world is seen as the *mental creation* of a deity; that is, a kind of *thought* in the mind of God. The universe begins as insubstantial imaginings—'illusions' in the Uitoto case; 'dreams' in the Arandan case; thought-up primordial 'waters' in the Hindu case—which then gain concreteness and solidity once the deity itself *enters the dream*—by waking up in it, in the case of the Arandan; by stamping on it, in the case of the Uitoto; or by birthing itself into it, in the Hindu case. The deity always undergoes a significant change in its state of consciousness—from dream or illusion to a lucid, self-reflective, deliberate state—once it enters its creation.

These motifs recur across time and cultures, the West being no exception. For instance, according to the Christian myth, God also enters His creation by being born into it as the Christ. The broader notion of a cosmic mind holding the world within itself as a thought is also present in Western mythology. Consider the following words of the *Corpus Hermeticum*, basis of the Hermetic myth that underlies Western esotericism:

> That Light, He said, am I, thy God, *Mind*, prior to Moist Nature ... *Mind is Father-God*. Not separate are they the one from other; ... He [God] *thinketh* all things manifest ... [and] manifests through all things and in all.[27]

Changes in the state of consciousness of such cosmic mind—dreamless sleep, dream and wakefulness—are integral to the cycle of creation according to many of the world's myths, as revealed in Joseph Campbell's monumental work on comparative mythology. Indeed, Campbell recognized a consistent message in many myths regarding the nature of reality and the process of creation. He called it the *cosmogonic cycle*, describing it 'as the passage of *universal consciousness* from the deep *sleep* zone of the unmanifest, through *dream*, to the full day of *waking*.'[28] In the waking state, creation is experienced as 'the hard, gross facts of an outer universe.' In the dream state, it is experienced as the 'fluid, subtle forms of a private inner world.'[29] In the dreamless sleep state, there is no experience as such and, therefore, only the *potential* for creation exists. The different phases of the cosmogonic cycle thus entail different states of cognition of the universal consciousness.

This is not to say that *all*—or even *most*—religious myths reflect the cosmogonic cycle, the notion that the universe is a kind of dream in a universal consciousness. Modern scholarly work has shown that religious mythology is varied and largely inconsistent.[30] Indeed, such inconsistency should come as no surprise: the briefest review of history and contemporary society already shows that the human mind is perfectly capable of generating baseless ideas, often dangerous ones. Mythology, as a human activity, couldn't be an exception to that. Not all religious myths—at least in their developed forms—fully resonate with the deepest intuitions of humankind, even when their original psychic seeds are genuine. Various mundane motivations play a role in the further development of myths, including human greed and drive to power.[31] But this isn't the point...

The point is that *some*—dare I say *many*—religious myths, originating in cultures separated by abysses of space, time and language, somehow reflect surprisingly similar themes and ideas. And although comparing myths can inadvertently imbue them with generic meanings they didn't have in their local historical contexts,[32] the similarities here aren't generic or simple. They are highly specific and sophisticated. The world as the mental activity of a deity that becomes lucid within its own imagination certainly isn't a view you would expect to arise by mere coincidence all over the world. Neither is it a vague generality created artificially by comparison. Somehow, peoples separated by half the circumference of the globe and thousands of years have, through their religious myths, arrived at specific, refined, surprisingly similar cosmologies. This, in itself, already raises interesting questions regarding the origin of the commonalities (more in the next chapter). The most urgent and important of all questions, however, is whether this largely shared cosmology is true. *Are these religious myths in some way true?* This is what we must now address.

A common motif across many traditional religious myths is the notion that the world is the imagination of a divinity. The divinity then enters its own imaginings, taking on a lucid, self-reflective state of awareness within it. It is this that brings concreteness to an essentially dreamed-up universe.

Religious myths: either true or irrelevant

When we were children, before we conceptualized the notion of 'truth,' we were able to derive great excitement and meaning from fantasy and imagination. How many a rainy afternoon have we not spent daydreaming amazing stories? Can you still remember how that felt? Our imagined stories were no less significant and evocative than any real event, simply because we hadn't yet learned to differentiate between these two categories. Both real events and fantasies were, for our younger selves, simply *experiences*. But things changed later in life. Once we began to conceptualize a boundary separating truth from untruth, we became unable to derive any excitement or significance from what we saw as mere fantasy. If you are a culturally-acclimated human being, this will still be the case for you today.

And that's the challenge we have to face before we are able to allow religious myths to enrich our lives again: *we can't take seriously that which we don't consider true.* How can an inconsequential fantasy influence our emotional and intellectual lives? We aren't children anymore. If a religious myth is just a fable it can't possibly count, can it?

The Arandan and Uitoto face the exact same challenge: their religious myths would also die out if they weren't believed. However, unlike traditional cultures, the intellect has become the dominant psychic function in our society. That's the difference between them and us. We don't just take our intuitions at face

---

Religious myths are powerless if they aren't seen as true. But unlike traditional cultures, we subject our mythical intuitions to the scrutiny of reason. Therefore, if our lives are to be colored by religious myths again, it is imperative that we rationally understand how and why they can be true.

value anymore—as the Arandan and Uitoto do—but subject them to the tyrannical scrutiny of reason. Therefore, *it has become indispensible for us to rationally understand how and why a religious myth can carry truth.* Without this understanding, the myth is dismissed by the intellect—bouncer of the heart—thereby losing its colors and becoming irrelevant to us.

Mere allegories?

Because traditional religious myths admittedly can't carry *literal* truth, our instinctive explanation for their sophistication and mutual consistency is to think of them as *allegories* for some kind of advanced cosmology. After all, it's pretty safe to say that Karora didn't literally rise from the soil and that Nainema didn't literally spit the jungle into existence. But to say that these myths are *just* allegories wouldn't do justice to the power they hold in their respective societies. To the Uitoto, the trees of the forest *really* grew from the saliva of Nainema. To the Arandan, the Ilbalintja Soak was *really* formed when Karora arose from the ground. If their myths were seen as mere allegories, they wouldn't have the power to flood the entire world of the Arandan and Uitoto with transcendence, as they do. The Ilbalintja Soak wouldn't be sacred. The trees of the Amazon jungle wouldn't have the significance of divine secretion. *Something glaringly essential is lost when we reduce religious myths to just allegories.*

Corbin pointed out that 'allegory is a more or less artificial representation of generalities and abstractions *which can be perfectly well grasped and expressed in other ways.*'[33] As such, allegories are quickly categorized by our intellects as marginally useful little stories that aren't *really* true after all. They just indirectly point to a truth that—we assume—can ultimately be described in some direct, explicit, accurate and precise way; that is, in a *literal* way. Immediately, we start investing the whole of our intellectual and emotional energy in searching for this direct representation of the truth, dismissing the allegory as a super-fluous intermediary step. We say to ourselves: 'Nice allegory, but what is it that is *really* going on?' As such, allegories cannot carry the power that we now reserve for literal truth. Religious myths seen as mere allegories cannot provide us with the context, perspective and meaning we crave in modern life. They cannot restore the transcendence and mystery of the world. They become merely 'a mode of thought that eventually needs to be abandoned for the clean lines and straight thinking of pure reason,'[34] in the words of Jeffrey Kripal.

Yet, despite lacking literal truth, religious myths have been the engine of human psychic life for almost the entire length of our history and pre-history combined. Whence do they derive their undeniable force? Here is a conundrum that isn't easy to solve. Patrick Harpur has probably made the best recent attempt at tackling this in his excellent books.[35] But his overarching conclusion—as much as it may be correct—is ultimately unsatis-fying: he argues that there is *a subtle, roundabout way of seeing reality* according to which the distinction between literal and allegorical truth disappears, and that religious myths should be interpreted in that ambiguous way. Harpur brilliantly uses poetry, psychology, philosophy and a whole arsenal of schol-arship to try and coax the reader toward his elusive but intriguing viewpoint. I, however, believe that the conundrum can be unpacked and made sense of in a fully explicit and declarative manner. Instead of elusive and ambiguous ways of seeing, I believe we can positively state, logically and coherently, in what precise manner religious myths can hold actual truth.

The key to solving this riddle lies in realizing that truth is not

---

The truth carried by religious myths is much more than merely allegorical, yet not literal.

---

restricted to only two categories—literal and allegorical—as implicitly assumed above, but that there is a third and essential category: *transcendent truth.* We will explore this in the next chapter.

Chapter 3

The truth of religious myths

For thousands of years, traditional cultures the world over have taken religious myths seriously, not only as an integral part of their lives but as the very basis and guiding principle of their existence. As David Leeming put it, religious 'myths have had significant power to move people. Societies have defined themselves by, committed themselves to, and even been willing to kill and be killed in support of their myths.'[36] Clearly, our ancestors believed in the truth of their religious myths unreservedly. Were they merely naïve and unenlightened or did they benefit from a subtle perspective that we have lost? What is the nature of mythical truth and why have we become so blind to it in our culture?

Language and thought

Underlying our contemporary attitude toward religious myths is the hidden but far-reaching assumption that *all relevant truths about reality can be directly captured by the intellect in the form of language constructs*. In other words, we take it for granted that, if something is *true*, then it can be *said*.

By 'language' I don't mean merely English or Chinese, but a system of *signs* for the representation and manipulation of information about the world. Language represents the *images* of consensus reality—lions, wildebeests, rocks, hills, etc.—with signs like written words, sounds and other labels.[37] It then combines these signs through a set of rules, called a *grammar*, so to represent the *interactions* found in consensus reality.[38] This way, language allows us to create an *internal model* of the world within our intellects. Examples of language in this general sense include not only English and Chinese, but also mathematical notations, computer codes, sign language, etc. As the basis of our internal models of reality, *language underlies the way we reason and delineates the boundaries of what we consider possible.* The Greeks were on to this, for their word for 'word'—λόγος (*'logos'*)—also means 'reasoning.'

Indeed, Noam Chomsky argued that our ability to use language is not just learned, but enabled and conditioned by pre-existing, hardwired structures in the human brain. Language isn't arbitrary: it is what it is because we are what we are. Before being a tool for communication, *language mirrors the very way our intellects process information about reality.*[39] This is not so surprising if you consider that the vast majority of our use of language is internal: we talk to ourselves much more than we talk to others. *We reason in language.* As Ian Tattersall put it, 'it is virtually impossible to imagine our thought processes in [the absence of language], for without the mediation of language those thought processes would be entirely intuitive.'[40] Our ancestors could only begin to communicate in our unique human way after biological hardware that enabled *a linguistic style of thought* had evolved in their brains, an idea confirmed by paleoanthropological data.[41] Our reasoning and our language overlap and co-define each other. 'Language is generated by the intellect, and generates the intellect,'[42] said Abelard, expressing a fundamental *circularity* whose profound implications we will explore in Parts II and III of this book.

For this reason, we have now become so accustomed to judging reality linguistically that we assume all relevant truths to be amenable to direct representation in language. In other words, we assume that if something cannot be unambiguously *said* then it cannot be *true.* We often judge people to be wrong simply because they cannot articulate their position coherently in words. How open are we, really, to the idea that there are essential aspects of reality that cannot be unambiguously repre-sented in any language?

Yet, there is no reason to believe that language is sufficient to capture all relevant truths. As Alan Watts put it, it's a mistake to think 'that one can make an informative, factual, and positive *statement* about the ultimate reality.'[43] After all, how plausible is it that the information processing apparatus of a mere primate would have evolved to articulate *all* reality? Indeed, the operations of the human intellect are based on what Chomsky has called a 'universal grammar,' a structured template for manipulating information. Chomsky went as far as to assert that 'the study of universal grammar ... is a study of the nature of human intellectual capacities.'[44] It is preposterous to think that such a template would mirror within itself all the dynamics of nature. Why would it? 'Things are not as graspable and sayable as on the whole we are led to believe; most events are unsayable, occur in a space that no word has ever penetrated,'[45] concluded Rilke.

Truth doesn't care about the limits of human language. It is what it is. Therefore, there almost certainly is much about reality that we cannot make sense of in words or other notations; many *truths* that cannot be unambiguously *said* and hence *reasoned*. These are *transcendent truths*, for they escape the boundaries of logic, time and space enforced by our universal grammar. And it is in regard to transcendent truths, as we soon shall see, that religious myths play an irreplaceable role. Indeed, while discussing the 'incommunicability of the Truth which is beyond

---

Because our self-reflective reasoning is constructed in language, we assume that if something cannot be unambiguously said then it cannot be true. But truth does not care about the limits of human language. There are many natural truths that cannot be said and, hence, reasoned. These are transcendent truths.

---

names and forms,' Joseph Campbell wrote: 'whereas the truths of science are communicable, ... *mythology* and metaphysics are but guides to the brink of a *transcendent* illumination.'[46]

The obfuscated mind

The boundaries of language and of the intellect, as we've seen in the previous section, are co-extensive: the intellect cannot go where language cannot take it. And most of us know how limited language is—despite the magnificent attempts of poets—in expressing the subtleties of human feelings, let alone the broader truths of reality. 'The categories of human thought ... so confine the mind that it is normally impossible not only to see, but even to conceive, beyond the ... phenomenal spectacle,'[47] continued Campbell.

Still, the human mind is not limited to the intellect. Where the intellect stops *intuition* picks up. We can *sense* truth even if we cannot *articulate* it in words or *derive* it from logical schemes. Unreliable as this sense may be, it is our only link to a broader reality.

The intellect resides in what depth-psychology calls the 'ego,' that part of our thoughts, feelings and perceptions that we are self-reflectively aware of. But underneath our self-reflective selves there is an unfathomably broader mental space that depth-psychology has come to call the 'unconscious,' the wellspring of intuition. As explained in an earlier work,[48] the term is actually a misnomer: the 'unconscious' mind is merely an *obfuscated* part of consciousness. Terminology aside, however, what matters here is the existence of a broader, intuitive part of mind underlying the ego. From this point on, I will call it the 'obfuscated mind.'

Today's neuroscience has produced strong empirical evidence that, like the ego, the obfuscated mind can also acquire, process, store and retrieve information, exhibiting a surprisingly broad range of cognitive functions.[49] Indeed, the presence of an obfuscated mind much broader and more powerful than the ego is an empirical fact that confronts every depth-psychologist, every day, in the therapy room. So the questions of real relevance here are not about whether the obfuscated mind exists, but: How does it operate? What can it know about nature that the intellect cannot? And how can we establish communication between the intellect and the obfuscated mind?

As a cognitive domain that transcends the intellect, *the obfuscated mind does not operate according to linguistic constructs.* In other words, it does not process information according to a logical, algorithm-like universal grammar. Instead, evidence from depth-psychology shows that the obfuscated mind operates *symbolically.*[50] Unlike a *sign*—such as a word, acronym or label—which merely *denotes* something well defined and circumscribed, a *symbol connotes* a deeper, subtler, broader idea or intuition. In the words of Corbin, 'a symbol is a primary phenomenon (*Urphänomen*), unconditional and irreducible, the appearance of something that cannot manifest itself otherwise to the world where we are.'[51] As such, the symbolic obfuscated mind is less constrained in the way it organizes its cognitive processes than the linguistic intellect.

We can experience the amazing latitude of symbolic cognition when we dream: as expressions of the obfuscated mind, dreams unfold in a much broader space than that delineated by rationality and physics. They don't 'make sense' in the way our rational thoughts do because they refuse to be bound by the constraints of logic, time and space normally enforced by grammatical rules. Scenes change suddenly and discontinuously; events don't obey ordinary cause-and-effect relationships; contradictions and cognitive dissonance abound; etc. Yet, dreams have great power to reveal *truth* about our inner states, conveying their meaning through indirect, seemingly absurd but strongly evocative symbols. This, in fact, is the whole basis of dream analysis in depth-psychology.[52]

As argued carefully in an earlier work, I believe that the

logical constraints of the human intellect are very useful but ultimately arbitrary.[53] After all, one cannot logically argue for the absolute validity of logic without begging the question. The obfuscated mind, for not being restricted to such arbitrary constraints, can embody a much greater range of cognition than the intellect. Its symbolic character should be regarded, according to Carl Jung, as an ancient mode of thought that has been superseded—or rather, obfuscated—by the relatively recent acquisition of linguistic thinking.[54] Clearly, our intellect—insofar as it enables deliberation, premeditation, evaluation of scenarios, planning, communication, etc.—offers immense practical survival advantages when compared to the earlier symbolic mode of thought. And evolution favors survival, not *per se* a broad cognizance of the underlying nature of reality. Hence, it isn't at all surprising that the intellect has become so dominant in our species, pushing our symbolic mode of thought down to seeming unconsciousness.

Yet, the depth, breadth and flexibility of the ancient obfuscated mind may represent a huge and untapped potential in every human being; a resource anchored much closer to the primordial truths of nature—like the roots of the tree growing out of Karora's divine head—than the later-evolved intellect. Modern life, with its relative comfort and security, is changing our priorities as a species. While practical needs like finding food and evading predators ruled the lives of our ancestors, modern humans are increasingly preoccupied with the bigger questions: Where did we come from? Where are we going? What is life? What are we supposed to do in it? What is the meaning of it all? The possibility that presents itself to us is that our neglected obfuscated mind—with its deeply rooted, unfathomably broader, but purely intuitive apprehension of reality—could offer us answers.[55] *Could it give us access to transcendent truths?* Could we ease our modern anxieties and rediscover the meaning of life by tapping into this ancient umbilical-chord that keeps us connected to the ground of existence?

> Truth can be intuited even when it cannot be articulated in language. Such intuition is rooted in our broader obfuscated mind, which can apprehend—in symbolic ways—aspects of reality beyond the grasp of our self-reflective thoughts and perceptions.

Transcending the intellect

I believe we can.

Many of the neuroses that plague the lives of modern humans—from anxiety to depression—are often fed, if not caused, by a confined, claustrophobic and ultimately unsubstantiated interpretation of consensus reality; that is, by a deprived myth derived from grammatical rules. The depressed person sees no meaning in life largely because the small box of her linguistic thinking limits her view of what life is. The anxious person fears self-destruction largely because her linguistic understanding of her own identity is confining.

But the *trans*linguistic, transcendent truths of nature hold the promise to liberate us from these artificial confinements, for they surpass the boundaries of logic, time and space enforced by grammatical rules. They inoculate against existential despair. That the intellect can't access these transcendent truths does *not* mean that our broader obfuscated mind can't either. As a matter of fact, both the long history of religious epiphany[56] and over a century of depth-psychology[57] suggest strongly that it *can*; that the obfuscated mind *can* intuitively recognize transcendence, offering us our best chance of deliverance from the clutches of deprived myths.

Indeed, the evocative power and remarkable sophistication of so many traditional religious myths can only be attributed to their origin in the obfuscated mind, which intuits aspects of reality unreachable by the intellect. These myths weren't thought through deliberately, but *sensed*. Their intricacies weren't composed through steps of reasoning, but arose spontaneously from attempts to *describe* the underlying structure of reality, which their originators could *intuitively apprehend*. This explains how cultures with limited intellectual development could produce such astoundingly refined cosmologies. It also explains how these various cosmologies ended up being so mutually consistent: after all, we all *share* the same reality that the myths attempt to describe. In a nutshell, despite the radically different geographical, historical and cultural contexts of different traditional peoples, they were intuitively 'looking at,' and trying to describe, the same phenomenon. In arguing this, I am largely echoing Jung's views, which were extensively substantiated in his own work and those of others after him.[58]

The conclusion here is inescapable: *to restore meaning to our lives, we must develop a close relationship with the transcendent truths symbolically unveiled by the obfuscated mind in the form of religious myths.* After all, 'Every positive statement about ultimate things must be made in the suggestive form of myth,' said Watts.[59] He was right, because 'Myth is a true story ... a story about reality.'[60] Of course, true religious myths are *always* symbolic, since they emerge from obfuscated regions of mind like our nightly dreams.[61] But their symbolisms 'are neither contrivances nor mere fables; they are not raw primitivisms either. They are hard-won intuitions of something before form,'[62] as Richard Grossinger put it.

Establishing communication between the self-reflective intellect and our obfuscated mythical cognition can help us ease our modern anxieties and rediscover the meaning of life. By listening to what the obfuscated mind has to say, and then taking it seriously, we gain access to a broader, less claustrophobic apprehension of reality, life and human identity: an apprehension of transcendence. And although this transcendent view is not *literally* true, it is potentially *truer* than anything our intellects could possibly come up with. After all, as argued above, there is no literal articulation of the transcendent truths that offer the only way to escape existential despair. As such, *the symbolic religious myths produced by the obfuscated mind aren't merely roundabout ways to refer to something literal, but the only pointers we have to a form of salvation.* They aren't less precise and redundant alternatives to literal explanations, but the only fair way to capture and communicate the transcendent aspects of reality. When seen this way, religious myths take on the power of literal truth: in the absence of the latter, *they become the most direct, explicit, declarative, accurate and precise utterance of the truth.* If transcendent truths are to be uttered at all, they can only be uttered in the form of religious myths. Anything else would simply be false or vastly incomplete.

Many religious myths reflect a culture's intuitive apprehension of transcendent aspects of reality. They aren't merely roundabout ways to refer to something literal, but the most direct and accurate utterance of transcendent truths. A religious myth is symbolic—never literal—because it emerges from the obfuscated mind.

A daring proposal

All this said, there is a fact we must face. We may intellectually understand and accept the nuances of the three categories of truth discussed above—literal, allegorical and transcendent—but *emotionally* things are pretty binary: we either believe a religious myth or we don't. And if we don't, the myth loses all of its power. I thus propose that, *if a religious myth resonates deeply with your inner intuitions and survives a reasonably critical assessment of its depth, then you should emotionally*—though not intellectually—*take it onboard as if it were literally true.* The religious myth that resonates the strongest with your obfuscated mind should inform your *emotional* life—again, not your intellectual life—as if it were the literal truth, even though you'll know rationally that it isn't. I am thus advocating a deliberate, lucid split or dissociation between your emotional and intellectual attitudes. The way to achieve it is to remind yourself constantly that *there is no better description of transcendent truths than the religious myth that resonates with your heart.* Therefore, the logical way to go about life is, ironically, to buy into your heart-chosen myth with reasonable but not excessive intellectual oversight. The intellect is a valuable adviser but a lousy king.[63]

I make this proposal because I believe it to be more in accord with reality than the alternative. Since religious myths are the best representations of transcendent truths, dismissing them as mere fictions actually takes us farther away from what is really going on than taking them onboard as if they were literally true. This was Nietzsche's mistake when he declared God to be dead.[64] Overwhelmed by late nineteenth century rationalism, he rejected the religious myth of an anthropomorphic God, omniscient overseer of human life. But, with this reasonable rejection of the literal interpretation of a symbol, he denied *all* transcendent aspects of reality.[65] Is this denial less false—or even less naïve—than the divine symbol taken literally?

Another example should make my point clearer. The Pueblo—a native people of North America—believe they are the offspring of Father Sun. According to their religious myth, the Pueblo's rituals are essential to help their father cross the sky every day. Were they to stop performing their sacred rituals, the Pueblo believe the sun would stop rising in ten years and darkness would befall the world.[66] Notice that, if we allow this myth to penetrate our minds deeply enough, it is possible to intuitively *sense* surprising wisdom in it. Indeed, traditionally the sun has symbolized the lucid, self-reflective human intellect. 'How naturally we imagine our own capacity to know and to create, as the bright sun of consciousness,'[67] says *The Book of Symbols*. Depth-psychologists also consider the sun to be a symbol of the ego or intelligence, as opposed to instinct.[68] As such, a life lived with the attention and deliberateness with which one performs a sacred ritual ensures that the sun of self-reflective awareness continues to rise and illuminate the world every day. This is, in a very limited sense, what the Pueblo's religious myth seems to hint at. And isn't it a fact that only through the human capacity for self-reflection can nature become aware of itself? Isn't it a fact that, without the light of our lucidity, nature would remain shrouded in the darkness of instinct? The religious myth brings the transcendent aspects of these facts forcefully into the daily world of the Pueblo, making it alive and relevant in a way that our detached, conceptual explanations could never do. Indeed, at the very moment that I attempted to *explain* the Pueblo's myth conceptually, by rationally interpreting its symbolism, I killed something crucial about it; I killed its immediacy and aliveness. 'Oh, that's what this myth means! It's *just* an allegory of self-reflection after all.' And kaboom! In one fell swoop, the transcendent truth suggested by the myth is lost from sight. Can you sense what I mean? Only when emotionally taken in as though it were the literal truth, *and therefore dispensing with further elucidations and conceptual interpretations*, does the religious myth allow the Pueblo to *feel* their true role in the natural order of things. Wouldn't they find themselves farther removed from the truth if they dismissed their myth and believed instead that their lives served no purpose?

Because an intellectual inaccuracy is unavoidable whether we *emotionally* take the symbolism of religious myths literally or dismiss them, the lesser inaccuracy is the logical way to go. Transcendent truths cannot be grasped directly and explicitly, so rejecting religious myths for the sake of a non-existing literal alternative is simply *irrational*. The dilemma here isn't comfortable, but we must bite this bullet. If we don't, we will be condemning ourselves to being forever insulated from a deeper reality and, therefore, effectively living out our emotional lives according to falsehoods and artificial constraints. How smart is that?

For you to be able to embrace my proposal, you will need your intellect to grant itself rational permission to *step out of the way and make space* for your wiser obfuscated mind to co-direct your relationship with reality. My attempt so far in this book has been to help you grant yourself this permission, allowing religious myths to color your emotional life without excessive intellectual judgment. I want to help you *emotionally* believe your chosen religious myth as fully as you believe any literal truth; and as fully as the Pueblo believe that they help the sun rise every day. This, in fact, is what it means to have faith. *Faith is the sincere* emotional *openness to the transcendent truths connoted by a story, beyond the superficial, literal appearances of the story's denotations*. And, as argued above, it is the absence of faith that is irrational.

Yet, I know that the symbolic images used in traditional religious myths defy our rationality too drastically, making it impossible for us to take them in as if they were the literal truth. How could any person in contemporary Western civilization take seriously the idea that animals and human beings sprouted *literally* from the navel and armpits of Karora? How could any one of you, dear readers, take seriously the notion that the trees of the Amazon jungle grew *literally* from Nainema's spit?

Plausibility is key for the images used in any religious myth. And plausibility changes with the zeitgeist and the views of a culture. For the Uitoto, the idea of trees growing out of divine saliva is entirely plausible. For our culture, obviously it isn't. Plausibility is important because it allows the intellect to relax in the *possibility* of truth. Anything implausible automatically triggers rational defenses, preventing the religious myth from penetrating past the intellect so to reach the deeper, emotional mind.

For my proposal above to be realistically applicable to a broader segment of society, we need modern formulations of religious myths; formulations that use plausible contemporary images, more amenable to intellectual tolerance, given what we think to know today about nature and its mysteries. The images of traditional myths were appropriate for cultures without the scientific understanding of the world that we possess today. We need new images, new representations consistent with our contemporary knowledge and intellectual ethos. This is what I will attempt to achieve in Part III of this book. For now, though, a word of caution is in order.

> Emotionally, we either believe a religious myth or we don't. If we don't, the myth loses the power to bring transcendence into daily life. I thus propose that, if a religious myth resonates deeply with your intuitions, you should emotionally—though not intellectually—take it onboard as if it were literally true.

The danger of fundamentalism

My proposal is that you allow your chosen religious myth to inform your *emotional* life as though it were literally true. However, I am *not* suggesting that you *intellectually* take it to be the literal truth. Doing so is tantamount to denying transcendence altogether, since it implicitly assumes that the corresponding truths can be accurately, unambiguously and completely captured in a language-based narrative. Moreover, taking a religious myth to be the literal truth at an intellectual level plants the seed of fundamentalism. This has been the source of unimaginable suffering and destruction throughout history. Let us elaborate on it with an analogy.

If you illuminate a solid cylinder from its top, it will project a shadow in the shape of a circle. If you illuminate the exact same cylinder from its side, its shadow will look like a rectangle. See Figure 1. Both the circle and the rectangle are equally valid projections of the cylinder, conveying *true* information about it. The fact that the rectangle is completely different from the circle—an apparent contradiction in the flat world of shadows— implies no conflict in the world of the solid cylinder. In 3D, the differences between 2D shadows are easily reconciled.

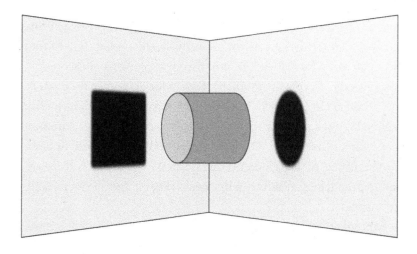

Figure 1. A solid cylinder and its shadows.

A transcendent truth is to our intellect like a solid cylinder is to its shadows. The same transcendent truth can, in principle, 'appear' to the intellect in different and apparently contradictory forms, like circle and rectangle. *The symbolisms of different but valid religious myths are the shadows of transcendent truths.* They are genuine, fair representations of those truths in just the same way that the circle and the rectangle are both genuine, fair represen- tations of the cylinder. The fact that a given religious myth apparently contradicts another does not necessarily imply that one of them is invalid, for exactly the same reason that the shadow circle does not imply that the shadow rectangle is invalid.

When proposing that you *emotionally* take your chosen religious myth in *as if* it were the literal truth, I am attempting to honor the fact that the shadow circle—or the rectangle, as the case may be—is a valid and fair representation of the transcendent cylinder. In other words, *it is really true*. The shadow circle conveys valid insights about the cylinder, which are essential to inform our emotional lives. *Cynically dismissing all religious myths is tantamount to closing one's eyes to the shadows projected by truth.* By doing so, one willingly ignores the genuine insights that shadows convey, an attitude somewhat akin to that of the clergy who refused to look through Galileo's telescope.

However, if you *intellectually* take your religious myth to *be* the literal truth, *you will be closing your eyes to the cylinder!* You will be taking a shadow to be all there is to reality and dismissing that which is its source. This is as unfair to the transcendent truth as dismissing all religious myths; perhaps worse. In both cases, one is practicing voluntary blindness; closing one's eyes to God, so to speak.

Moreover, if one grants validity only to the world of shadows, a logical implication is that shadows with different shapes cannot be concurrently true. Since the transcendent reality—the place where these differences are reconciled—is intellectually dismissed, the differences in shape must imply true contradictions. In the absence of the cylinder, if the circle is true then the rectangle must be false, and vice-versa. Here fundamentalism is born: 'I know that *my* religious myth—my chosen shadow—is right so *yours* can only be wrong.' When the Christian myth is honored by being *emotionally* taken in *as if* it were the literal truth, Christians live lives of meaning and transcendent significance, escaping the madness of a materialist society and coming closer to truth. When it is *intellectually* taken to *be* the literal truth, countless innocent people die burning at the stake or at the point of the crusader's sword. Perhaps even worse, millions wither slowly in the meaninglessness that results from forced 'conversions.'

Cynicism and fundamentalism are the two sides of one coin. Both practice voluntary blindness toward transcendent truth: one by refusing to acknowledge that shadows convey *valid* insights about it, and the other by taking a shadow to be the sole and complete truth. My proposal in the previous section is thus not meant as a nod to fundamentalism. Allow me to exhaust this important point.

Because of its very nature, there are no arbiters of mythical veracity other than intuition. The validity of a religious myth is not decidable by the intellect. We may each see a different but equally valid projection—or shadow—of a transcendent truth in the form of the myth that best resonates with our hearts. As such, it is hopeless to try to identify a fully objective, dispassionate criterion for judging which myths are valid. Fundamentalism is untenable because it depends on there being just such a fully objective standard of transcendent truth.

Does it mean that all religious myths are equally valid at a transcendent level? Of course not. A shadow in the form of a pentagon is always invalid as a projection of a solid cylinder, whichever way one illuminates it. As a matter of fact, a brief look at the metaphysical hysteria reigning at the fringes of society today shows that many of the cosmologies being promoted are internally inconsistent and lack the depth to resonate with our hearts. Moreover, as discussed earlier, the developed form of many traditional religious myths isn't grounded in genuine intuition alone, but also in shallower human drives like greed and fear.

I am, thus, *not* saying that there is no way to evaluate the validity of a religious myth. We will always have our own *sincere* intuition—the sense of the heart—to do so. The difficulty, of course, lies in telling real intuition—emerging from the depths of the obfuscated mind—from shallow self-deception, like wish fulfillment and gullibility. Many fall victim to self-deception and, I'm afraid, there are no surefire recipes to avoid it. Ultimately, we are each responsible for the sincerity, attention and discernment with which we listen to the whispers of our obfuscated mind.

In addition, it is conceivable that the comparative study of religion, as professionally done in academia, could *help* us recognize true religious myths by identifying the symbolic patterns typical of genuine intuitive insight.[69] Through complementing our personal intuition with collective validation, this could ease the individual burden we now carry in navigating our religious life. However, as long as academia—plagued as it is by the deprived myth of materialism—insists on rejecting even the possibility of transcendence, the burden will remain on each of us individually.

> Allowing one's chosen religious myth to inform one's emotional life as though it were literally true does not mean that one should take the myth, intellectually, to be the literal truth. Doing so plants the seed of fundamentalism.

Religious myth and language

Let us try to summarize and put in perspective some of what has been discussed so far. See Figure 2. The figure is divided vertically into outer (above) and inner (below) realms. Two concentric circles are shown. The inner circle represents our self-reflective intellect—operating according to language constructs—paired with the world of ordinary images and interactions, like lions, wildebeests, lions eating wildebeests, etc. The outer circle represents the obfuscated mind—operating according to symbols—

paired with a world of transcendent meta-images. Unlike the images of consensus reality, these transcendent meta-images have no form: they are ineffable idea gestalts, not perceptual representations.

In the same way that only some of the conceivable interactions among ordinary images are empirically verifiable consensus facts, only a subset of all conceivable meta-images is actually true. These transcendent truths are recognized by the human mind as outer realities, as though captured by a sixth sense utterly incommensurable with the other five.

There are five different chains of dots in Figure 2, illustrating the basic categories of language constructs:

Chain 1-2: *lies, ordinary fictions and factual errors.* Here, an ordinary statement of language (1) denotes an ordinary image interaction (2) that is not a consensus fact. An example would be to say that 'the Earth is flat,' a simple factual error.

Chain 3-4-5: *allegories.* Here, an ordinary statement of language (3) denotes an ordinary image interaction (4) that is not, but does connote, a consensus fact (5). A famous example can be found in Shakespeare's play *As You Like It:* 'All the world's a stage, And all the men and women merely players.' Clearly, the world isn't literally a stage and not everybody is an actor. But the world is indeed the space wherein we all express ourselves as living beings and fulfill our roles in life.

Chain 6-7: *literal truths.* Here, an ordinary statement of language (6) denotes an ordinary image interaction that is a consensus fact (7). An example would be to say that 'the Earth is a spheroid.'

Chain 8-9-10: *transcendent fallacies* or *false religious myths.* Here, a mythical statement of language (8) denotes an ordinary image interaction (9) that is not a consensus fact, but does connote a transcendent meta-image (10). This transcendent meta-image, however, is not a transcendent truth.

Chain 11-12-13-14: *true religious myths.* Here, an intuition emerging from the obfuscated mind (11) inspires the intellect to produce a mythical statement of language (12) denoting an ordinary image interaction (13). This ordinary image interaction is not a consensus fact but does connote a transcendent truth (14). Clearly, true religious myths aren't allegories (chain 3-4-5).

Figure 2 lays out a succinct template that captures, in a nutshell, the most important notions discussed. It is worthwhile to contemplate it for a moment, so to try and see its broader implications. We will return to this template shortly.

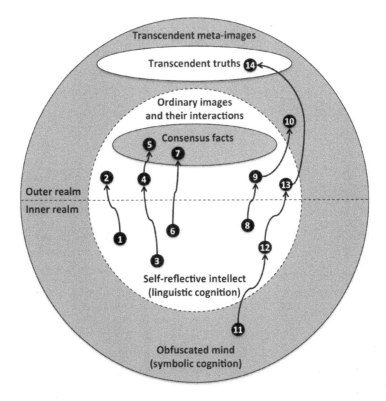

Figure 2. Mind and world.

Is the universe itself a form of language?

We have seen that true religious myths point to transcendent truths through symbolic stories. None of these stories, when taken as a whole, corresponds to a consensus fact. They, therefore, are not literally true. See Figure 2 again. For this reason, we can call such mythical stories *quasi-fictions*.[70]

Now, notice that the *basic images* in these quasi-fictions—the building blocks of the stories—are, in themselves, consensus facts. It's just their *particular interactions* that are not. For instance, the story of a tree growing up to the sky from Karora's head is a quasi-fiction. It may evoke a transcendent truth but does not correspond to a consensus fact: no tree has ever *grown from* the head of a buried deity to *reach* the sky. But the basic images used in the quasi-fiction—the tree, the head, the sky—are themselves consensus facts: trees do exist; heads do exist; the sky does exist.

Again: it is the *particular interactions* between the basic images of a religious myth—the tree *sprouting from* a head and *reaching* the sky—that do not correspond to consensus facts. The *basic images* themselves—the tree, the head, the sky—do.

Clearly, the basic images of consensus reality provide the building blocks not only for compound consensus facts, but also for religious myths that evoke transcendent truths. *The building blocks of facts and religious myths are the same.* This may sound like a casual and insignificant point, but it suggests an astounding possibility: Could the ordinary events of life themselves be pointing to transcendent truths? Could nature be *connoting* something fundamentally beyond or behind what it seems to *denote*?

It is curious enough that, in the context of religious myths, the images of consensus reality can be so effective in evoking transcendent meta-images. The entire field of mythology attests to this amazing fact and a quick look at a symbol dictionary will make it abundantly clear.[71] But it doesn't stop there: our nightly dreams, incredibly insightful as psychology has found them to be,[72] are also built from consensus images borrowed from our waking lives. Even the mere fact that *we sleep and dream*—believing the dream to be real while we are in it—seems suspiciously like a hint about the transcendent nature of existence, if you remember our earlier discussion about the cosmogonic cycle. Moreover, we can effectively use ordinary images to convey our deepest transcendent intuitions. Case in point: in my earlier book *Why Materialism Is Baloney* I used the images of whirlpools, quicksilver, dreams, obfuscated stars in the noon sky, mutually-facing mirrors, and so on, to convey subtle metaphysical views. I found these images to be unreasonably suitable for such purpose. Why is consensus reality filled with images so appropriate for making sense of itself on a metaphysical level? Similarly, spiritual teachers and gurus have always made liberal use of consensus images to communicate their insights: onions to represent the nature of the ego ('you peel its layers looking for its core and, at the end, nothing is left'), waves in the ocean to represent the underlying unity of nature ('we are no more separate from the rest of nature than a wave is separate from the ocean'), etc.

The proven effectiveness of the images of consensus reality in evoking transcendent meta-images is non-trivial. In principle, there should be no reason for nature to be like that. The fact that it is is cumbersome to make sense of, *unless consensus reality itself is attempting to evoke something transcendent;* unless it is trying to say something deeper about itself through symbolism. 'Holy art Thou, O God ... *of whom All-nature hath been made an image.* ... Holy art thou, transcending all pre-eminence ... unutterable, unspeakable,' sings the Hermetic myth.[73] Sri Nisargadatta Maharaj, a twentieth century Indian sage, was less-than-cryptic about this idea: 'When you see the world you see God. There is no seeing God apart from the world. Beyond the world to see God is to be God,' he stated.[74] Nisargadatta's words echoed the teachings of Hindu saint Ramakrishna about a century earlier.[75]

Figure 3 maps these ideas onto the previous template. As

suggested by the figure, *consensus reality may be a form of symbolic language attempting to point at something else.* This 'something else' may be trying to reach out to us by appealing to our interpretative capacities. It may be posing the question: 'Here is consensus reality, the best representation of myself that I can produce. Can you figure out what it *really* means?' The question

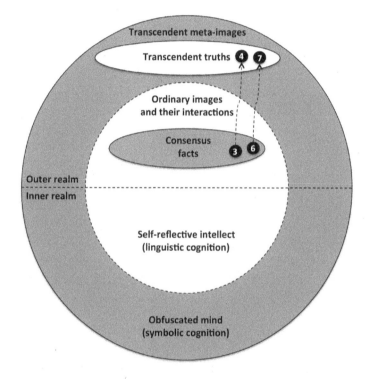

Figure 3. Consensus reality as a symbolic language pointing to transcendent truths.

isn't necessarily rhetorical or redundant, for the 'something else' may not know the answer. In fact, *we* may be the means through which it hopes to solve the riddle. *We* may be nature's best shot at coming up with the answer. *We* may be the ones responsible for helping the sun of self-reflective awareness to rise and illuminate this conundrum. For all we know, there is no other game in town. As the Pueblo myth so powerfully illustrates, the human responsibility in the dance of life may go far beyond our intellect's wildest guesses. If we fail to *observe* our rituals with sincerity and attention, the sun may no longer rise and darkness may befall the world forever. 'Contemplator of God's works did man become; he marveled and did *strive to know their Author,'* continues the Hermetic myth.[76]

The proven effectiveness of the images of consensus reality in evoking transcendent ideas is non-trivial. It is as though consensus reality were a symbolic language connoting something beyond or behind itself, which may be trying to reach out to us.

Chapter 4

Myth and no-myth

Earlier, I've said that it is nearly impossible to live life without a myth, for an on-going effort at interpreting consensus reality is part-and-parcel of the human condition. Yet, throughout much of history, there have been spiritual traditions whose aim has been precisely that: to reach an interpretation-free state of awareness; a state of pure observation, without commentary. Among these traditions one can count Zen Buddhism, Advaita Vedanta, Dzogchen and certain Western variations. Collectively, these traditions today are usually lumped under the term 'nondualism.' I will call them the traditions of *no-myth*, so to emphasize their contrast with what we have been discussing thus far. In the West, the traditions of no-myth roughly correspond to what has been called the *'via negativa'*—theologies of negation that attempt to characterize transcendence by stating what it is *not*—as opposed to the *'via positiva'* of mythology.[77]

There is an obvious justification for no-myth traditions that is entirely consistent with—and, in fact, emerges naturally from— everything we have discussed earlier: because transcendent truths cannot be rationalized in words, no religious myth can be *literally* true. As such, all religious myths are *literally* false. It is easy to see how this realization could have led entire spiritual traditions to a complete rejection of the intellect and all myths. Clearly, the motivation behind such rejection does not contradict the *non-literal* truth of religious myths that we have been exploring in this book. Nonetheless, it is also clear that the outright exclusion of all myths implies, on the face of it, a clear conflict with the role and value of mythology. This ambiguous interplay between myth and no-myth traditions is prone to misinterpretation, requiring the more in-depth analysis that is the purpose of this chapter. Before we proceed, however, some brief clarifications are necessary.

First, it would be simplistic and false to conclude that the traditions of no-myth are exclusive to the East or that mythical traditions are exclusive to the West. Many Christian mystics— like Dionysius the Areopagite, Meister Eckhart, Johannes Tauler, Heinrich Suso, Jan van Ruysbroeck, etc.—echo no-myth approaches, whilst many Eastern religions—Hinduism, Tibetan Buddhism, Zoroastrianism, Mandaeism, etc.—are rich in myths.

Second, what follows isn't intended as a thorough or scholarly review of the ways in which the traditions of myth and no-myth can help one achieve transcendent insight. It also isn't intended as a complete review of the subtle complementarities between myth and no-myth approaches. My intention here is to briefly *suggest* the intertwining roles of myth and no-myth, as well as their potential pitfalls, in the search for the transcendent truths of nature. This book—a book about religious myths—would be omissive without it. Moreover, this chapter is heavily colored by my own personal experiences, as you will soon notice. This isn't the most scholarly way to approach the subject, but it is certainly sincere, genuine and vivid.

The traditions of no-myth

A passage by Adyashanti describes well the interpretation-free state of awareness that no-myth traditions seek to achieve:

> The mind compulsively *interprets* what it is aware of (the object) in a mechanical and distorted way. It begins to *draw conclusions* and *make assumptions* according to past conditioning. ... In true meditation, the emphasis is on being awareness; not on being aware of objects, but on resting as primordial awareness itself. ... An attitude of open receptivity, *free of any goal* or anticipation, will facilitate the presence of *silence and stillness.*[78]

Versluis' characterization of the *via negativa* echoes this: it 'is not concerned with the symbolism and meaning of nature so much as with the sheer transcendence of gnosis.'[79]

Notice how this seems antithetical to religious mythology. Instead of seeking to interpret the images and interactions of consensus reality (the 'objects' or 'symbols') to derive meaning and emotional significance from them, the emphasis is on relinquishing all effort of interpretation. Instead of seeking to achieve the goal of cracking the riddle of creation, the emphasis is on abandoning all goals. Instead of actively engaging with the cognitive activity of the obfuscated mind to understand its insights, the emphasis is on silence and stillness. So, do the traditions of no-myth fundamentally contradict the importance and value of religious myths? No, but this is probably the most delicate and easily misconstrued point of this book. So take a deep breath and bear with me.

In the traditions of no-myth, the emphasis is on stopping the effort to interpret consensus reality, thereby relinquishing all myths. Instead of actively engaging with the symbolic activity of the obfuscated mind to understand its insights, the emphasis is on silence and stillness.

Transcendence with no-myth

The essence of the no-myth traditions is to free the human being from the myriad little myths that imprison us in intellectual cages of delusion. Not every myth is a true religious myth, mind you. Most people—and I am no exception to this—instinctively run an arsenal of delusory codes for interpreting the world, which arise out of past conditioning. If I was conditioned to think poorly of myself, I might interpret the way someone looks at me as a sign of disdain, while the person might have, in fact, looked at me with shy curiosity. My false interpretation of a consensus fact—the particular way the person looked at me—arises from a conditioned, delusory myth of self-worth. If I was conditioned to think of the world as a dangerous and malevolent place, I might interpret an offer of help from a stranger as a threat, while the stranger might have, in fact, genuinely wanted to be of service. My false interpretation of a consensus fact—the offer of help from a stranger—arises from a conditioned, delusory myth about the nature of the world. And so on. Much of what we think to be part of consensus reality is, in fact, delusional interpretations generated by these conditioned myths. The no-myth traditions seek to help us free ourselves from their tyranny.

The most damaging delusory myth most of us adopt has to do with the relationship between outer and inner realms. As I related in an earlier book,[80] one of my strongest childhood memories is of a period of a few months during which I slowly accepted the notion that I was separate from the rest of the world. I still remember how weird this notion felt to me at the time. Apparently, I had always only existed inside my own skin; I wasn't, and had never been, the rest of the world around me; the trees, sky and other people had never been part of me. How could that possibly be? It violated my most innate intuitions. Yet, obviously it was the case, wasn't it? I remember literally getting a cold shiver down my spine every time I thought of it, so alien the idea was. Until one day it didn't feel strange anymore. Right there and then, a delusory myth caught hold of me through conditioning.

The delusory myth of personal identity and separateness is at the root of human suffering. *It is also at the root of our loss of contact with transcendence.* The intellectual reasons I believe this myth to be entirely delusory have been expounded in my earlier books *Why Materialism Is Baloney* and *Brief Peeks Beyond*. Those interested in the argument can consult those books. The point I want to focus on here is this: by helping one drop the delusory myth of personal identity and separateness, the traditions of no-myth also bring a form transcendence back into one's everyday life, just like religious myths do! After all, if one no longer feels limited to the ego and the body, one automatically transcends ordinary human boundaries. Indeed, *much of what we refer to as 'the human condition' is itself a deprived myth that, if abandoned, opens space for a spontaneous reconciliation with timelessness and boundlessness.* In this particular sense, the traditions of myth and no-myth ultimately lead to the same destination through different roads.

This is not all I have to say about the dichotomy of myth versus no-myth. It isn't even the most important point yet. But before I advance my argument further I want to elaborate on a concrete, illustrative example of how myth and no-myth can lead to the same destination.

> By enabling one to drop the delusory myth of personal identity and separateness, the traditions of no-myth also help bring a form of transcendence back into one's everyday life, just like religious myths do.

Advaita Vedanta and Christianity

There is a striking analogy between, for instance, Advaita Vedanta—a tradition of no-myth—and Christianity—a highly mythical tradition—when it comes to the manner in which they help an individual relate more harmoniously to reality. Before you feel compelled to point out how these two traditions differ dramatically in their respective outlooks, let me emphasize what I said: the analogy I see is *in the way they help an individual relate more harmoniously to reality,* not in a similarity of outlooks.

As we've seen earlier, a major source of human suffering is

the claustrophobic interpretation of the world entailed by the deprived myth that we are separate from the rest nature—that is, *that we are our egos*. It is this interpretation that leads to the existential despair discussed in Chapter 1. Indeed, suffering arises from the ego's inability, *yet compulsive need*, to control the world. If it could dictate nature's behavior, we would all be happy tyrants. Naturally, the ego is well aware that it cannot have everything it wants or avoid all that it doesn't want. But it can't stop trying either! Hence, the ego is constantly at war with what is, was and could be. This is why we suffer. Advaita Vedanta and Christianity help us tackle this fundamental cause of suffering in surprisingly analogous ways.

Advaita aims to stop all suffering by dis-identification with the ego. In other words, an Advaita practitioner seeks to drop the myth of identification with his own thoughts, emotions, beliefs and personality. The practitioner *has* thoughts, but he *isn't* those thoughts; he *has* feelings, but he *isn't* those feelings; etc. A successful Advaita practitioner will identify himself only with pure awareness: an impersonal, interpretation-free witness. He will still maintain an ego, but instead of believing himself to *be* the ego, he will *use* the ego as a tool for interacting with the world. At the moment this state of 'enlightenment' is achieved, suffering—though not necessarily physical pain—stops. In a strong sense, the ego is demoted from king of the hill to a small, limited, yet useful servant of impersonal awareness.

Now let's look at Christianity. Christians also suffer because of the inability of their egos to control the world: they can't have all they want, they can't avoid all adversity and they can't stop death, no matter how hard they pray. Their myth offers a way to deal with this dilemma through a form of surrender to a higher power: they place their fate 'in the hands of God,' as former American president Jimmy Carter said upon announcing his cancer diagnosis. *By handing over its responsibilities and struggles to a higher power, the ego withdraws from its war against reality.* As a consequence, it also finds itself demoted from king of the hill to a small, limited, yet useful servant of something universal. Do you see the correspondence with Advaita? In the inner realm, the lessening of a tremendous burden is achieved in both cases, as if a huge load were lifted off of one's shoulders. The futile struggle against reality stops.

Advaita seeks to achieve this result by the rejection of every myth: it entails no narratives or theories of any kind. Its masters simply try to point the way for you to *drop* the myth of identification with the ego. Instead of trying to *describe* what enlightenment is, they focus their attention on helping you *experience* enlightenment directly. As such, Advaita has appeal to me as a skeptic empiricist. It soothes my instinctive fear of falling prey to wish fulfillment. The price, however, seems to be a kind of dryness and aloofness that may come across as non-empathetic. As humans, we crave empathy and reassurance, which is natural and legitimate. Moreover, dis-identification with all thought and emotion may end suffering, but is it really natural, given that thought and emotion are so inherent to the human condition?

Christianity, on the other hand, achieves an analogous result through a plethora of narratives and symbols. Instead of the barren landscapes of Advaita, it provides one with an incredibly rich and meaningful myth that speaks directly to the obfuscated mind.[81] Empathy, compassion and reassurance abound. Instead of the elusive concept of impersonal awareness, Christianity offers the idea of a transcendent divinity incarnated as a flesh-and-blood man. How much easier it is for the ego to surrender to such a concrete father figure, handing over its struggles to Him, instead of accepting itself to be a mere illusion! The price of this richness and accessibility, however, is the difficulty faced by any rational person to accept the narratives of the Christian myth uncritically enough. And make no mistake: the power of the narratives is entirely dependent on their being believed. 'A myth can only "work" when it is thought to be truth, and man cannot for long knowingly and intentionally "kid" himself,'[82] said Watts, an Episcopal priest who knew this problem well. One must, somehow, muster enough *faith* in the Holy Trinity for it to be of any help in achieving the surrender of the ego. This isn't trivial in today's cynical and overly-intellectualized cultural ethos.

Clearly, Advaita and Christianity represent different trade-offs. They may appeal to different people with different proclivities. But they aren't dissimilar in at least the one aspect discussed above. This alone shows how myth and no-myth can, despite apparent contradictions, lead to the same destination.

Finally, notice that, although I've been using Christianity and Advaita as examples, the point is more generic. Consider, for instance, Islam: the very word 'Islam' means 'surrender;' to surrender and submit oneself to a universal will—the will of God—much beyond the ego's petty desires. Here is a religious myth that results in over one and a half billion people worldwide prostrating themselves to a power beyond the ego; not one, but five times a day. It's easy to see how this, too, reflects the parallel discussed above.

Both Advaita Vedanta (no-myth) and Christianity (myth) help ease suffering by enabling one to drop one's futile struggle against reality. Advaita does this by dis-identification with the ego. Christianity, by surrender to a higher power. Indeed, this parallel goes beyond Advaita and Christianity alone.

The pitfalls of no-myth

The potential pitfalls of religious myths are well known and publicized in our culture. We have already discussed them earlier: when one adopts a religious myth *intellectually* as the *literal* truth, one not only loses sight of the transcendent reality one seeks, but also stokes the fire of fundamentalism. Moreover, the seeming implausibility of religious myths often renders them unpalatable, given our culture's excessive emphasis on the intellect. However, the traditions of no-myth also have subtle and less-publicized pitfalls. Below, in the interest of balance, I will dare suggest what these may be.

It is as striking as it is undeniable how conducive the human organism is to the myth of separateness. Whatever the ultimate truth may be, we clearly *seem* to be discrete individuals, separate from the rest of nature. If, in reality, this is not so, then we are left with two alternatives: either the human organism evolved the tendency for this delusion by accident, or the delusion is a side-effect of some other evolutionary pressure.[83] Watts offers us a clue:

> One can only attempt a rational, descriptive philosophy of the universe on the assumption that one is totally separate from it. But if you and your thoughts are part of this universe, you cannot stand outside them to describe them. This is why all philosophical and theological systems must ultimately fall apart.[84]

He eloquently expresses the essence of the no-myth traditions: separateness is a delusion and, therefore, all myths ultimately fall apart. There is an obvious validity to what Watts says,[85] but I believe he misses a crucially important point.

The human intellect does have the unique ability to 'stand outside' its own thoughts in the sense that it can *think about its thoughts*. We can also stand outside our emotions in the sense that we can *ponder our emotions*. We can even stand outside ourselves in the sense that we can contemplate our situation in the world as if we were looking at ourselves from the outside. This capacity is what we call *self-reflective awareness* and it is essential for making sense of nature.[86] Without it, we would be completely immersed in the turbulent waters of instinct, unable to even ask ourselves what's going on. Only through self-reflective awareness can we raise our heads above the water and lucidly try to steer our way. Therefore, if it is true that the images of consensus reality point to a transcendent truth—as suggested in Figure 3—then our capacity for self-reflection is nature's only chance of solving the conundrum. Think about this for a moment: without the capacity for self-reflection embodied in us, nature would stand no chance of groking itself; it would never be able to raise its head above the waters of its own instinctive unfolding.

Now, this uniquely human capacity seems intimately tied to our tendency to think of ourselves as discrete entities, separate from the rest of nature. *At the very moment that we become able to 'stand outside' our own thoughts and emotions, we also become able to 'stand outside' the rest of nature.* Do you see how these things come together? Whatever evolutionary pressure pushed the human organism towards self-reflection also rendered it vulnerable to the myth of separateness. Perhaps this delusory myth was never the point. Perhaps the delusion of separateness is merely an unwelcome but natural side-effect.

Be it as it may, a potential pitfall of the no-myth traditions is the temptation to throw away the baby with the bath water: to reject, along with the myth of separateness, the value of self-reflection for interpreting the phenomenal world, simply because they seem to come together. Moreover, because we cannot derive meaning from the outer realm without interpreting it, *by rejecting interpretative effort the no-myth traditions may also mislead us towards the conclusion that consensus reality is meaningless.* These potential pitfalls were clear, for instance, in a 1936 dialogue between a truth-seeker and Sri Ramana Maharshi, a sage of the no-myth traditions. The truth-seeker asked: 'Should we not find out the ultimate reality of the world, individual and God?' to which Ramana Maharshi replied:

These are all conceptions of the [delusory separate] "I." They arise only after the advent of the "I-thought". Did you think of them in your deep sleep? You existed in deep sleep and the same you are now speaking. If they be real should they not be in your sleep also? ... So these are *only* your conceptions.[87]

Hence, the 'ultimate reality of the world' is *'only'* a conception of the delusory separate 'I.' It is easy to conclude from this that self-reflective inquiry about the world is futile. Personally, I do not think that Ramana Maharshi—or any other truly enlightened sage, for that matter—ever meant it quite this way. I believe this is a misunderstanding arising from the ambiguities of language, as well as the specific context of the original dialogue. Whatever the case, however, the potential for such misunderstanding is blatant.

Those seduced by this line of thought reckon that consensus reality is a pointless, useless drama; a cosmic mistake of sorts. They reckon that nothing in consensus reality is important or means anything. Therefore, nothing in it needs to be reflected upon. They see all consensus images as mere illusion, dream, *'maya;'* nothing we need to pay careful attention to. They overlook the possibility that *the transcendent truth may only be able to express itself through the illusions it generates.* They fail to see that, even though our nightly dreams are illusions (no, you didn't really fall from a building last night), they do symbolically reveal something intimate and true about us (perhaps you are afraid of letting go or anxious about losing control).

Even if consensus reality is indeed an illusion, why does the illusion look and feel like *this*, instead of something else? What does *this*—in all its details and nuances—say about the fundamental nature of whatever is generating the illusion? Do you see what I am trying to suggest? Something beyond our egos must be giving rise to the illusion of consensus reality, in the same way that a loudspeaker gives rise to sound. For the same reason that the sounds produced by a loudspeaker say something about the loudspeaker's structure—even though the structure is incommensurable with the sounds—the illusions we call consensus reality may be saying something about a transcendent truth. If they are, it is certainly not futile to actively engage our capacity for self-reflection and inquire into the images of the world.

A potential pitfall of the no-myth traditions is the failure to see that not only may illusions carry symbolic truth, they may embody the *only possible* expression of transcendence. Those who fail to realize this close their eyes to the clues that nature so laboriously makes available to us. They forget Nisargadatta Maharaj's revealing words quoted earlier: 'When you see the world you see God. There is no seeing God apart from the world.'[88] Or even Ramana Maharshi's paradoxical words: 'The world is illusory. Brahman alone is real. *The world is Brahman.*'[89] If the universe is essentially an assemblage of symbols, it is up to us to make something out of it through attentive observation and self-reflection. What is the symbolic narrative we call 'life' trying to say? What does it suggest about the transcendent character of the loudspeaker generating it? If our capacity for self-reflection is nature's only chance to address these questions, dismissing the illusion is a nature-denying tragedy.

> The no-myth traditions may reject self-reflective interpretations of the world along with the myth of separateness. They may fail to recognize that the illusion of consensus reality may be the symbolic expression of transcendence. If so, self-reflection is crucial for groking the symbolism.

Myth and no-myth working together

All this said, let us also not make the opposite mistake. It is a fact that most of us are constantly consumed by the myriad delusory, deprived myths that distort our apprehension of consensus reality, starting with the myth of personal identity and separateness. *It is important to drop these pernicious myths, lest we become unable to see the symbols of consensus reality for what they really are.* Without dropping the delusions, our vision remains blocked and distorted. Unable to see the symbols clearly, what chance do we have to properly reflect upon them and articulate new, more powerful myths? In this sense, the no-myth traditions are essential for the advancement of religious myths. Indeed, pre-literate cultures like the Arandan and Uitoto aren't as severely victimized by the myth of separateness as our Western culture, embodying instead a more collective identity, more integrated with their natural environment. Maybe partly for this reason, their mythology is disproportionately sophisticated for the relative simplicity of their culture.

Moreover, it is also a fact that the intellect alone can never deliver transcendent truths, as discussed extensively in the previous chapter. Insofar as the no-myth traditions help us put our intellect in its proper place—that of servant, not of ruler— they help us attune to our true, deepest intuitions. This, too, is essential for healthy myth-making.

Myth and no-myth can be complementary. The traditions of no-myth help us put the intellect in its proper place and attune to our mythical intuition. They also help us unblock our view of the symbols of consensus reality, so we can reflect upon them more clearly and advance religious myths.

The true value of self-reflection

I've emphasized the importance of our unique capacity for self-reflection in interpreting the symbols immanent in consensus reality. The idea, as illustrated in Figure 3, was that the images and interactions of consensus reality are themselves pointing to transcendent truths. As such, it is our role as human beings to engage our capacity for self-reflection and attempt to unveil those truths. To do so, we need to bring our deepest obfuscated intuitions up into the field of self-reflection, where they can then be properly elaborated so as to produce answers.

But there is a problem: self-reflection is largely an *intellectual* capacity. At the very moment that we bring an originally obfuscated intuition up into the field of self-reflection, we place it in the intellect and, therefore, confine it to language. And since language cannot capture transcendent truths, the whole exercise seems to defeat itself. If we try to apply self-reflection to a transcendent idea, we end up losing its very transcendence through the filter of language; we end up with a well-elaborated circle, but miss the cylinder altogether. Does this mean that our capacity for self-reflection is, after all, useless for decoding the symbols of consensus reality? Does this mean that the no-myth traditions are, after all, right in dismissing the intellect? No, but to see how and why we need to flip our perspective by 180 degrees.

The true value of self-reflection is not in answering, but in asking. As we've seen above, the self-reflective but language-limited intellect will never be able to produce the transcendent answer to the riddle of life. *But by progressively refining the way the riddle is posed — that is, the way the questions are asked — the intellect can nudge and guide the obfuscated mind toward increasingly more insightful answers.* Indeed, the limitation of the obfuscated mind is not its ability to arrive at answers: as argued in the previous chapter, its range of cognition is much broader than that of the intellect. The limitation of the obfuscated mind is that, because it lacks self-reflection, *it simply doesn't occur to it to ask the questions.*

Here is a way to think about this: when you are dreaming, it simply doesn't occur to you to ask self-reflective questions that

74

could help you navigate the dream: 'How did I end up here? What am I doing? Why am I doing it? Where can I go next?' And so on. Instead, you simply remain immersed in the twists and turns of the dream, uncritically and unquestioningly, like a leaf in the wind. This happens because, while in a regular dream, you lose your ability to self-reflect; you lose the ability to stand out of yourself and evaluate your situation critically. My claim is that the obfuscated mind is just as uncritical and unquestioning as the dream state. We know this because, after all, *dreams are expressions of the obfuscated mind.*[90] As such, by its very nature, the obfuscated mind can't stand out of itself; it doesn't occur to it to ask the deeper questions about the nature of self and world.

That's why the obfuscated mind needs the self-reflective intellect to nudge and guide it toward answers. *For as long as the right questions aren't asked by the intellect, the ultimate answers of life and reality will remain elusive.* And here is where we, self-reflective human beings, may have a crucial role to play: to ask the questions that will evoke the deepest transcendent answers, thereby making them a living reality. Only then will nature truly figure out what's going on. And to properly play our role, we need to engage our capacities for attentive observation and self-reflection, otherwise we won't know what questions to ask. 'Asking the proper question is the central action of transformation ... The key question causes germination of consciousness. The properly shaped question always emanates from an essential curiosity about what stands behind. Questions are the keys that cause the secret doors of the psyche to swing open,'[91] wrote Clarissa Estés.

This is the natural way the linguistic intellect and the symbolic obfuscated mind spontaneously cooperate. The intellect self-reflectively contemplates its circumstances and asks progressively more refined questions, while the obfuscated mind—nudged along by these questions—reacts intuitively with symbolic answers. As a matter of fact, this is how every creative person ordinarily operates in any area of intellectual activity, from science to business: first, the intellect contemplates the problem and iterates upon the right questions to ask. Then, you must stop thinking, so the questions have a chance to sink into the obfuscated mind. Once they do, inspiration suddenly strikes, as if out of nowhere. Don't you recognize this in your own personal experience? If you do, it's because this is the natural manner in which the human mind operates. The natural role of self-reflection—even in ordinary situations—is to ask the right questions, as opposed to composing creative or original answers through mechanical steps of reasoning. Of course, the answers are just as good as the questions asked, so self-reflection remains just as important as if the intellect constructed the answers itself.

If the questions sink in, the obfuscated mind always reacts with answers: it is a mental reflex. But for as long as these answers remain there, in the obfuscated mind, they are of limited value to ordinary life. Their true impact is only realized when we intuitively and emotionally *experience* them with less obfuscation. And since answers to the ultimate questions of life and reality are always intrinsically transcendent, *the only way to reduce their obfuscation is to frame them in the form of a religious myth.* So here we come full-circle: if consensus reality is a symbol of something transcendent, the only way to unveil the symbol's meaning is, again, through religious myth. *Our myth-making capacity may be our key role in the dance of existence.* Only through advancing myth may we be able to ensure that the sun continues to rise every day.

The true value of intellectual self-reflection is not in answering, but in asking the right questions. By progressively refining the questions, the intellect can nudge and guide the broader obfuscated mind toward increasingly more insightful answers.

Consensus reality evoking religious myths

Figure 4 summarizes all these ideas in our familiar template. A lucidly observed consensus fact (1) triggers the self-reflective intellect into stating a critical question in language (2). This is a question we ask ourselves without being able to compose a satisfying intellectual answer. Instead, the question sinks in and pokes the obfuscated mind into spontaneously reacting with a symbolic answer (3), which—if we are attuned and receptive—percolates up into the intellect in the form of a language narrative (4). This language narrative evokes ordinary images and respective interactions (5) that are *not* consensus facts. Instead, the images and interactions connote a transcendent truth (6). The whole chain 1-2-3-4-5-6 is, thus, *a religious myth evoked by consensus reality itself.* As such, consensus reality isn't inherently meaningless or purposeless, as the traditions of no-myth may inadvertently suggest. On the contrary: it is a symbol actively engaging our self-reflective intellect to generate the right questions and, through them, our myth-making obfuscated mind to unveil the answers.

Consensus reality is trying to get us to ask the right questions. Dramatic life events are forceful, maybe desperate attempts to lead us to these questions. A tremendous mystery unfolds in front of our senses every waking hour of our lives; a mystery more profound, more tantalizing, more penetrating and urgent than any novel or thriller. This unfolding mystery is nature's challenge to us. *Are we paying enough attention to it?* Or are we,

---

Consensus reality is trying to get our intellects to ask the right questions, so to poke the obfuscated mind into unveiling the deepest transcendent truths in the form of religious myths. As such, our myth-making capacity may be nature's only chance to grok itself.

---

instead, cavalierly dismissing the whole thing as meaningless illusion?

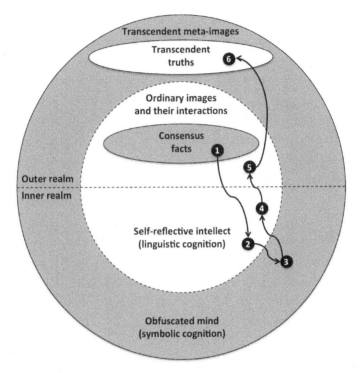

Figure 4. Consensus reality evoking a religious myth.

Breaking through religious myths

There is another sense in which the traditions of myth and no-myth can arrive at the same destination. As we've seen, a true religious myth indicates the way to transcendent truths. It isn't the moon, but the finger pointing at the moon. Some of us—the cynics, literalists and fundamentalists—stay fixated on the finger, never looking at what it is pointing at. Others take the hint and discover that beautiful celestial body reigning over the night sky. *But a few go beyond watching and visit the moon itself.* These latter ones actualize an intrinsic potential we cannot ignore. It is very hard to describe this potential in generic terms, so I will relate a personal story instead.

I was raised in a largely Catholic extended family and exposed to the Christian myth and liturgy from childhood. Concurrently, I was also strongly influenced by science and the scientific mentality, thanks largely to my father. As a child, the apparent contradictions between these two worldviews didn't bother me. However, as I grew up and became more critical, things changed. By the time I went to University at seventeen, I was already dismissing the Christian myth as mere fiction and continued to do so for many years thereafter. The scope of my interest in the Christian world became reduced—or so I told myself—to the history and architecture of Europe's medieval churches. Yet, this modest interest was enough to maintain a tenuous, delicate link to the myth.

Each time I went to a church and watched the faithful in prayer, I caught myself wondering how the Christian myth could have such a strong hold in the souls of so many otherwise rational people. It didn't make sense to me and the whole thing felt like a puzzle I couldn't solve. As my interest in, and knowledge of, psychology grew, my curiosity in this regard became even more acute. 'How? Why? What is it in this myth that has such a grip in the mind of Western civilization?' To simply dismiss the whole thing by labeling it 'delusion' would be—or so I felt—a lazy and unsatisfying way out. It would represent a puerile refusal to acknowledge an undeniable and rather remarkable psychosocial *fact*, so one wouldn't need to understand it. With the risk of sounding arrogant, I was too thoughtful to take such a dull-witted exit.

One day, I had an experience that answered all those questions to my own satisfaction. I happened to be visiting one of Europe's oldest and largest churches: Cologne Cathedral, in Germany. I had no specific agenda during my visit. I was just there, absorbing the 'vibe' of that amazing place. As it happens, my gaze got caught by the large crucifix above the golden shrine

Figure 5. The shrine of the Three Kings behind the altar of Cologne's Cathedral, Germany.

of the Three Kings (see Figure 5). There was the figure of a man, nailed to a cross, in a dramatic depiction of great human sacrifice. At once something flipped inside me, like a sudden shift of perspective: *I had gotten it.* I had been suddenly 'carried over'[92] directly to the transcendent cognitive space the icon was pointing to all along. I *knew* what the Christian symbolism was attempting to convey. 'The Event of the symbol is a stunning, unexpected moment when something ... in the world takes your breath away,'[93] explained Cheetham quite accurately. Could I articulate my epiphany in language? I could try, but I know that it would be completely misunderstood, no matter how carefully I chose my words. I know it because *I* would misunderstand it completely if someone else tried to describe it to me. The insight escapes language and can only be conveyed—precariously as it may admittedly be—through the religious myth. All I can say is this: that sudden epiphany confirmed the validity of the Christian myth to me and, *simultaneously*, shredded it to pieces. It was an 'Aha!' moment that, while making clear *why* the Christian myth is what it is—it simply couldn't be any different—it also showed that the truth has *very little* to do with the myth *as expressed in words*. Although this may sound like a contradiction, my living experience wasn't contradictory at all: it made perfect sense at a non-intellectual, heart-felt level. I had glanced at the cylinder beyond the shadows.

The experience I am trying to describe wasn't rapture or ecstasy. It was simply an *insight of understanding* that escapes the boundaries of the intellect and resolves paradoxes; a syzygy or *coniunctio*, as Jung called it.[94] It was like a subtle but powerful *shift of perspective* that instantly placed me where the myth had been pointing to all along. In my childhood I could see the moon; in my early adulthood I could only see the finger pointing at the moon; but, during that fleeting moment in Cologne Cathedral, my cognition left the firm earth of the intellect and *I was on the moon*.

I could only characterize this experience as serendipitous grace. Other than to say that the religious myth—by pointing— somehow helps create the *conditions* for the experience, I don't know how or why it actually happens. I only know *that* it happens. Either way, here is the point I am trying to make: when the experience does happen, *the religious myth dissolves itself* like clouds dissolve as they surrender their rain. After all, once on the moon, one no longer needs to follow the pointing finger. If anything, *one finds the finger pointing directly at oneself!* In the template of Figure 2, it is as if one's cognitive vantage point shifted from the intellect (12) to transcendence itself (14); from the earth to the moon.

It is this graceful self-dissolution of a religious myth that brings us back to the traditions of no-myth. In both cases, there are no narratives left to speak of, but only a direct, living, transcendent experience of truth. Yet, as discussed earlier, this transcendent experience is usually short-lived. It certainly was for me and I don't know anyone who lives permanently on the moon. Therefore, *even for those lucky souls who receive the grace of experiencing a transcendent truth directly,* the religious myth remains an important reminder; an important link to transcendence that infuses meaning into earthly life after one's cognitive vantage point returns to the intellect. The pointing finger now says: 'Look! You've been there! Never forget what you knew to be true then!'

And as for those still to leave the earth for the first time, the religious myth allows them to know that the moon exists. It allows them to contemplate the *true* beauty and transcendence of the moon from a distance, even if only with their peripheral vision. The clearest view possible, as we've seen, is achieved when one takes the religious myth *emotionally* onboard *as though* it were the literal truth. This is well worth the effort. After all, being able to watch the moon from the earth, although admittedly not the same as being on the moon, certainly allows for a much broader and truer view of *reality* than spending a lifetime staring at the ground. Moreover, who knows when serendipitous grace might strike?

A religious myth can create the conditions for a direct experience of a transcendent reality. If and when the experience actually happens, the myth dissolves itself. But once the experience is over, the religious myth remains an important link—a reminder—between ordinary life and transcendence.

PART II: Truth

These things never happened, but they always are.
Sallust

Chapter 5

The quest for truth

You've just finished reading Part I of a book that deals largely with religious myths. Why have you read it? What made you pick up this book? Why are you interested in religious myths to begin with? What is it about religion that has so powerfully drawn the soul of humankind for so many generations?

The answer is the innate, irresistible intuition most of us share that religious myths can point the way to a truth beyond the appearances of ordinary life; a truth that promises to liberate us from existential despair. The very existence of religious myths reflects humankind's archetypal quest for liberation.

Yet, because of the elusive nature of truth, the successful truth-seeker needs to negotiate his or her way through a vast tangle of subtlety, nuance, self-deception and paradox. So before we begin to talk about the destination—that is, about truth itself—let us illustrate the nature and challenges of the path in the form of a *myth* (What other format could be more appropriate?). This will give us intuitive context and set the stage for everything that follows.

The myth below is the story of Castor and Pollux, twin brothers that couldn't be more different. Their epic journey mirrors aspects of ourselves as we seek liberation. Indeed, Castor and Pollux live within me as they probably live within every human being who is sincerely engaged in this ultimate quest. By hinting at the very questions we will soon be facing, I hope their story will prime you for the remainder of this book.

The seer

Castor and Pollux sailed far, to a distant island beyond the boundaries of maps, in search of Phineus, the seer. Upon arriving, exhausted but exultant, they immediately sought an audience with the famed blind prophet. Pollux, carefully trying to disguise his identity as son of Zeus—who had caused the blindness of Phineus—was the first to speak:

—Greetings, wise seer. My brother Castor and I are on a quest for truth. But we know not which course to pursue. Bewildered as we are by the myriad myths of man, we humbly plea for your guidance.

Phineus looked over the two brothers with compassion. He knew the inevitability of what was to follow. After a long sigh, he replied:

—There are only two authentic paths to truth, young seekers. Man has no shortage of myths at his disposal. If his true motivation is to find peace, he must search for the myth that resonates with his heart and make it his life and reality. This, the path of the heart, is legitimate and true to man's nature.

He paused, knowing full well what he was about to do to the son of his nemesis:

—The other path is one on which many truth-seekers before you have found their demise. It is the path of the absolute: the rejection of every myth in the quest for a truth as pure and untarnished by the touch of man's thoughts as a buried jewel in the bowels of the Earth. This path requires the rigorous cleansing of raw experience from the narratives constantly woven and projected by the intellect. Behold, for he who finds and polishes this jewel will know the absolute truth!

Castor—whose mother, like Pollux's, was Leda, but whose father was the mortal king Tyndareus—interjected:

—How do we know which path to choose, great seer?

Phineus:

—Find out what is your deepest, most uncritical, most sincere motivation, young seeker! What does your heart truly yearn for? Peace?

And then, turning slightly to glance at Pollux, he continued:

—Or the absolute truth? Listen to your heart and, above all, be honest to yourself. This is the most intimate of all quests. In its pursuit, you cannot deceive anyone but yourself.

Pollux and Castor, confused but resigned, thanked Phineus and returned to their ship. The darkness of the night had already descended upon them.

The choices

On the deck of their ship, bathed by the light of many stars— Gemini particularly conspicuous above their heads—Castor shared his thoughts with his brother:

—I must be honest about my most sincere motivation, brother. Truthfully, what I seek is peace. The confusion, doubts and insecurities of life corrode my very soul. If I can find safe haven in a myth whose validity my heart can accept, there my quest will end.

Pollux:

—I respect the sincerity of your choice, brother. But truthfully, no myth can sooth my heart. I must know what *is*, not the narratives woven by my own thoughts or the thoughts of lesser men.

The brothers then parted ways, each pursuing the path dictated by his heart.

Castor's quest

Having scoured the known world for the many myths and traditions of man, Castor failed to find the peace he yearned for. He did find a handful of myths that resonated deeply with his heart, but how could he surrender to a myth while knowing that it was just a narrative, a story? How could his heart be soothed by something he knew fell short of a direct depiction of the absolute truth?

Castor, diligent and attentive as he was, could observe his own intellect in the process of weaving narratives—arbitrary explanations for the harsh realities of life—whose true motivation was to sooth his suffering. The narratives were self-created wish-fulfilling devices. Castor was aware that he was trying to trick himself. But how could the trick have any effect upon one who knew how it was done?

Pollux's quest

Having spent years in seclusion in some of the most isolated islands of the Aegean carefully observing the dynamics of his own mind, Pollux sought diligently to separate the jewel of immediate experience from the pollution of explanations and predictions. He saw through the many layers of narrative-making: stories built on top of stories, all ultimately resting upon unexamined assumptions and circularity. He realized that removing the narratives was like peeling an onion: there was always another, more subtle layer underneath.

In his quest, he tried to find the most basic, raw factors of reality: he had a body; that seemed free of narratives. His bodily sensations in the present moment seemed as close to an apprehension of the raw truth as he could get. The past and the future were just stories. Extrapolating this line of thinking, he concluded that only a newborn baby could experience the absolute truth, before any narrative had a chance to contaminate its sense of reality. As a grown man, such a state was not available to Pollux, but it suggested to him that an absolute truth did exist. His ultimate goal was there, just tantalizingly out of his reach.

Yet, upon further reflection, Pollux began to question his own conclusions. The possibility of narrative-free cognition in a newborn was itself a narrative; a story constructed by his intellect, since he could not experience the state of being a newborn in the present moment. Could there really be such a thing as raw cognition without narratives? Was the mind of a newborn truly story-free, or was it simply *in the process* of weaving its first stories *as* it perceived the world for the first time? Was perception fundamentally concurrent and co-dependent with the narratives that gave it context? Could anything—anything at all—be perceived without being couched in an explanatory narrative, chaotic and inconsistent as it might at first be? Pollux realized that he was forever locked in the story-making processes of his intellect. *Even his search for truth was a story.*

The meeting

After many years, the brothers met again on the deck of their trusted ship. As it floated gently on calm night seas, under the light of the full moon, Castor offered:

—Brother, I have failed in my chosen path. The soothing power of myth needs permission from the intellect to be accepted as truth. Without such permission, it is sterile. Knowing, as I do, that narratives are not the absolute truth, my intellect cannot give my heart permission to bask under the light of its chosen myth. I cannot find peace. For this reason, wise brother, I shall follow your example and pursue your path toward the absolute!

To which Pollux, in horror, replied:

—Seek not through my path, brother! It is a hall of mirrors. Nothing absolute will you find there; only reflections of yourself, layered in exquisitely subtle veneers. The intellect is an unstoppable narrative-making machine of unfathomable power. It constructs our entire world, like a cocoon that we end up inhabiting. In my search for the intellectual ideal of an 'absolute,' I have only found my own limits.

The brothers sighed as they gazed at the moon. In quiet desperation, Pollux concluded that their quest had been doomed from the start; and there was nothing to be done. He, the immortal son of a god, was defeated. But he said nothing to his brother. 'Damned be you, Phineus,' he whispered to himself instead.

The dreams

That night, they fell asleep on the deck of their ship. Pollux dreamed of Phineus. In the dream, Phineus sat by a rich banquet table, indulging his appetite and laughing hysterically at Pollux's predicament. Phineus had taken revenge on Zeus simply by telling the truth when requested to do so. What an ironic twist of fate, Pollux thought, as he descended into a domain of restless hopelessness.

Castor, in turn, dreamed that he was swimming naked in the sea, under the moonlight. He swam effortlessly, drifting along as if one with the waves. He could feel the water caressing his skin. There were no narratives... only curious, unreserved communion with the sea, the moon and the fresh air, as if they were aspects of himself he'd just been rediscovering. In the dream, he found his peace.

Chapter 6

Deconstructing truth

We usually take the meaning of the word 'truth' for granted. Part I of this book is guilty of this sin: we've freely spoken of not one but *three* kinds of truth—literal, allegorical and transcendent—without stopping for a moment to consider what the very concept of truth actually entails. We've concluded that many religious myths point to transcendent truths, but never questioned what it means for something to be true in the first place. Dictionary definitions aren't sufficient, for the question here is much deeper than mere semantics: *What hidden, unexamined metaphysical assumptions do we make when we think of truth?* Turning our attention to this question, as we are about to do, can open Pandora's proverbial box by deconstructing the foundations of our view of reality.

Three culturally sanctioned concepts of truth

It's prudent to start from the beginning: whatever else it may be, 'truth' is surely a *concept* of the human intellect. This concept isn't at all essential for experience: a five-year-old can have a rich life without it, freely conflating what we adults call reality and imagination. But after infancy, developing the notion of truth helps us to categorize experiences and organize our actions. What is entailed by this notion? What do we actually have in mind when we talk of truth? As it turns out, there are at least three different things we commonly mean by it, motivated by our cultural ethos.

The first culturally sanctioned concept of truth has to do with the validity of *perceptions* in the *present moment*. It entails that our perceptions are true only if they correspond to states of affairs that exists now, independently of our subjective inner lives. For instance, my experience of seeing daylight at noon is true because it corresponds to the presence of the sun in the sky out there. But schizophrenic hallucinations are untrue because they exist only in the subjective inner life of the schizophrenic. Notice that the mind-independent state of affairs that a true perception supposedly corresponds to must exist in the present moment, simultaneously with the perception itself. After all, the vivid re-experiencing of an episodic memory is not a true perception, for it does not correspond to a thing or event out there in the present moment. Let us call this first concept of truth *'perceptual truth.'*

The second culturally sanctioned concept of truth has to do with the validity of *explanations*, whose essential elements are *inferred past causes*. For instance, suppose that a person visits her doctor presenting a skin rash. Based on the rash's appearance and the patient's memory of a recent walk in the woods, the doctor infers that a now-invisible insect bite was the cause. After a few days, the rash clears by itself. Since this is the outcome expected in cases of mild insect bites, can we then say that the diagnosis was true? Not really: it is conceivable that the rash was caused by exposure to a chemical, cold weather, or even by clothes rubbing on the skin. In all these cases, rashes also tend to clear on their own. We can only assert that the doctor's explanation was true if it corresponded to past causes that existed independently of the doctor's conjectures: in this specific case, an actual insect piercing the patient's skin just prior to the onset of the rash. In other words, a true explanation is supposed to be more than just a story that happens to be fully consistent with the present; it must also correspond to a past state of affairs independent of subjective, internal conjectures. Notice that what we call episodic memories are, in essence, elements of our explanations for the present moment: they, too, are only considered true if corresponding to past states of affairs outside mind. Let us call this second concept of truth *'explanatory truth.'*

The third culturally sanctioned concept of truth has to do

with *predictions* and deals with *future possibilities*. For instance, imagine that Italian seismologists detect earth tremors in Sicily, suspecting that Mount Etna is going to erupt once again. A first team of seismologists runs the measured data through a first computer model and concludes that Etna, despite the tremors, isn't going to erupt any time soon. A second team then runs the same data through a second model and concludes that Etna is indeed going to erupt within a week. Imagine that the models of both teams, though different, are theoretically sound and internally consistent. Nonetheless, if Etna actually erupts within the week, only the second team's conclusion will supposedly have ever been true. Indeed, a true prediction requires more than just theoretical soundness and internal consistency: it must also correspond to a future state of affairs independent of subjective, internal expectations. Let us call this third concept of truth 'predictive truth.'

In summary, perceptual truth entails that an internal, subjective perception is true only if it corresponds to a present external state of affairs. Explanatory truth entails that an internal, subjective explanation is true only if it corresponds to a past external state of affairs. And predictive truth entails that an internal, subjective expectation is true only if it corresponds to a future external state of affairs.

Truth is a concept of the human intellect that arises after infancy. There are three culturally sanctioned concepts of truth: perceptual, explanatory (which includes memories) and predictive. They are meant to correspond to present, past and future external states of affairs, respectively.

The subjectivity of the past
All three culturally sanctioned concepts of truth require that

there be mind-independent states of affairs that our subjective inner states correspond to. But can this be the case when it comes to the past?

Think about it. Where is the past? It exists only as memories and inferences, which are inherently subjective: they aren't 'out there' but 'in here.' If you now play a video of an old family holiday on your computer, the watching of the video may be present perception, but the holiday itself is *still* just a memory. Look around you: Where is the holiday? It isn't out there, is it?

Even your conviction that your memories are true is itself subjective. You may proclaim that you know with 100% certainty that you had fish for dinner last night, but the memory of the dinner and your conviction that it corresponded to a mind-independent state of affairs are still entirely in your mind. Where else could they be? The dinner isn't out there right now and neither is your conviction in its mind-independent reality. If they exist at all, they can only exist in your mind. Can you take the dinner and the conviction in your hands right now and show them to me? You see, I am not saying that your memories are *false*—I will soon argue that this assertion is as meaningless as to claim that they are true—but that they are *subjective*.

Our confidence in the objectivity of the past arises from our subjective, intellectual models of reality. These models take our memories and perceptions as inputs and then interpolate a chain of causal links between them, so to couch the present in a coherent, reassuring and actionable context. This way, when you find yourself in a meeting room surrounded by colleagues, intellectual models of reality in your mind take your recent memories—like having driven to work in the morning and having gotten a meeting invitation from your boss yesterday—and string them together so to make sense of your perceptions in the meeting room. This linear and coherent chain of connected events is a mentally constructed *story* that reassures you and allows you to take appropriate actions. Imagine how disorienting it would be if you found yourself in a meeting room having no idea how you got there or why you were there! Your intellectual models often even *infer* past events that you don't remember at all, but which are necessary to cover eventual gaps in the storyline: you may not remember this particular morning's drive to work, but of course it happened; how else could you have gotten there, right?

Fundamentally, thus, what you call the past is the output of your intellectual models of reality. And since the models themselves, as well as the memories that feed them, are subjective, the past can't be anything other than subjective, no matter how plausible or even certain you believe it to be. Even your conviction in the objectivity of the past is a subjective result produced by these subjective models of reality. It can't be anything else.

The past is a mental, intellectual construct meant to give context to your present perceptions. There has never been a moment in your entire life in which the past has been anything else; I challenge you to find one.

Again, I am not saying that this mental construct is false; I am saying that it is a *mental construct*. It can be very easy, due to the subtlety of the topic at hand, for you to read into my words more than what I am actually saying. Therefore, I am choosing my words very carefully and ask that you follow them with attention. At this point, what I am *not* saying is probably as important as what I *am* saying.

If the past is entirely subjective, it follows that *there can never be explanatory truths*. We can never say that any explanation is true in the culturally sanctioned sense, for the past is *always* already gone; it's never out there. The best we can ever say is that the explanation is *consistent* with memories and present perceptions, like the doctor's diagnosis was consistent with the then-present perception of the rash and the patient's memory of a walk in the woods.

Because of our cultural conditioning, this idea may be tough to swallow at first, so let us dwell on it a little longer. You may claim, for instance, that if the doctor had subjected the patient to a conclusive battery of tests—biopsies, blood work, whatnot—the status of the past would be objective. We would be able to look at the test reports *now*, in the present, and know that the diagnosis of an insect bite was true. So explanatory truths are possible after all, aren't they?

Of course not. Even in this case, it would still be our intellectual models of reality that, based on subjective memories (the recall of the patient's symptoms) and present perceptions (the examination of the test reports), would produce the subjective conclusion that the patient really had an insect bite. Our confidence in this conclusion would arise solely from our subjective, intellectual inability to envision any other coherent story to connect memories to present perception. But that says nothing about the mind-independence of the conclusion. At best, it only says something about the limitations of our intellectual models. We aren't seeing the insect pierce the patient's skin right now, are we? The event exists only as an *inference* of and in the mind. It isn't out there no matter how plausible the inference. To say that the test reports *prove* that the rash was really caused by an insect bite *is just a story*, no matter how appealing. As a matter of fact, at this point even the rash is just a story, a memory in the mind. What else could it be? Where is the rash now? Where is the insect? Where is the past? Can you point at them and say 'There they are'?

Our mind generates, based on our intellectual models of reality, the stories we call the past. Moreover, we know that the mind is innately incentivized to construct these stories so 'to preserve a coherent personal narrative,'[95] which reassures us by strengthening our sense of personal self. Clearly, then, the coherence and plausibility of our image of the past, no matter how compelling, are at least suspicious as evidence for objectivity. After all, we construct this image *so to* make it coherent, plausible and reassuring to ourselves. Our commitment to the objectivity of the past arises, thus, from self-validating mental processes. It survives because of our inability to notice how we deceive ourselves; our inability to become lucid of the many nuanced layers of our own mentation.

Explanatory truths require mind-independent past states of affairs that are never really out there, for the past is *always* a mental construct. All bulletproof rational arguments for believing certain explanations are also subjective, arising from our intellectual models of the workings of nature. No matter how much we want to project our stories onto the outside, the truthfulness of any explanation will always reside in our inner lives alone. It has nowhere else to go.

Recall Joan Didion's words quoted in Part I: 'We tell ourselves stories in order to live. ... We live entirely ... by the imposition of a narrative line upon disparate images.'[96] Indeed. *All explanations are myths whose truth-value we assign subjectively.* They are true only insofar as we say that they are true. They are stories we conjure up and tell ourselves in order to make sense of the disconnected, context-free phantasmagoria of present perception. It makes no sense to proclaim any explanation for the present to be *objectively* true. And since the concept of falsity is simply the opposite of that of truth, it makes no sense to proclaim any explanation to be objectively false either. The attempt to attribute *objective* truth or falsity to any explanation is as nonsensical as the attempt to attribute marital status to the number five:[97] it simply

---

The past is a mental construct generated by subjective, intellectual models of reality fed with subjective memories and present perceptions. It isn't anywhere out there but an internal myth meant to give context to present perceptions. Thus, there can be no explanatory truths.

isn't applicable. All we can hope to establish is whether an explanation is *consistent* with memories, present perceptions and our intellectual models of reality.

The subjectivity of the future

Naturally, the same goes for the future: Where is it? It exists only as a subjective expectation. No matter how sure you are of what is going to happen in the next minute, you can't point at it and say 'There it is, the future!' It's just an image in your mind. What else could it be? Where else could it exist? Moreover, it's even cliché to say that the future is unpredictable. You may be sure that you will still be sitting where you are in the next minute but, for all you know, there may be an earthquake and your location may forcibly change. The future is always just a subjective expectation in your mind, never a mind-independent state of affairs somewhere out there.

We constantly tell ourselves the 'story of the future' because doing so is essential to the continuance of life. Without this story, we would literally grind to a halt. Why move the fork to the mouth if you haven't got a story running in your mind predicting that you will get food once you complete the motion? Why do anything or go anywhere if you haven't got a story that tells you where you will eventually arrive and what you will find there?

The future is a mental, intellectual construct meant to give perspective to your present actions. There has never been a moment in your entire life in which the future has been anything else; I challenge you to find one.

Therefore, there cannot be predictive truths, for they require mind-independent future states of affairs that are never really out there. The future, after all, *never* comes; otherwise it wouldn't be the future. *All predictions are myths whose truth-value we assign subjectively.* They are true only insofar as we say that they are true. They are stories we conjure up and tell ourselves in order to motivate action in the present. The best we can ever say is that a prediction is *consistent* with intellectual models, memories and present perceptions, like the predictions of *both* teams of seismologists regarding Mount Etna's eruption.

You may claim that, although it is strictly impossible to assign objective truth to a present prediction, in some future moment we will be able to look back and assert retroactively whether the prediction was true. For instance, one week in the future we should be able to tell for sure which team of seismologists made the correct forecast about Etna. The problem is that this very scenario *is also a prediction*. It only exists in your mentation. You are *imagining* this future moment when the truth-value of the seismologists' forecasts can be assigned in a non-subjective manner. Your mind is using an *imagined* future scenario to reinforce its own conviction in the objectivity of another *imagined* future scenario. The whole thing is circular.

Moreover, even if you were to eventually arrive at this hypothetical future, by then the original prediction about Etna's eruption would be just a *memory;* a subjective image woven in a mental narrative meant to couch your perceptions in a subjective context. You would exclaim: 'Aha! Etna is erupting just as they predicted!' But where would the original prediction exist at that moment? What else would it be but a subjective recollection that reinforces the storyline playing out in your mind at that moment? You see, we are prepared to imagine even the *memories* we would have in a hypothetical future, in order to reinforce our conviction in the objectivity of that hypothetical future. But how could *imagined future memories* possibly count as evidence for the objectivity of the future?

The sophistication and skill with which we trick ourselves in these circular cognitive games is dazzling. We *imagine* a future wherein we *remember* a past wherein we *predicted* a future that matches the future we are now imagining. From this tortuous intertwining of *imaginings* we conclude that the future and the past must exist, well, *objectively*, even though all the while we've never left the present. Wow! Do you see how we create past and future out of thin air? What an amazing trick of conditioned cognition this is! *Past and future are myths: stories in the mind.* If you truly grok this, you will be dumbfounded. When I finally did—which happened while I was sitting with friends in a restaurant—I was somewhat catatonic for a half hour, which made for some understandable gossiping around the table. You see, we believe so unreservedly in having pulled ourselves up by our own bootstraps that it stuns us to realize we actually never have. As discussed in Part III, it is this unreserved belief that creates our ordinary experience of life. But I digress.

What matters for now is this: whichever way you look at it, if you remain attentive to the many nuanced layers of your own cognitive processes, you cannot escape the inherent subjectivity of both past and future. Explanatory and predictive truths are thus mirages. They don't exist. We only ever live in the present. And it is in the present that our limited awareness of our own cognitive processes perpetuates the illusion of past and future.

The future is a mental construct generated by subjective, intellectual models of reality fed with subjective memories and present perceptions. It isn't anywhere out there but an internal myth meant to give perspective to present actions. Thus, there can be no predictive truths.

There is only ever the present

The past is *always* gone and the future *never* comes. There is only ever the present. Have you ever left the present in your entire life? Even if you had a time machine to visit the 'future,' during your visit the 'future' would be your present. You cannot escape the present; ever; not even theoretically.

Past and future exist only as mental explanations and predictions, images in the mind. *But these images are experienced in the present.* Pause and consider this. There has never been a single moment in your entire life in which the past or the future existed as anything other than images experienced in the present. Any other conclusion is simply the subjective output of an intellectual model of reality—no matter how plausible—not a mind-independent fact.

Forever locked in the now, we subjectively *project* a past backwards and a future forwards. See Figure 6. But even those projections exist only insofar as they are experienced in the present. Past and future, at bottom, are simply particular *qualities* or *configurations* of certain present experiences: the past corresponds to the qualities of remoteness and finality, while the future corresponds to fuzziness and openness. It is our intellect that mistakes these different qualities of *present* experience for an objective timeline extending back and forth. Past and future are merely concepts arising from cognitive confusion.

> Past and future exist only as mental explanations and predictions, images in the mind projected backwards and forwards. But these projections are experienced in the present, for there is only ever the present. Our intellect mistakes particular qualities of certain present experiences for a past and a future.

Figure 6. Past and future are subjective projections of present mentation.

The intangibility of the present

Having concluded that only the present still stands a chance of really being out there, independently of our subjective mentation, we are left with the question: Where exactly is the present?

We could say that the present is today, while the past is yesterday and the future is tomorrow. Yesterday is a memory and tomorrow is an expectation, so both exist only in mind. But today is really out there, isn't it? Well, if you come to think of it, today is quite a long period of time. Within today there is last hour, this hour and next hour. Last hour and next hour can only exist in mind. Only this hour is really out there. Or is it? Within this hour there is last minute, this minute and next minute; and so on. You get the picture.

We could say that the present is a *very short* moment squeezed in between a growing past and an approaching future. But even that wouldn't be satisfactory: How short is it exactly? After all, even very short periods of time still contain past and future. If you try to pin down the present moment by exclaiming 'Now!' it's already gone into the past by the time your tongue begins to move.

The present is *infinitely* short unless we choose to believe the theoretical, abstract limits imposed by current physics. In this case, the shortest possible interval of time is supposed to be the so-called Planck time, denoted t_P:

$$t_P \approx 0.0000000000000000000000000000000000000000001$$
second

If you try to develop a felt intuition for how short this is, you will quickly discover that you can't. It is inconceivably shorter than the ranges of time you have any familiarity with and could use as references for comparison. Yet, the present cannot be any longer than one Plank time. As such, however close to *nothing* you may imagine the present to be, *it's a lot closer*. From an intellectual standpoint, the present is thus *intangible*. See Figure 7.

Now, since perceptual truths must correspond to present states of affairs, they can only exist within this intangible moment. They are, at best, inconceivably fleeting. The overwhelming majority of what we consider 'true' is conjured up by the mind in the form of explanations (projected past) and predictions (projected future). Most of what we experience in our life thus consists of our own internal storytelling. *The bulk of life is entirely mythical.*

The present is an intangible moment squeezed in between a growing past and an approaching future. Therefore, perceptual truths are, at best, an inconceivably fleeting part of the experience of life. The bulk of life consists of internal myths.

Figure 7. The intangible moment we call the present.

The cognitive 'big bang'

Despite its intangibility, all of existence must fit within the present moment, for the present is all there ever is. Even the past and the future, as myths experienced in the present, exist within it. Thus, out of the quasi-nothingness of the now somehow comes *everything*. 'Form is emptiness, emptiness is form,' says the *Heart Sutra* of Buddhism.[98]

The present moment is the cosmic egg described in so many religious myths,[99] which we briefly discussed in Part I. It is a *singularity* that births all existence into form. It seeds our mind with fleeting consensus images that we then blow up into the voluminous bulk of projected past and future. These projections are like a *cognitive 'big bang'* unfolding in our mind. They stretch out the intangibility of the singularity into the substantiality of events in time. But unlike the theoretical Big Bang of current physics, the cognitive 'big bang' isn't an isolated occurrence in a far distant past. *It happens now; now; now.* It only ever happens now.

This is a subtle but crucial point: the cognitive 'big bang' is not a process unfolding in time. Rather, *it's a qualitative pattern of distribution of mental contents across the map of human cognition.* This complete pattern exists now and only now. Mental contents close to the central singularity have the qualities we associate with the present: immediateness, vividness. Contents distributed across the periphery of awareness have the qualities we associate with the past or the future: remoteness, fuzziness. Nonetheless, each of these mental contents is a particular reflection of the central singularity on the mirror of human awareness. There is nothing else they *could* be.

The past and the future are thus projected images—symbols, icons—of the intrinsic, timeless attributes of the singularity; of the intangible essences contained in the cosmic egg. There is nothing else the past or the future *could* consist of. Myths are the form taken by these symbolic projections of intangible essences. No wonder that physicists ended up conceiving of a Big Bang: it is a 'true' myth as an *icon*—a reflection—of the now, not an explanatory truth in the culturally sanctioned sense. Analogously, in the words of Wittgenstein, the myth of 'Christianity is not ... a theory about what has happened or will happen to the human soul, but a description of something that actually takes place in human life.'[100]

Existence only appears substantial because of our intellectual inferences, assumptions, confabulations and expectations. What is actually in front of our eyes *now* is incredibly elusive. The volume of our experiences—the bulk of life itself—is generated by our own internal myth-making. We conjure up substance and continuity out of sheer intangibility. We transmute quasi-emptiness into the solidity of existence through a trick of cognitive deception where we play both magician and audience. *In reality, nothing ever really happens*, for the scope of the present isn't broad enough for any event to unfold objectively. That we think of life as a series of substantial happenings hanging from a historical timeline is a fantastic cognitive hallucination. Roger Ebert's last words, illuminated by the clarity that only fast-approaching death can bring, seem to describe it most appropriately: 'This is all an elaborate hoax.'[101] And who do you think is the hoaxer?

> The present moment is an intangible singularity containing all existence. It seeds a cognitive 'big bang' unfolding in the human mind, whereby intrinsic attributes of the singularity are symbolically projected onto past and future, in the form of myths. These myths conjure up the volume and substantiality of experience.

The subjectivity of all concepts of truth

We have now refuted explanatory and predictive truths, and confined the potential existence of perceptual truths to an intangible singularity called the present moment. But is even this intangible present really independent of mind?

Like explanatory and predictive truths, perceptual truth is also contingent on the dichotomy inside/outside. A perception is true only if it corresponds to a present external state of affairs,[102] so there must exist something 'outside.' And by 'outside' I mean an objective world independent of consciousness, wherein states of affairs would still exist and develop even if no conscious entity were observing them.

Clearly then, perceptual truth is contingent on the validity of a metaphysical abstraction: a world independent of consciousness. The problem is that such a world is merely a hypothesis, for the only reality we can ever know is that of subjective experience.[103] We *infer* a world outside experience in an attempt to *explain* present perception, but—as we've known at least since Kant—the reality of any world beyond the subjective contents of perception is fundamentally inaccessible to us.[104] As such, the concept of perceptual truth is inextricably linked to an abstract hypothesis formulated by, and residing entirely within, thought. In other words, *perceptual truth is as subjective as explanatory and predictive truths*. All three rest on intellectual projections.

Perceptual truth depends on a metaphysical abstraction: a hypothetical external world independent of consciousness. All three culturally sanctioned concepts of truth thus rest on intellectual projections. The very foundations of truth are inherently subjective.

The circularity of space-time

I've argued that the existence of a world independent of consciousness is an inference, a hypothesis. We can never be sure that it is really there. Now I'd like to take this reasoning one step further: there are strong signs that, in fact, it *isn't* there.

The fabric of this hypothetical world outside consciousness is what we call space and time. They make up the scaffolding where supposedly objective things and events hang from. But what is space? What is time? Try to state in words what time is. You may say: 'Time is the interval between two events.' But 'interval' is just another word for 'time.' As such, this definition is circular and says absolutely nothing; it contains no new information. It's like saying that high speed is the quality of being fast. If you try it, you will soon discover that it doesn't matter how much effort you spend, you will never find a strictly non-circular definition of time. Go ahead, give it a go. Even dictionary and textbook definitions are broadly circular, simply hiding their circularity under indirection and the use of synonyms. These indirections create the illusion that we know what we are talking about when, in fact, we haven't got a clue. 'What, then, is time? If no one ask of me, I know; if I wish to explain to him who asks, I know not,'[105] admitted Saint Augustine. You see, *if you can't even define time, how do you know it's out there? What is it that supposedly is out there?* In recognition of this conundrum, there is even a formal articulation of physical theory that excludes time altogether.[106]

The same thing applies to space. Take a moment and try to define space without direct or indirect, narrow or broad circularity. Definitions like 'Space is the distance between two objects' simply hide the circularity through the use of synonyms: 'distance' is just another word for space. We all take space and time for granted until we try to tell ourselves what they are. We then discover that, despite the fact that we seem to inhabit them, they can't be defined without reference to themselves. They arise magically from self-reference, like Brahman hatching from the cosmic egg that Brahman Itself created (pause and give some thought to the symbolism here). Space and time are like ghosts that vanish into thin air every time we try to grab them. Their 'form' is 'emptiness' referring to itself in a kind of cognitive short-circuit.

Indeed, *if you can't tell yourself what something is, then it's most-likely an illusion resulting from a cognitive short-circuit;* it isn't really out there. More specifically, I suggest that space and time are language ghosts. They only seem to exist as independent entities because we conceptualize them in words. Here is an analogy to help you see what I mean: if you close your left hand into a fist, you can point at it with your right hand and say 'Here is a fist!' Linguistically, the fist is treated like a standalone entity, which you can move around and point at. But when you suddenly open your left hand, where does the fist go? Does it just magically dematerialize? You see, we just named a particular *configuration* of a hand and confused it linguistically with an independent object. I suggest that we make a similar mistake when it comes to space and time. These are names we give to certain *configurations* of subjective experience, not independent entities out there. They refer to *qualities* of experience, not the scaffolding of a world outside consciousness. And if the scaffolding isn't there, the objective world that supposedly hangs from it right now can't be there either.

> Space and time supposedly form the scaffolding of a hypothetical world independent of consciousness. But we cannot define space or time without circularity. They are language ghosts. The hypothetical world outside mind isn't there.

Brief recapitulation

We've discovered so far that unexamined intellectual projections, based on hidden circular reasoning, lie at the root of our belief that an objective, standalone reality grounds truth. Everywhere we've looked we've found only circularity and projections: in the past, present, future and space itself. They are all stories — *myths*, though not religious ones — we tell ourselves. Once we've redirected our attention to our own cognitive processes and unmasked their self-validating nature, the objectivity of the world vanished into thin air. We've realized that, through the fantastic trick of self-reference, our thoughts make the intangible phantasmagoria of present experience feel like a substantial external world unfolding across space and time.

Evidence for non-objectivity

My strategy so far has been to appeal to your direct experience of both the world and your own cognitive processes to instigate skepticism about an objective universe. I've tried to coax you into the personal, heartfelt insight that a great many things we take for granted are cognitive illusions. But if you are well acclimated to our contemporary cultural ethos, your next question will be: 'What about objective evidence for or against a world independent of consciousness? Can it be *proven* or *disproven*?'

In a sense, the essence of my argument so far has been precisely to raise doubt about anything allegedly independent of consciousness, *including so-called objective evidence*. Be it as it may, I will acquiesce to the cultural conditioning here because, as it turns out, objective evidence shoots itself in the foot. The latest experiments in the field of quantum mechanics have rendered all but untenable the notion that there is anything objective at all.

For instance, Kim and others have shown that observation not only determines the world perceived at present, but also *retroactively* changes it, so that its history becomes consistent with what is measured now.[107] This suggests that the world is merely a self-consistent myth constructed in the mind. Moreover, it further substantiates our earlier discussion that explanatory truths are entirely subjective. Gröblacher and others have also shown that the world is either entirely in consciousness or we must abandon our most basic intuitions about what objectivity means.[108] Their work is probably the most compelling to date in refuting the notion that reality is 'out there,' as opposed to 'in here.' Lapkiewicz and others have shown that, unlike what one would expect if the universe were independent of mind, the properties of a quantum system do not exist prior to being observed.[109] This suggests that things only exist insofar as they are experienced. Ma and others have again shown that no naively objective view of the world can be true.[110] Finally, as I was writing this book, two new results emerged: first, a group of scientists in Australia confirmed, through yet another, more sophisticated experiment, that the universe really does not exist except insofar as it is observed.[111] Then, physicists in the Netherlands performed the most rigorous experiment yet, closing a number of possible loopholes. The respected scientific journal *Nature* even called it the 'toughest test yet.'[112] Unsurprisingly by now, their results further confirmed the outcomes of earlier experiments.[113]

Even before most of the studies I've just cited had been carried out, renowned Johns Hopkins physicist and astronomer Prof. Richard Conn Henry had already seen enough. Back in 2005, he published an essay in *Nature* claiming that 'The universe is entirely mental. ... There have been serious [theoretical] attempts to preserve a material world—but they produce no new physics, and serve only to preserve an illusion.'[114] The illusion he was referring to was that of a world outside consciousness.

The bulk of my earlier writings focuses on explaining, rationally and in an empirically honest manner, how we can reconcile our sense perceptions with the notion that the world isn't 'out there' but 'in here.'[115] In fact, in Chapter 2 of my previous book *Brief Peeks Beyond* I went as far as listing the sixteen best arguments against this notion and refuting them one by one. But my goal with the present work is not to repeat my case or embark on an argumentative and abstract intellectual trip. I want to remain focused on helping you inquire critically into the many subtle layers of your own cognition, for nothing more is needed to expose our culturally sanctioned delusions. The only point that needs to be stressed here is this: the seeming independence of the world from consciousness, if pursued diligently to its ultimate implications, contradicts itself from within and then implodes. The universe seems to be inherently a phenomenon of and in mind; an internal story; a myth. In Western philosophy, this is known as the metaphysics of *idealism*, according to which the universe consists solely of *ideas* in consciousness.

Significantly, *idealism is precisely what many of the world's religious myths have been hinting at for thousands of years*, as discussed in Part I. In the Arandan, Uitoto and Hindu myths we explored, as well as in the Hermetic myth that underlies Western esotericism, the world is seen as the mental activity of a cosmic mind. As a matter of fact, the sophisticated Vedanta school of Hinduism states explicitly and unambiguously that all phenomena unfold in consciousness alone.[116] The same notion is found in Buddhism, particularly the Yogācāra School.[117] Even the Christian New Testament hints at this in a magnificently symbolic way when John the Evangelist writes: 'In the beginning was the Word, and the Word was with God, and the Word was God. ... Through [the Word] all things were made.'[118] 'Word' here is a translation of the original Greek Λόγος (*Logos*), which also means reasoning or thought. So through *thought* 'all things were made.'

Kripal states that '*Logos* here does not refer to some form of rationalism or linear logic, but to a kind of cosmic Mind, universal intelligence, or super-language out of which all that is emerges and takes shape. *Logos* is not human reason here. It is "with God." It *is* God.'[119] Yet, John has the *Logos* incarnate as a man, Jesus.[120] So this 'cosmic Mind' is *also* the *human* mind. The *Logos* is *also* human reasoning because God was *also* the man Jesus. Indeed, as we've seen in Part I, the *words* of language are the form and manifestation of *human* thought.

Ponder about this for a moment: just as John's *incarnated Logos* makes all things, the cognitive 'big bang' resulting from *human reasoning* (*logos*) creates the substantiality of the universe across space and time through a trick of self-reference. As God is born within His own creation as the Christ, Brahman is born in primordial waters from the cosmic egg—the *singularity*—that Brahman Itself created, subsequently uttering 'the Word' to bring forth the world's substance. The self-referential, circular character of the process and its parallels with the cognitive 'big bang' are even more striking here.

And it goes on and on: Nainema breaks into his own illusion to *spit*—a movement of the mouth, like the utterance of words— the *substance* of the forest into existence, while Karora wakes up within his own dream to experience, by *eating*, the *substance* of the animals sprouted from his own navel. Do you see how different peoples have been trying to suggest the same subtle cosmology through the symbolism most evocative to their respective cultures? *The world we ordinarily experience is a mental creation.* Its concrete form arises out of emptiness through cognitive self-reference, a process whose inherent circularity makes you believe that you were born in the world. *But it is you, through your human thinking, who is creating the whole of it now; now; now.*

To be more generic, let me again cite the work of scholar of comparative mythology Joseph Campbell. It reveals that, when looked at closely, many of the world's religious myths suggest that the universe isn't 'out there;' that it is, instead, a kind of dream in a transpersonal cosmic mind,[121] just as maintained by idealism. Where does this leave us as far as our concepts of truth and the way they inform our lives?

The latest experiments in the field of quantum mechanics have rendered all but untenable the notion that there is anything objective at all. Significantly, this is entirely consistent with many of the world's religious myths, which suggest that the world is a self-referential mental creation.

The false idols of truth

Clearly, our culturally sanctioned notions of truth are

meaningless concepts, idols of delusion. We've been chasing ghosts, mirages conceived and maintained entirely in the human intellect through circular reasoning and projections. This delusion pervades the way we relate to each other and the world. It underlies everything, from ethics to legislation, from trade to the economic system, from politics to war, from science to religious dogma, from our neuroses to street revolutions. In all these domains we scramble to find external references to ground the truth of the matter. A meaningless quest this is. We've become completely entranced by our own projections and lost ourselves in a hall of mirrors. Alarmingly, we can no longer even *conceive* of reality without these projections. Just consider your own thoughts as you read my words. You may be thinking: 'Bernardo claims that it is true that there is no truth, which is self-contradictory!' You see? Because I've denied all *external* truths, you may have concluded that I've denied reality itself.

The ghost didn't exist when we were infants. We didn't ask ourselves whether something was true or not, illusion or not. We didn't even know what these questions meant. We simply experienced what was there to be experienced. There were no external arbiters determining the 'validity' of our experiences—what could that even mean anyway?—for the experiences simply *were*. Can you still remember that simple, unpretentious state of mind? If you can, I encourage you to invoke it again, for it contains the key to our inquiry here.

The problem is not our experiences. The problem is what we make of them with our intellect. Instead of contemplating our experiences in an open and self-reflective manner, trying to sense their *symbolic meaning* in a way analogous to how a therapist analyzes dreams, we continuously search for external references in a futile quest to determine their 'validity.' In doing so, we close ourselves up to reality and proceed to tirelessly chase our own tails. You see, *there is nothing more to the world than experience itself.* What meaning can there be in trying to determine the 'validity' of an experience?

When we had unsettling dreams as children, our parents would try to reassure us with that fatidic statement: 'Forget about it, *it was just a dream!*' That was a seminal moment in the process of our entrancement. It was then and there that we began to learn that an experience is either bigger than ourselves—the 'real world out there'—or so insignificant that it should be dismissed without a thought. It was then and there that we began to slice away huge chunks of our mental lives and throw them in the garbage bin, while elevating other chunks—the ones that weren't *just* dreams—to the status of oppressive external tyrants. A huge fault line cracked open through the center of our mind, like a bleeding wound from which most of us never recover.

'It was *just* a dream' is probably the most pernicious, damaging thing that good, well-meaning parents say to their children. It inculcates the notion that each and every experience is to be categorized as either *nothing* or *other*; that each and every experience must either be killed or exiled. By doing this, we surrender intimacy with our own lives and become estranged from ourselves. The insanity here is plain to see: an experience is never nothing; it comes from somewhere; it is formed and arises in some way; it reveals something; it is an integral part of nature at some level. And an experience is never an external tyrant: Where else could it exist if not in ourselves, the experiencers?

Notice that the compulsion to either deny or externalize the reality of an experience is a neurotic form of self-protection. It is motivated by a deeply ingrained fear to realize and acknowledge who or what we really are. Whether we reject or project the reality of an experience, we isolate ourselves from it. We avoid responsibility for it. Perhaps most importantly, we circumvent the need to identify with it. But in doing all this we become, at best, small and insignificant ourselves: What is left for us to *be*? Ironically, thus, our neurotic attempt at self-preservation is precisely what causes the existential despair from which we succumb, as discussed in Part I. This is our present dilemma. We have internalized so deeply the reflex to first *categorize* before *acknowledging* experience that it has become automatic. Unthinkingly, we spend much of our cognitive resources adjudicating 'validity' instead of heeding the symbolic messages that reality holds about ourselves. We are busy checking the provenance of the envelope instead of reading the letter. This is an arbitrary game and a tragedy unique to the modern and contemporary ages.

No, I am not suggesting that we abandon our critical thinking. I am simply proposing that we redirect it towards fruitful goals. Using our critical intellect to create excuses for discarding or alienating experiences is a counterproductive denial of reality and ourselves. After all, experience is the only reality we can ever know and it is integral to who or what we are. *We should redirect our critical abilities towards reflecting upon the symbolic, iconic meaning of our experiences,* not artificially categorizing them according to the rules of some game. We should be busy looking for the right questions to ask, not passing arbitrary judgment.

How much of our life do we miss out on because of the delusory idols of external truth? How much of our inner realm do we neglect because of its alleged frivolousness? Those hypnagogic and hypnopompic images, feelings and insights that come to us on the edge of sleep: they are forgotten within seconds because, well, they are just nonsense anyway; they can't correspond to anything 'out there,' where all truths supposedly lie. The unusual, surprising associations that arise in our awareness in moments of quiet contemplation: we don't waste time with them because, well, what significance could they have anyway? The alien landscapes of thoughts and impressions we traverse just after orgasm: no more than the inconsequential gimmicks of an indulged organism. The mind-boggling alternative realities of psychedelic trances: just chemicals. The richness and emotional charge of our daydreams and fantasies: just *nothing*. And so down the drain go the most transcendent moments of our lives and aspects of ourselves; precisely those that could offer us a passage—elusive and brief as it may be—to visit something beyond the ordinary human condition and sooth our existential despair. We have been educated to dismiss the natural paths to transcendence.

Our delusions about the nature of truth are the single most important reason for the loss of vibrancy of religious myths worldwide. Because most of the events portrayed by these myths cannot correspond to anything we consider possible in a world outside mind, they are condemned to irrelevance. Yes, there is no external, mind-independent reality to religious myths; not to a single one of them. *But there is no external, mind-independent reality to anything else either.* The only meaningful way to conceive of truth implies that truth is *internal*, not external. Realizing this is probably one of the most urgent and critical challenges humanity faces at the present historical nexus.

Without an external reality, our culturally sanctioned notions of truth are meaningless concepts. They fallaciously suggest that an experience is either *nothing* or *other*; that it must be either killed or exiled. So we surrender intimacy with our own lives and become estranged from ourselves.

Chapter 7

Truth, myth and world

After extensively elaborating on religious myths in Part I, we have now also addressed the idea of truth in some depth. Moreover, it has become clear that our conclusions regarding the nature of truth have significant implications as far as the nature of the world itself is concerned. In this chapter, we will delve further into this multifaceted relationship between truth, myth and world. We will do it one facet—one step—at a time and tie it all together at the end of the chapter. At that point, it should become clear to you how deeply intertwined these three ideas are.

The world as true myth

An inescapable implication of our conclusions so far is that the bulk of the world is a collection of narratives experienced in mind according to linguistic patterns. In other words, *the world is made of myths*, though not necessarily religious ones.

Indeed, as we've seen, the past is a story we tell ourselves in order to give context to present perceptions. Even the partial consensus that emerges in society about past events is a story, since it results from instances of linguistic communication such as history lessons at schools, newscasts, personal memories shared in conversations, etc. Moreover, the vivid recall of episodic memories doesn't change the inherently mythical character of the past. After all, memory recall is experienced *in the present*. If you close your eyes right now and relive your first kiss, your experience will take place *now*, not in the past. That this present experience *corresponds* to something in the past is itself a story—a myth—we tell ourselves, whether true or false. It can't be anything else. The same goes for historical artifacts in, for instance, museums: we perceive them in the present. That they come from the past is a story—an explanation—whether true or false. The past is always a myth.

Likewise, the future is a story we tell ourselves in order to give perspective to present actions. What else could it be? Even the partial consensus that emerges in society about future events is a story, since it results from shared models of reality communicated through language. In other words, we predict the same future only insofar as we tell each other the same myths about how the world works.

Only the present moment, which we share by directly co-perceiving images, can escape the mythical framework of language. However, as discussed earlier, the present is an elusive, intangible singularity. As such, the experiential bulk of human life is a collection of stories, myths. *Whether we live in transcendence or existential despair is simply a matter of which type of myth—religious or deprived—predominantly composes our world.* Whichever the case, we always live in a myth that can be neither confirmed nor disproven by reference to states of affairs outside mentation.

Clearly, then, dismissing myth is tantamount to dismissing life. The very essence of what it means to be a human being alive in the world is the linguistic hallucination that creates that world. There is valid information in the hallucination for the same reason that there is valid information in a nightly dream. Although the dream is entirely conjured up in mind, it does reveal—if interpreted properly—something true and significant about the dreamer: his or her drives, desires, fears, traumas, etc.[122] It couldn't be any different, since the dream is an expression *of* the dreamer. Analogously, lies—which are by definition untrue—betray something true about the aspirations and insecurities of the liar. For instance, a teenager who lies about his sexual exploits gives away not only his sexual insecurities, but also his inner need to be accepted by others. So the lie does ultimately reveal significant truth about the teenager, if only we know how to read it. Even an entirely fictional novel is bound to suggest something true about its author, since the novel is an expression *of* the author. So you see, that something is fictional, hallucinated, conjured up or 'hoaxed'—to use Roger Ebert's chosen word—does *not* mean that it can't ultimately reveal important truth. The hoax is bound to betray the nature of the hoaxer, if only we inquire into it through the right angle.

Myth—and therefore life itself—is how the 'hoaxer' symbolically projects out its nature, so it can perceive these projections as seeming objects and thereby inquire into itself. Without the projections self-inquiry would be impossible, for the same reason that you can't see your own eyes without a mirror. The hallucination we call the world—including its history—consists of symbols of the intangible nature of mind reflected on the mirror of human awareness. These symbolic reflections are the 'correspondences' between the natural and spiritual worlds insisted upon by Swedenborg.[123] The projected symbols betray something about mind in the same way that a lie betrays something about the liar or that a dream betrays something about the dreamer.

Dismissing myth is tantamount to dismissing life, for the bulk of our world is made of myths, whether religious or deprived. The world consists of symbols of the nature of mind projected out and reflected on the mirror of human awareness, so to enable self-inquiry.

Consensus reality without external truth

We've concluded earlier that there is no standalone reality outside mind to ground the truth of any explanation, perception or prediction. But the absence of external truth does not change the fact that experience exists *as such*. Whether grounded in external truth or not, experience isn't nothing. It occurs and is the only reality we can ever know for sure. For instance, when you fantasize about a new romantic partner, there clearly is an experiential reality to your fantasies, even though there is no external truth to them. You may even get aroused during your reveries. In this sense, *the absence of external truth does not refute reality, insofar as experience is real as such.*

But to leave it at this would equate the world we perceive through our five senses with quirky fantasies. We would be left with no basis to distinguish between a football match witnessed by thousands and a schizophrenic vision; after all, both are experiences. Do we live in a universe in which these things are equivalent? Of course not. There obviously is a difference between sense perception—the 'consensus images and interactions' I talked about in Part I—and fantasies. It's just that the difference isn't what our culture takes it to be: if you reflect upon it carefully, you will see that *the only difference between sense perceptions and private reveries is the degree to which the experience is shared across individuals.* Consensus images are largely shared across individuals, while your nightly dreams and daytime fantasies aren't. Our culture takes this simple observation and extrapolates it to a gigantic and unjustified metaphysical abstraction: a whole universe independent of mind.

While rejecting a universe outside mind we do not need to reject the undeniable fact that certain experiences are shared while others aren't. It is this fact that allows us to still differentiate consensus reality from fantasies without any need for external arbiters of truth.

Now, notice that only perceptions (present) seem to be intrinsically consensual, while explanations (past) and predictions (future) tend to vary from person to person. Most people can easily agree about what is in front of their eyes right now, but will tend to disagree about how or why it got there, or where it will go next. If several people stand before the great pyramid in

Giza, they will likely all agree that there is a large stone building in front of them (perception), but will disagree about how, why, when, or by whom it was built (explanation). They will agree that the Egyptian desert feels hot and dry right now (perception), but are likely to disagree about how it will feel in ten thousand years (prediction). These disagreements arise from differences in each person's intellectual model of reality and the memories—books previously read, prior visits to construction sites, etc.—that feed this model. Only raw perceptions seem to escape idiosyncratic intellectual modeling and remain conducive to consensus.

But if the only point of generalized agreement were perceptions, consensus reality would be elusive to the point of not being there. After all, the present is an intangible singularity. Since we all seem to share the same world, there has to be a broader cognitive space—beyond just perceptions—wherein consensus can arise naturally. And indeed there is.

Notice that *the closer to perception an explanation—including memories—or prediction lies, the higher is its potential for consensus.* For instance, if you and I watch an athlete slip and fall while running on a wet track, we will agree not only that there is an athlete lying on a wet track (perception), but also that water on the track caused the athlete to fall (explanation including the memory of the fall). The consensus between us will be due to the fact that the explanation lies very close, in the map of cognition, to the singularity of the present moment. Similarly, if you and I watch a waiter drop a glass of wine while approaching a table in a restaurant, we will agree not only that there is a waiter walking and a glass of wine in the air (perception), but also that a fraction of a second later the glass will hit the floor, break and spill the wine (prediction). The consensus between us will be due to the fact that the prediction lies very close to the singularity of the now. This way, consensus reality is a cognitive space not only comprising, *but also surrounding*, perception. It exists as a kind of glow around the center of the cognitive 'big bang.' See Figure 8.

The diffuse boundaries of consensus don't extend much beyond the singularity. A week after the fact, I may feel sure that the athlete slipped because of a misstep and not even remember that the track was wet. And you may disagree with me about it. Similarly, I may anticipate in my imagination that the waiter will immediately clean up the mess after the glass breaks, while you may anticipate in your imagination that he will first go back to the bar and fetch another glass for his patron. The potential for an experience to be shared dissipates fast as it is projected further away from the center of the cognitive 'big bang.'

Narrow and diffuse as the boundaries of consensus may be, they still play a crucial role: the experiences that fall within them gain the formidable weight of a collective reality. *Consensus experiences live in a transpersonal cognitive space, instead of an individual mind.* It is this collective momentum that motivates us to attribute more reality to shared experiences than to private reveries. And the closer to the center of the cognitive 'big bang' the experience lies, the higher is the momentum. The intangible singularity is the source of all shared experiences, the unifying nexus of our respective lives.

This way, the experiences we ordinarily look upon as real are simply the *consensus* images around the center of the cognitive 'big bang.' They are collective in nature and, as such, reflect the activity of a common, transpersonal root underlying all cognition. On the other hand, what we ordinarily look upon as confabulation are experiences we project onto the periphery of awareness in the form of explanations and predictions.

> For not refuting experience, the absence of external truth does not refute reality. What we call consensus reality is a cognitive space of shared experiences surrounding present perceptions.

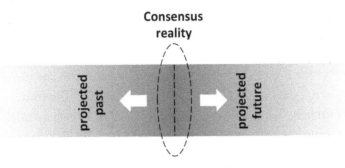

Figure 8. Consensus reality is a cognitive space surrounding
present perceptions.

The mythical origin and fate of the world

As briefly discussed earlier, it is our delusional concepts of truth
that lead us to mistakenly belittle religious myths: since the
entities and events they portray cannot correspond to mind-
independent facts, religious myths are considered untrue and
thus irrelevant. But as we've seen, there are no such things as
mind-independent facts to begin with. The basis we thought we
had for differentiating religious myths from any other myth,
including the best scientific theories, is just not there. All myths
equally lack correspondence to facts outside consciousness.

One may still try to set religious myths apart from scientific
myths by pointing out that, even in the absence of an objective
world, we still have the momentum of *shared, consensus perceptions* as a criterion of differentiation. Myths that correspond to
consensus perceptions—such as the immediate outcome of
experiments—can be considered more valid than myths that
don't, this being where science has an overwhelming edge. Such
is indeed a sound differentiation—and the only one that saves us
from the chaos of relativism[124]—but its scope of applicability is
more limited than most people realize. After all, the cognitive
space of consensus is confined to the surroundings of the singularity we call the present moment.

Notice that most religious myths are, in fact, *explanations* and *predictions.* They try to make sense of life by couching present perceptions in a *transcendent context.* They try to give meaning to life by offering present actions a *transcendent perspective.* Because they deal with the primordial origin and the ultimate goal of existence, the events portrayed by religious myths are supposed to take place in an often-distant past or future, respectively. As such, in both cases the mythical events fall outside the boundaries of consensus.

The rise of Karora from the ground and the consequent formation of the Ilbalintja Soak are projected too far into the past for any consensus criterion to be applicable. The only thing that motivates us to deny their reality is our intellectual model of the workings of nature. It is this model that forces us to subjectively infer that Karora's rise *couldn't* have happened. But the inference isn't consensual. Many Arandan surely don't agree with it!

Similarly, the Christian myth of the Rapture predicts that, during the second coming of Christ, chosen human beings will be lifted into the air to meet Jesus. These events are projected too far into the future for any consensus criterion to be applicable. The only thing that motivates us to deny their reality is our intellectual model of how nature operates. But this model isn't consensual. Many Christians surely don't agree that the Rapture is impossible!

Remember: I'm not suggesting that even the best religious myths are objectively true. What I am saying is that it is nonsensical to attribute either objective truth or objective falsity to them. There are no external, mind-independent states of affairs to ground the attribution either way. Any judgment of the validity of religious myths is subjective. Moreover, they are projected too far outside any reasonable range of consensus for their validity to be grounded on joint perception by multiple observers. So any judgment of their validity is not only subjective, but also largely personal.

One cannot hope to overcome this inherent subjectivity by

crafting ever more refined models of reality, any more than one can hope to fly by crawling in ever more refined ways. No matter how strong one's conviction is in one's model of reality, the model is still mental and non-consensual. One cannot pull oneself up by one's bootstraps.

Even if you see and concur with what I am arguing here, chances are that your intellect will soon have the irresistible urge to dive right back into the culturally sanctioned 'story.' You will lose the thread of what I am saying and re-immerse yourself in your intellectual model of reality: 'This cannot be so. Our scientific theories are validated against concrete data. We run experiments to check their validity. These experiments are repeated and confirmed across time and space. One cannot compare these models to empirically baseless religious myths. They are just not the same thing.' It all sounds so persuasive, doesn't it?

The thing to remember here is this: explanations and predictions are but reflections of the intangible singularity on the mirror of present awareness. There is nothing else they *could* be. And since the singularity is mind itself, *explanations and predictions are symbols of the nature of mind.* Some of these symbols—like the Big Bang of modern cosmology—are shaped to be consistent with our current, subjective models of reality. Others—like Brahman hatching from the cosmic egg—aren't. *But it is only their symbolic content that carries any significance, not their consistency with circular linguistic models.* After all, there is no such a thing as the *literal* truth of any explanation or prediction, for the past and the future are just mental projections experienced in the present moment. 'There never was a creation. Rather, there is a continuous creating going on,'[125] remarked Campbell. Realize, thus, the futility of wrestling with the question of objective truth when it comes to *any* creation myth, scientific or otherwise. See that the only real value of any explanation or prediction is *symbolic* and that the only meaningful way to interpret them is as *icons of the now.* 'Creation myths ... describe not the origin of our cosmos, but the origin of man's conscious awareness of the world,'[126] observed Marie-Louise von Franz. As a matter of fact, the symbolic similarity between the Big Bang of modern cosmology and Brahman's hatching from the cosmic egg is striking. But unlike the implicit suggestion of Carl Sagan in the original *Cosmos* series,[127] the Hindu myth isn't merely some kind of lucky allegory for the Big Bang. These two myths aren't pointing at each other but at a third and ineffable element: the structure of human cognition in the present moment. *The significance of both myths lies solely in how they symbolically portray what is happening in your mind now; yes, right now.* Anything else is just culturally sanctioned cognitive delusion.

If, after this reminder, you still find yourself immersed in the cultural 'story,' the alternative is to go back and try to find the thread of my argument again. Because of cultural conditioning, we are all subject to the enormous gravitational pull of this 'story.' You may follow my argument along each step of the way until a small, intruding thought suddenly pulls you right back to where you started. It's like slipping and falling back to the bottom of the hole of cultural conditioning before you manage to climb out completely. But if I were to follow you down the hole and engage you there, on the terms, assumptions and internal logic of the cultural game, I wouldn't be of any help to you. Any discussion at that level would just reinforce the 'story,' because it would be inherently circular like our 'definitions' of space and time, as well as the linguistic operation of the intellect. You must find the thread and pull yourself up again.

So here is my suggestion: whenever you fall back to a conditioned intellectual model, return to Chapter 6 and re-read it while constantly comparing its arguments to the conditioned model. Try to hold the cognitive dissonance of this comparison in awareness as you read. By staying with the corresponding psychic tension, you will notice that the apparent paradoxes and contradictions slowly begin to dissolve. You will gain insight into more and more nuances and, at some point, clarity will dawn. You will then have climbed out of the hole and the horizon will present itself to you in all directions.

With this newfound clarity and perspective, you will *know* this: to find and live the transcendent truth portrayed by religious myths, we must not look 'outside,' for there is no such a place. The 'outside' is nothing more than an abstraction of the intellect. We must look where *all* reality resides: our own mind, profound aspects of which are given symbolic expression in the form of religious myth.

> Religious myths are, by and large, explanations and predictions. They do not correspond to facts outside mind, but neither do scientific cosmologies. The only value of any religious myth or scientific cosmology is symbolic. The only meaningful way to interpret them is as icons of the now.

How religious myths reveal internal truths

If there is no external truth, then the transcendent truths pointed to by valid religious myths can only be *internal*. They are the truths of our own nature, not of an outside reality. And our own nature is clearly transcendent, for *that which conjures up time and space through a trick of circular reasoning cannot itself be bound by time or space.*

You may recall the epiphany I related in Part I, which I had while contemplating a beautiful crucifix in Cologne Cathedral. Well, on that occasion I suddenly recognized that the man hanging from the cross is each and every human being. His sacrifice is *our* sacrifice: we are all hanging from the self-conceptualized cross of space, time, confinement and impermanence. His divine nature is our true nature as timeless mind taking particular, seemingly limited perspectives within its own dream. That Christ is both God *and* the Son of God born into God's creation is a hardly disguised way to express this symbolically. *We* are Brahman hatching from the cosmic egg now; now; now. 'Atman [the personal self] is Brahman,'[128] concludes the Vedanta School of Hinduism.

My feeble attempt to word my epiphany isn't really the point. I am just trying to illustrate how an involuntary shift in cognitive perspective can suddenly reveal that religious myths aren't about external events, but about us as creative consciousness. The transcendent truths these myths point to are the truths of our own nature, for there's nothing 'out there.' And it is the religious myths themselves that prime us for this realization. God's birth in the world as the Christ, Brahman's self-creation through the cosmic egg, Karora's rise within his own dream, Nainema's incursion into his own vision, all illustrate the self-referential nature of reality and, therefore, the internal character of truth. The finger has only ever pointed at ourselves. True religious myths can thus help us *live* the deepest transcendent truth by reminding us of our intimate kinship with it. Working with and within the phantasmagoria of symbolic projections of mind, the myths help us eventually turn our gaze inward, to the projector.

One might object to this by pointing out that many religious myths promote the worship of external agencies: deities, angels, saints, etc. This may seem to contradict the idea that the myths point inward. However, remember that these seemingly external agencies are—like everything else in life—*symbols* of our own inner nature projected outward. 'The gods are real, but they are not as real as the Self, of which they are temporary projections,'[129] wrote Kripal, describing certain Hindu comparative practices. A minor instance of this kind of projection can even be caught at work when we, for instance, colloquially refer to our own neuroses as assailing 'demons.' Thus, *what seems to be the worship of external agencies is, in fact, a conversation with estranged aspects of ourselves through symbolic proxy.* In this context, the myths still point inward: if we can't turn our head back to look at ourselves, we can at least project our inner essence out so to face ourselves head-on. As Swedenborg put it, 'One should not omit the practice of external worship. *Things inward are excited by external worship.*'[130]

There is also another way in which religious myths can reveal truth: by *cancelling out the implications of deprived cultural myths.* Take the modern myth of materialism, for instance: it states that the real world is outside and independent of consciousness, and that consciousness is generated by particular, transient configurations of matter. There are two peculiar things about it: the first is the abstract *inference* of a world outside consciousness, which is fundamentally beyond knowledge. The second is the *implication* that consciousness, as a secondary phenomenon of matter, is limited in both time and space. Notice further that it is this very implication that obscures the transcendence of our lives. Thus, by believing in a deprived myth, we lose touch with our own transcendent nature. Here is where even the most seemingly naïve religious myth can play a valuable role.

For instance: the seemingly naïve substance dualism of the Abrahamic myths, which postulate an eternal immaterial soul next to a material body, *cancels out* the transcendence-denying implication of materialism. Never mind the fact that an immaterial soul floating in space and time is just as abstract and unprovable an idea as a material world outside mind; the point here is the myths' balancing counter-perspective, which gives us a chance to remain open to the internal truth of transcendence. The 'soul' of the Abrahamic myths isn't a literal truth, but a *symbol* of a timeless inner reality.

This second role of religious myths is vital under a cultural ethos dominated by redundant, inflationary inferences and circular systems of thought. As such, it is absurd to say that modern civilization no longer needs religious images: the very opposite is the case. Never before have we been in as dire a need of religious symbolism, liturgy and iconography as today. True religious myths negate the implications of delusions—implications that would otherwise obscure transcendence—helping us stay open to the mystery of our own nature and the possibilities it entails. This openness is, in fact, the true meaning of *faith*. The importance and validity of religious myths has thus nothing to do with an objective truth somewhere 'out there.' That the contemporary anti-religion movement[131] focuses precisely on combating the *literal* validity of religious myths misses the point rather spectacularly.

There is a third and equally essential role religious myths can play in helping us come closer to truth. Ordinarily, most of us are locked inside what I've earlier called 'the hole of cultural conditioning.' This 'hole' entails self-reinforcing, circular patterns of thinking—intellectual models—that prevent us from becoming lucid of the many layers and nuances of our own cognitive processes. They blind us to the simple, transcendent truth of our being. Yet, not all intellectual models inside the 'hole' are equivalent: some swirl very close to the bottom in their circular, self-referential flow of linguistic cognition, while others swirl higher up. For instance, both the metaphysics of materialism and idealism—the notion that the world is made up entirely of ideas in transpersonal consciousness—are intellectual models inside the 'hole,' since both assume space and time in a linguistic description of reality. However, materialism makes more unnecessary, fictional postulates and abstract inferences. This extra ballast weighs it down and drags it much deeper in. Consequently, there are *better* and *worse* myths in the 'hole' of conditioning: worse myths drag you down while better myths lift you up to the edge of the 'hole'—the 'brink of a transcendent illumination,'[132] in the words of Campbell—maximizing your chances of escape. This is where religious myths come in again.

As discussed in the previous chapter, many religious myths, by suggesting that reality consists entirely of ideas in a cosmic mind, are symbolic articulations and enrichments of the metaphysics of idealism. This is the case for the Hindu, Arandan, Uitoto and Hermetic myths we looked at. Even the Christian philosophy and theology of Swedenborg are, if one looks carefully, eminently idealist.[133] These idealist myths may not go as far as denying the existence of space and time in an internally consistent manner—after all, the concepts of space and time are built right into language itself—but they do lift us up to the edge of the 'hole,' the brink of illumination. They are *better* myths that bring us as far as language can go, minimizing the distance we have to jump in order to finally escape conditioning. By legitimizing transcendence, they free us from the intellectual chains that could otherwise keep us shackled to the bottom.

As discussed in Part I, the full realization of transcendence is a kind of quantum leap: it happens spontaneously, suddenly, in one swift movement without any apparent cause. It's a kind of grace. But if we are running intellectual models that anchor us to the bottom of the 'hole' of conditioning—like the deprived myth of materialism—we give grace no chance: the distance to the edge of the 'hole' remains just too great to jump. These bottom-dwelling models prevent escape because they deny the very *possibility* of transcendence, closing us up in a bubble of cynicism. True religious myths, on the other hand, acknowledge transcendence and foment the openness—the *faith*—that is *precondition* to the final leap to freedom. They bring us to the edge of what can be achieved within the framework of language, space and time, priming us for grace. This, in a nutshell, is the third way in which religious myths can nudge us ever closer to truth.

In conclusion, true religious myths can help bring transcendence into our lives, thereby delivering us from existential despair, in three ways: first, by helping us turn our gaze inwards to realize the truth of our own nature; second, by projecting symbols that cancel out the implications of deprived cultural inferences and abstractions; and third, by lifting us up to the edge of the 'hole' of cultural conditioning, from which grace can help us take the final step to freedom.

> Since there is no external reality, religious myths can only point to internal truths. They reveal our transcendent nature, for that which conjures up time and space cannot itself be bound by time or space. Religious myths also cancel out the transcendence-denying implications of cultural abstractions and lift us up to edge of the 'hole' of conditioning.

Religious institutions

I feel forced to briefly digress at this point, so to prevent misunderstandings of my position. My emphasis on the importance of true religious myths in contemporary culture and society should not be construed as blanket support for religious *institutions* and their actions. Although it is hard to imagine how religious myths could retain vitality without some form of institutional support, it would also be naïve to deny the defacement, abuse and misappropriation of religious mythology at the hands of institutions.

Indeed, religious myths have been routinely hijacked and corrupted for political and economic gain. They have been misused to establish and maintain the power of clergy. They have been abused as instruments of oppression and social control. Inconceivable harm has been done in their name, as any cursory reading of history will show. This doesn't eliminate the intrinsic validity and importance of true religious myths discussed earlier, but it must be acknowledged. Acknowledgement, after all, is the first step towards healing.

It is not too difficult to spot the misuse of religious mythology.

The essence of a myth lies in its symbolic pointing at the internal truths of cognition; truths that are *inside* us, not in the world 'out there.' As such, the relationship between true religious myths on the one hand, and codes of external conduct on the other, is indirect and ancillary at best. So when religious myths are used as justification for arbitrary morals—meant to tell people what to do and not to do—suspicion is justified. When a house of worship begins to resemble a court of law, where the emphasis is on passing judgment and casting blame, one must wonder.

Moreover, by pointing at the inner truth of each person, true religious myths also contradict any alleged need for intermediaries or translators of any kind. The myth only has vitality if we develop a direct, personal, intimate relationship with it. No one can explain to us what the myth means since, as we've seen in Part I, its meaning transcends words. 'Make sure that your religion is a matter between you and God only,'[134] advised Wittgenstein. So when religious myths are used to legitimize the power of people who place themselves between transcendence and us, the motivations for this must be questioned. When clergy become dictators instead of symbols of, and guides to, our own inner wisdom, something isn't quite right.

Because *living* the transcendent truth of a religious myth is a subtle and very personal phenomenon, not conducive to the gathering of adoring crowds, religious institutions often try to 'translate' the myth into pre-packaged dogmas that can be doled out like pills and practiced blindly like calisthenics. We are told that if we simply *believe* the simple formula handed down to us we will attain transcendence—'salvation' in Christian terminology—after death. This, of course, is very convenient for the institutions. But if transcendence could be directly captured in simple words and beliefs, we wouldn't need the iconography of the myths to begin with. We wouldn't need *religion* to begin with. As a matter of fact, dogmas anchor us to the bottom of the 'hole' of cultural conditioning; *religious conditioning* in this case. They prevent the quantum leap that could lead us to the realization of our true, transcendent nature. Dogmatic belief isn't faith and, in fact, *contradicts* faith: one who spouses an arbitrary set of rules closes himself up to the possibility of living transcendence.

As any human activity, institutions are prone to corruption by the greed, insecurities, prejudices and maliciousness of egos. Therefore, one should not confuse religious myths with the activities of religious institutions. The true myth precedes any institution in its psychic purity and authenticity. It precedes any moral or behavioral code. In an ideal world, religious institutions would do no more than nurture the purity of their myth in altruistic fashion. In reality, however, they often behave like parasites, hijacking the innate psychic force and appeal of the myth for selfish gain.

Mind you: I am *not* against moral codes. Morals are not only useful, but also indispensable for a productive life in society, ensuring that we all have the opportunity to express ourselves in the world. What I am against is the flattening of the unfathomable cognitive dimensions of a true religious myth into a mere moral system. In my view, doing so is an illegitimate attempt to tap into the appeal of the myth for social control. Moreover, legitimate moral systems don't require religious myths *per se* as underpinning: secular underpinnings and justifications can be perfectly appropriate and sufficient.

To be clear, I don't deny that one can legitimately derive personal morals from one's felt understanding of a religious myth. For instance, it's perfectly valid, in my view, that a Christian adopts the moral principle of non-violence inspired on Christ's 'turn-the-other-cheek' example. But for these morals to be alive and authentic, they have to arise *spontaneously* from one's own intimate, *personal* relationship with the myth. Only then can they actually reflect the living mythical essence, which always points inwards. Standardized moral codes defined and packaged by institutions and enforced by decree are not only artificial and dead, they conceal the message of the myth behind a veil of arbitrary conventions. Authentic moral principles are a natural *consequence* of the personal assimilation of a true religious myth, not the other way around. Nobody can gain a genuine, vibrant, living understanding of a religious myth merely by following a code of behavior.

Finally, I am not against religious institutions as such. Much to the contrary: *in principle*, I think they can be of great service if their actions honor the purity of the myth. Indeed, as suggested above, without some form of institutional nurturing I don't think religious myths can survive and thrive in society. However, in my view, a legitimate religious institution will focus on *making the images of the myth alive through ritual*, not on laying down dogmas and codes of behavior. Its clergy will serve merely as *actors* in a symbolic ceremonial drama, not as authoritarian intermediaries between people and transcendence. Its messages will center on evoking inner truth, not on judging the 'world outside.' In Christian terms, my ideal Church would be centered on liturgy. Its sermons would repeatedly tell the Christian myth in as evocative, nuanced and alive a manner as possible, not pass judgments. Confession would be a ritual of self-inquiry lovingly facilitated by sensitive and supportive clergy, not a trial.[135] Churches would be wombs of warmth, safety, tolerance and unconditional love—just as illustrated by the life and message of the Christ—not chambers of blame, guilt, shame or control.

Having developed this disclaimer to my own satisfaction, let's now rejoin the main thread of this chapter.

One should not confuse religious myths with the activities of religious institutions. The true myth precedes any institution in its psychic purity and authenticity. It precedes any moral or behavioral code.

Bringing it all together

At this point, we've already seen through the illusion of a world outside consciousness. We've also realized that myths not only can point to the transcendent truths of mind, they also *constitute* the world of our ordinary experience. Therefore, it's time we revisited and updated our understanding of the relationship between mind and world, as originally discussed in Chapter 3 and summarized in Figure 2.

Instead of a world outside consciousness, what we actually have is a universal consciousness, which I'll henceforth call 'mind-at-large.' The world we live in can be thought of as a *collective dream* grounded in mind-at-large. Just as it happens in an ordinary dream, we believe we inhabit the world and we can't control it at will. Unlike an ordinary dream, however, the dream of consensus reality is shared across individuals.

An individual mind is formed when a segment of mind-at-large collapses into itself, creating a point of dense, highly localized cognitive activity. This *singularity* subsequently gives rise to the cognitive 'big bang' discussed earlier. Each living being thus corresponds to one among countless such singularities in mind-at-large. A metabolizing body is simply what the singularity looks like from the outside. As we've also seen earlier, traditional religious myths have symbolically described the cognitive collapse of a divinity as the formation of a 'cosmic egg.' Clearly, the cosmic egg and the local collapse of mind-at-large I've just described point to the same transcendent truth, so it's fair to borrow the mythical symbolism from now on. See Figure 9.

The formation of a cosmic egg creates a cognitive *boundary* between the inside of the egg—that is, the 'inner realm' of thoughts and emotions discussed in the very beginning of this book—and the mental activity in the parts of mind-at-large immediately surrounding the egg. It is this boundary that gives rise to sense perceptions: from the perspective of an egg, the

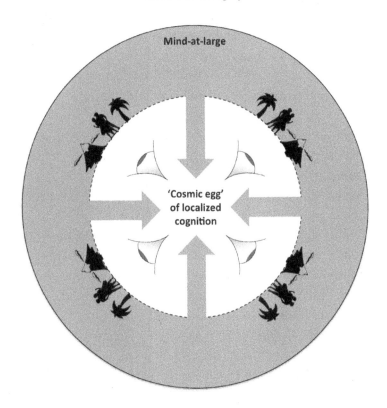

Figure 9. The cognitive collapse of mind-at-large and the rise of sense perception.

activity in the surrounding cognitive neighborhood is experienced in the form of images of an 'outer realm,' such as mountains, other people, trees, etc. Therefore, *the empirical world you see around you right now is simply your egg's view of mental processes unfolding in neighboring parts of mind-at-large.* See Figure 9 again. We all share the same world because, like islands in an ocean, our personal minds are surrounded by one and the same mind-at-large.

Unlike islands in an ocean, however, cosmic eggs aren't different or separate from mind-at-large. They are simply localized cognitive *configurations of* it. Therefore, beyond sense perceptions, we remain cognitively connected to all of mind-at-large at a foundational level. This is represented by the four grey arrows directly penetrating—in fact, forming—the cosmic egg in Figure 9. In Part I of this book, I've referred to this foundational connection as our *obfuscated mind*. And because the obfuscated mind can tap into non-local cognitive resources, its reach is much broader than that of the localized intellect.

Notice that Figure 9, despite being useful to illustrate the cognitive collapse discussed above, is rather incomplete. After all, there is more to our personal mentation than just perceptions: we also experience thoughts, intuitions and fantasies. Moreover, the history of mystical experiences shows that the boundary between the inside and outside of the cosmic egg isn't exactly sharp and definite: it consists rather of progressive levels of obfuscation. To address these points, consider Figure 10. Its shades of grey represent different degrees of obfuscation. Its four quadrants represent the different modalities of our personal mentation.

Figure 10 consists essentially of a revision of Figure 2 based on our latest insights. Let's cover it more systematically starting from the left-upper quadrant: when you look out to the world, what you see is the visible 'surface' of mind-at-large. Its mental activity is presented symbolically to you in the form of the images of consensus reality: mountains, trees, other people, etc. Your intellect then translates these intangible images into the myth of an objective and concrete world.

But the consensus images available to your five senses are not the only aspect of mind-at-large that you can 'perceive.' As discussed extensively in Part I, through the obfuscated mind we can gain intuitive insight into a transcendent reality. This means that we can have direct apprehension of deeper aspects of mind-at-large—aspects hidden under the visible surface of consensus images—without the intermediation of the five senses. As mythically described by Rudolph Steiner, 'Just as in the body, eye and ear develop as organs of perception, as senses for bodily

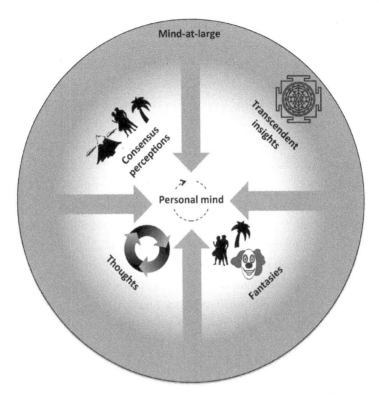

Figure 10. Mind and world, revisited.

processes, so does a man develop in himself soul and spiritual organs of perception through which the soul and spiritual worlds are opened to him.'[136] This form of 'spiritual perception' leads to, in the words of William James, 'states of insight into depths of truth unplumbed by the discursive intellect. They are illuminations, revelations, full of significance and importance.'[137] The right-upper quadrant of Figure 10 represents this. Notice that the transcendent insights so achieved, when translated into narratives with the help of the intellect, form the basis of true religious myths.

Transcendent insights *feel* like perceptions, in that the personal mind often has the impression that they come from outside. This is true in that the insights originate *outside the personal mind*, in the obfuscated cognitive regions of mind-at-large. However, you also have the ability to deliberately produce insights within your own personal mind: we call it *thinking*. As discussed in Part I, thoughts are circular patterns of association shaped according to a grammatical template. They arise and unfold entirely within the intellect, even when their original trigger is a perception or a transcendent insight. This is illustrated in the lower-left quadrant of Figure 10. It is in the form of thoughts that you create the myths of explanations and predictions.

As thoughts are the personal mind's analogues of transcendent insights, fantasies are the personal mind's analogues of consensus perceptions. You can confabulate images, events and scenarios in your mind that have no correspondence to consensus facts. These confabulations may even use certain building blocks co-opted from consensus perception—images like people or trees—but the way they are woven together is idiosyncratic. The lower-right quadrant of Figure 10 represents this. It is in the form of fantasies that you experience not only your daydreams, but also the images you attribute to past and future. And before you ask the question, allow me to anticipate it: memories are indeed fantasies. What else could they be? They certainly aren't present perceptions, are they?

The diagram in Figure 10 can be divided vertically into two hemispheres. The top hemisphere corresponds to 'perception' in a broad sense: the symbolic apprehension of mental activity unfolding *outside* the personal mind. The bottom hemisphere corresponds to cognitive activity arising *within* the personal mind itself. Similarly, we can also divide the diagram horizontally. In this case, the left hemisphere corresponds to the analytical interpretation of sensory data, or the 'left-hemisphere mode of thought' described by Iain McGilchrist.[138] The right hemisphere, on the other hand, corresponds to the noetic imagination, 'an extra-ocular organ of perception and knowledge.'[139] The noetic imagination can both symbolically *'perceive'* a transcendent order and *create* idiosyncratic experiences in the form of fantasies, it often being hard to differentiate between the two. It is this difficulty in telling personal fantasy from transcendent insight that lies at the heart of much of the metaphysical hysteria at the fringes of contemporary culture.

Implicit everywhere in the diagram of Figure 10 are our *emotions*: all four modes of cognition illustrated—perceptions, transcendent insights, thoughts and fantasies—evoke emotions in the personal mind, each in its own way. We are all familiar with the fact that our thoughts and perceptions can trigger strong emotional responses. For instance, negative thinking can trigger gloomy moods, while contemplating the beauty of nature can reverse them. But the same applies to the right hemisphere as well: transcendent insights can fundamentally alter our emotional state, with fantasies having a smaller but nonetheless significant effect.

Not only do the four modes of cognition illustrated in Figure 10 automatically trigger emotions, they also automatically trigger our myth-making capacities: the myth of an objective reality is triggered by consensus perceptions; true religious myths are triggered by transcendent insights; more ordinary explanatory and predictive myths are triggered by thoughts; and the myths of past and future are lived out in the form of fantasies. As a result, our entire cognitive 'space' becomes populated with myths, which gives substance to human life. These myths hint at the essential truths of mind: they reflect, in symbolic form, the underlying reality of whatever it is that we are. Our seemingly objective perceptions of the world reveal something true about the surface of mind-at-large, while true religious myths hint at its deeper, underlying layers. Perhaps most significantly, for embodying small-scale 'samples' of mind-at-large that we can demarcate and slide under the microscope of self-reflection, our personal thoughts and fantasies are uniquely conducive to lucid inquiry. As such, the myths of explanations, predictions, past and future, *when properly contemplated as symbols,* provide a unique window into something ineffable and otherwise impervious to self-reflection. This may be an important clue to the very meaning of human life.

Instead of a shared world outside mind, what we have is a collective part of mind that we don't identify with and cannot control. Our perceptions and transcendent insights originate from this collective part, while our thoughts and fantasies arise in our personal mind.

PART III: Belief

Some things have to be believed to be seen.
Ralph Hodgson

Before we begin Part III proper, a little introduction is in order. We've just seen that reality is a 'dream' of a disembodied universal consciousness, which we called mind-at-large. We, as individuals, are collapsed segments of mind-at-large that 'wake up'—become lucid—inside the dream. As illustrated in Part I, this is precisely what many of the world's religious myths have been saying for thousands of years. So what better way to elaborate further on these ideas than through a myth adapted to our contemporary language, sensitivities and cultural references? The final part of this book hence consists entirely of a modern religious myth, each chapter relating a part of its story. And, as is the case with any such myth, *what follows is much more than mere allegory.*

Unlike what people today normally associate with a religious myth, the one here is fairly down-to-earth and contemporary. Its cultural references are plausible and familiar to many. It entails no supernatural occurrences, no prophets and no saints. Anyone could be its protagonist. It is a myth of the recent past, not of distant events shrouded in vagueness and ambiguity. The story it tells is very close to us in both time and space. Indeed, even only a few pages into it, you may already question whether it is *religious* at all. Nonetheless, it perfectly fits the definition of religious myth given in Part I: a symbolic story that helps bring transcendence into everyday life.

When today's best-known religious myths were still recent—that is, thousands of years ago in most cases—they, too, sounded plausible to the people of the time. The romantic anachronisms we associate with these myths today are a later acquisition, which came—as discussed in Part I—at the cost of plausibility. My attempt in the remainder of this book is to recover some of that original sense of plausibility, intimacy and contemporaneity radiated by religious myths around the time of their inception.

The meaning and role of belief in our lives is explored in this symbolic narrative in both explicit and implicit ways. Besides addressing belief directly, whatever significance the myth will have in your life will itself depend on your belief in it. This way, the story intentionally flows back and forth between two different but intertwined levels of meaning. Will you believe this myth *as if it were literally true?* And if so, how will the myth's assertions about belief affect your relationship with it?

The story is narrated in the first-person because direct insight into the subjective perspective of its protagonist is essential to the myth's message.

Chapter 8

Ticket off-world

And there I finally was, comfortably but firmly strapped to a customized recliner made to perfectly accommodate my body shape. My head was tightly fastened to a rig that prevented it from moving. An eye mask and earplugs isolated my senses completely from whatever was going on around me. But I knew that the complex and rather large rig around my head was about to kick into operation, so it was comforting to know that I wouldn't be able to hear its rather disturbing hum. The nurse was probably already starting the carefully orchestrated series of intravenous infusions that would, together with the electromagnetic fields beamed directly into my head, completely change my sense of self and reality. From that moment on, and despite all the training I had undergone, I really had no idea what was going to happen. I felt that my whole life had somehow been about that very moment, everything preceding it mere preparation. With these thoughts rushing through my mind, I took a deep breath to try to relax and—as instructed—began counting down from ten. At around seven, I already knew that nothing would ever be the same again...

Joining the club

Some years earlier, I was just an ordinary, particularly young and naïve computer engineer working at an international research facility. Although I was rather good at what I did, I expected nothing of my future but a perfectly ordinary life. I was convinced that my story would unfold along all the predictable milestones: I already had a degree, a good job and was about to marry. The obvious next steps would be to buy a house, some dogs—err, cats—have children and finally retire in peace. I even thought myself lucky for being able to realistically look forward to all this, which, in hindsight, was pitiful. Little did I know what I was in for.

I was a specialist in Artificial Intelligence (A.I.) systems for data acquisition. My job consisted in designing and programming computers capable of processing information and adapting to changing circumstances in ways similar to how the human brain does. These computers would recognize changing patterns in hugely complex streams of data and then learn how to adapt to these patterns in order to achieve preset goals. This was pretty leading-edge work at the time, with very few commercial applications. My employer was an international, government-funded organization with enough resources and a sufficiently cocky attitude to try unlikely but promising new technologies. I was by far the youngest member of my team, enthusiastic and starry-eyed. I loved what I did, greatly enjoyed the company of my colleagues and was generally having a fantastic time. I think I radiated a kind of unthreatening, optimistic vibe that subtly made people want me around. I didn't know this back then; only in hindsight do I believe to discern this as a possible explanation for what followed.

It's not my intention here to recount details of my personal life, which are irrelevant in view of what I actually have to say. I am merely providing the minimum necessary background for you to understand how I came to be in the rather unique position to learn—or rather, *remember*—certain things about the nature of life and reality, despite being a very ordinary person myself. It is these things that I actually want to share with you. But before I can get to them, I need to relate just a bit more of my story.

One day—I still recall: it was an overcast early-spring morning—I received a phone call at home while brushing my teeth. This was highly unusual given the early time, since most of my friends and colleagues started their days even later than I did. I rinsed my mouth quickly, suspecting that it was something important, and picked up the phone. The female voice on the other side was polite but all business. She identified herself as a headhunter who had an interesting job opportunity to offer me. I told her I had no intention to leave my employer but she insisted, pointing out that I probably wouldn't need to give anything up and asking me to at least hear her out. That sounded reasonable and, partly persuaded by her charming voice, I figured I had nothing to lose. Over the next few weeks, I would have several meetings with her and several of her associates.

The alleged headhunter's name was Sophie. Disarmingly attractive and only a couple of years older than me, she was quite young for her role and responsibilities. Indeed, she was the key recruiter of a large, massively well-funded, yet completely stealthy project initiated by an unacknowledged club of (former) corporate leaders and high-net-worth individuals. Some would call this club a secret society, but the conspiracy connotations are totally inapplicable. I will refer to it simply as 'the Club.'

The Club had originally been formed in the late sixties by a group of successful bankers who were undergoing a kind of late mid-life crisis. These people—all males—had achieved everything they'd ever wanted in life. They had their mansions, yachts, supercars and whatnot. They had power, influence, trophy wives, but lacked one important element: their lives no longer had any meaning. Having realized all their material dreams, they no longer knew what they were alive for. Moreover, middle age and its usual ailments had begun to force them to acknowledge their own mortality. The message from their bodies was loud and clear: 'you aren't superman and you, too, are going to die.' Unable to believe the naïve religious myths they had grown up with, they wanted to find out whether there was indeed something after death; and if so, what. Their motivation to explore these questions was total—there was nothing else of interest in their lives—and their pockets very deep indeed. The Club was the way they found to pull their efforts and resources together to achieve critical mass.

Although most of the original founders had already died, the Club itself was now more active and better funded than ever, run by a new generation of leaders with the same profile and motivations of the founders. Some of the current leaders were actually sons and daughters of former leaders. They had re-organized the Club as a kind of meta-investment fund and management bureau interested in projects that would, from the point of view of the mainstream, probably be considered fringe and ridiculed. This, in fact, was the main motivation for the secrecy surrounding the whole enterprise. Open-minded as they were, these people still held highly visible positions in the corporate and political worlds. They had images to protect.

The Club's assets thwarted the budget of some small nations. Through third-party investment funds they controlled, the Club financed several external projects both at universities and private companies. Nothing could be easily traced back to them because of a network of intermediaries and foundations, even though everything was perfectly legal. Their key project, however, wasn't external: it was supervised directly by the Club's leaders and carried out mainly in Club-owned premises. Its codename— for reasons I never really understood—was 'Trilobite.'

Sophie's goal was to recruit me for a 'volunteer research associate' position in Trilobite. The work was directly related to my areas of specialization and, apparently, I had been recommended by people who knew me well in my professional capacity. My conclusion then, and still today, was that some of my colleagues or supervisors at work had some degree of involvement with the Club.

As the name implied, my work was to be officially carried out on a 'volunteer' basis, in my own free time and, to the extent possible, out of my own home through a virtual private network (the latter was pretty high-tech at the time). All necessary equipment—including a professional, high-end workstation and communication equipment—would be 'donated' to me by the Club. There would be no contracts of any kind and the Club would have complete deniability regarding my participation. The advantage for me was that I would not need to leave my day job. Indeed, as I would later learn, most of Trilobite's workforce was made up of part-time 'volunteers' like myself. Only a few staff positions—top scientists and managers—were occupied by people with a formal link to one or another of the Club's foundations and funds. Together, staff and volunteer associates were responsible for all the research and development behind Trilobite. The commodity work of implementation—of both hardware and software—was almost entirely contracted out to external firms. Each of these firms only ever saw small modules of the project, never getting a chance to understand how they came together or what ultimate purpose they served.

As for how the Club managed to attract volunteers, I can only speak for myself: my key motivation for having eventually accepted the job was the nature of Trilobite itself, as I am about to describe. The project was simply irresistible to me. I considered— and still consider—my participation in it the privilege of a lifetime. Yet, I also won't deny that volunteers were treated well by the Club in terms of in-kind contributions and intangibles. Being an associate made life easier and safer, especially when one was a young engineer just getting married.

Trilobite

Originally inspired by the psychedelic revolution of the 1960's, the Club had set up Trilobite to find more effective and controllable methods for accessing what was described to me as 'transcendent realms.' I once asked the project's Chief Scientist whether these were actual realities or just otherwise unconscious mental spaces. He replied by asking me, rather rhetorically, what the difference between the two was. I didn't quite get his drift at the time.

Anyway, the problem was that psychedelics, although providing unambiguously powerful effects, were unpredictable and impossible to control. The experience was also awkward to describe or make sense of afterwards. It was as if the subject's rational capacities for analysis and recall were switched off during the trance, rendering it impossible to articulate or bring back anything meaningful. Club founders had experimented with psychedelics but were highly frustrated by these short-comings. Their 'trips' had given them the certainty that there was something huge to be explored—potentially holding all the answers they yearned for—but tantalizingly out of reach. They wanted to find ways to enter the psychedelic realm for long periods of time, with their analytical and recall capacities somewhat preserved, and with some level of control over the themes and directions of the trip. Specifically, they wanted the trance to be conducive to intention: a goal or a question posed before the beginning of the trip.

The working hypothesis behind the inception of Trilobite was that everyday brain activity somehow restricted or blocked lucid access to these 'transcendent realms.' Club founders were galva-nized by Aldous Huxley's psychedelic-inspired description of the brain as a 'reduction valve' of otherwise unlimited consciousness—discussed in Huxley's famous 1954 book *The Doors of Perception*—and believed it to be rather accurate. Huxley's book, in fact, had been the basis for the foundation of Trilobite. The project's scientists were tasked, from the beginning, with finding ways to temporarily and selectively switch off specific parts of the brain in a coordinated manner, in hopes that this could eventually induce a controlled psychedelic trance. This seminal hypothesis was the guiding principle of Trilobite throughout its life and, as it turns out, a good-enough approximation of the facts. Indeed, time after time the hypothesis was confirmed in trials, at least at an operational level: things did behave *as though* a normal working brain were a reduction valve of consciousness, focusing our attention on what was important for the survival of the physical body but restricting our access to transcendent insight.

The scientists' initial attempts had focused purely on drug design. However, for many years little progress was made. To be sure, new and effective psychoactive agents were developed — some even found their way to the streets — but none that could deliver on the Club's key requirement: that of a controllable trip preserving one's analytical wits and memory access capacity. Early methods for synthesizing drugs were crude, severely restricting what could be achieved. And even as methods improved over the years, project scientists realized that drugs alone, no matter how well designed they were, could never give them sufficient granularity of control over the activity of different brain regions. Finally, they also realized that the subject's responses during the trance were dynamic, requiring the effect of the psychoactive agent to quickly adapt on-the-fly. This was impractical with drugs. The scientists' ultimate dream was to be able to selectively deactivate any individual neuron anywhere in the brain, at any time. Drugs alone simply couldn't do it.

It was only in the mid 1980's that project scientists began exploring another tool: exposing the subject's brain to electro-magnetic (E.M.) fields. Some guy in England had managed to control a subject's motor functions by applying these fields through the skull, so project scientists figured that they could push the technique further. The E.M. fields could disrupt activity in specific regions of the brain in a way that could be programmed and adapted on-the-fly. The theory was that one could manipulate the subject's state of consciousness with these fields, opening the 'gates of transcendence,' so to speak. The scientists also theorized that they could control the trance by, for instance, disrupting cyclical, self-reinforcing neural processes responsible for the notorious 'loops' of 'bad trips.' The whole thing was rudimentary back then, but it offered enough degrees of freedom for progressive refinement.

Through exhaustive and unbelievably expensive trial and error over many years, project scientists had converged on a mix-and-match technique that they called 'the Recipe.' It entailed three different elements: a carefully coordinated series of intravenous infusions that delivered different psychoactive drugs at specific moments (colloquially called the 'Juice Mix' among research associates); a programmed series of E.M. pulses at specific locations of the subject's brain (which we inaccurately called the 'Light Show'); and brain function measurement technology to monitor the subject's neural activity during the trance (the 'Telemetry,' also a rather inaccurate term that stuck). A custom-made computer coordinated all three elements. The Recipe had shown tremendous promise in trials carried out during the few years preceding my joining the project. This had motivated the Club to free up a seemingly unlimited financial line to, once and for all, have Trilobite deliver on its goals. Their efforts to get me onboard were a small part of this renewed push.

One of the key remaining technical challenges had to do with pattern recognition and control. This is where I came in. With their brain function measurement technology, project scientists could see and record the neural activity in a subject's brain with exquisite detail, but they hadn't yet developed a way to reliably *interpret* the patterns they saw. They didn't quite know what the Telemetry meant from the subject's direct subjective perspective; that is, what the subject was *experiencing* in association with the measured pattern of brain activity. To develop a tool to help figure this out was the first part of my team's task. The second part was to develop a way to translate this interpretation of the Telemetry into commands for adjusting the Juice Mix and the Light Show. The idea was to have a computerized system continuously observe the subject's brain activity and adapt both the cocktail of psychoactive drugs and the position and intensity of the E.M. pulses on-the-fly, so to steer the trance along paths predetermined by the subject's original intention.

Our general approach was to use offline data to train an A.I. system to interpret Telemetry. Trilobite had amassed a huge library of Telemetry recordings and corresponding trip reports, the latter written by the subjects shortly after their respective trips. With enough trip reports and Telemetry recordings we should, theoretically, be able to develop an A.I. system that could mine for correlations between the two and learn what patterns of neural activity corresponded to what types of subjective experience. Once the A.I. had learned enough, it could then be deployed 'live,' during a trip, so to help adjust the Light Show and the Juice Mix on-the-fly. There were huge problems, though: despite the thousands of trip reports and Telemetry recordings available to us, the data were, statistically speaking, extremely limited for our purposes. The complexity of neural activity and the variety of subjective experiences reported were such that orders of magnitude more data would be necessary for an ordinary A.I. to learn the correspondences. To compound the problem, the trip reports were not time-stamped: we didn't precisely know what segment of the Telemetry corresponded to what part of the subject's later narrative of his or her experiences. Fundamentally new technical insights were necessary to tackle these issues.

Even with these problems addressed, project scientists were aware that deliberate control of the trance could only be done coarsely, at the level of broad themes and directions. But that was enough. The Club's intent was to learn about the underlying nature of life and reality, so the system was meant to continually monitor the Telemetry to see if the trip was going in this general metaphysical direction. If not, it should calculate changes in the Juice Mix and the Light Show to put the trip back on the intended course.

Notice that the idea here wasn't to create an artificial virtual reality by manipulating brain function; in fact, that would have defeated the whole purpose of the project. As mentioned earlier, the hypothesis was that the trance gave subjects access to transcendent but *real* landscapes, where *real* answers to the biggest questions of life could be found. The goal of fine-tuning the Juice Mix and Light Show during the journey was merely to help an explorer *navigate* an unfamiliar terrain with some level of control, not to artificially simulate the terrain itself. Selectively *de*-activating certain parts of the brain was just a means to send people off to specific locations of a transcendent space, rather like Jody Foster in the movie *Contact* (there actually were some interesting rumors about the relationship between that movie and Trilobite, but that's not relevant here). There, they would hopefully find the answers and insights the Club sought.

Trilobite had an amazing team of carefully selected volunteer subjects to undergo the trips. We called them 'Explorers' and I was surprised to find the names of some well-known personalities among them: authors, scientists, filmmakers, spiritual teachers, artists, the lot. I wondered whether their celebrated creative power, insights and eloquence didn't arise, at least in part, from their secret Trilobite journeys. Be it as it may, the Explorers were handpicked for their uniquely varied background in mathematics and hard sciences, the arts, humanities, literature and poetry. The idea behind this careful selection was to send in people equipped to interpret and make some sense of the transcendent landscapes encountered. They should also be able to describe what they experienced with some clarity and consistency, which turned out to be quite difficult. The average person on the streets, as project scientists soon discovered, simply couldn't accomplish this.

The unfortunate implication was that there was no overlap between the team of research associates developing the Recipe— of which I was part—and the team of Explorers. The respective selection processes posed radically different requirements. As a member of the research team, I wasn't supposed to trip myself.

However, a few years into my tenure at Trilobite, we had managed to turn the Recipe into computer-controlled fine art. The system was playing like an orchestra. The increasingly coherent and tantalizing reports of Explorers emerging from their trips began to instill in me an irresistible urge to trip myself. I just had to know first-hand what the Explorers were talking about. And, as it turns out, I'd get my chance; in fact, many more than one.

Off to another realm

I did my work well at Trilobite. Even though my physical visits to Club premises were few and far between, because of constraints related to my day job and personal life, I was highly motivated and engaged in the project. This had given me visibility and earned appreciation from Trilobite staff. Indeed, after only a couple of years, I was already seen as a true member of the family. Being aware of this, there came a time when I decided to leverage my solid position in the project to—how should I put it?—*enrich* the modes of my participation in it.

Yes, I just wanted to trip. I needed to trip. My curiosity was becoming unbearable and Sophie was the person I chose to share my feelings with. Over the years, she and I had become friends— in case this word is applicable to people who see each other in person once or twice a year—so I felt comfortable opening up to her. As it turns out, she sympathized with my cause and brought it up for discussion with her management. The usual arguments against mixing roles were brought up, but I had one important thing going for me: *I was trusted.* I guess they figured that, in the worst-case scenario, my trip reports would be useless but at least I would be happy. For them, I guess this was simply a new way to compensate my efforts in the absence of a salary; another type of in-kind bonus, so to speak.

I had to undergo training and preparation before my first journey. This consisted in: multiple psychological and physical evaluations; a form of psychotherapy aimed at 'clearing the skeletons in the closet' (deeply-ingrained, unnoticed fears and traumas that could get amplified during a trip to the point of ruining it); tools for controlling the journey from within, like breathing techniques, self-hypnosis, visualization and the use of mantras; a mildly restrictive diet; and—most time-consuming of all—academic-level courses on philosophy, history, religious studies and mythology. Because of my background, no courses were required on math or sciences. Fortunately, the vast majority of this training could be done remotely, via self-study and guided live sessions on the Internet.

For the actual trips, however, Explorers needed to be physically present at the Club's main laboratory, where the rather large rigs required by the Light Show and Telemetry were located. Qualified nursing staff was also required for the application of the Juice Mix. Traveling to the lab's site, despite being demanding on my schedule and complicated to disguise as a regular business trip or vacation, was always very pleasant. It suffices to say that most Club leaders reside in a particularly beautiful, quiet and safe part of the world; and it was there that they set up their laboratory. Like several retired Explorers, I, too, dream of retiring there one day.

And so it was that, in the first years of the twenty-first century, I embarked on a series of journeys that would forever change not only my life, but my very sense of identity. At first, I had been scheduled to undergo only five journeys. However, the surprising results of my initial experiences triggered a process that would see me trip into transcendence more than two dozen times.

What nobody had anticipated was that, precisely for having intimate knowledge of the A.I. that automatically adjusted the Juice Mix and the Light Show during the journey, I was uniquely positioned to correlate the inside view of the trip with what the system was measuring and doing from the outside. This allowed me to optimize both the Recipe and my own mental states—the latter during the trip—so the A.I. would pick up my intentions and react accordingly. In essence, I could teach the A.I. new skills and then tell it, *from within the trip*, exactly what to do to help me steer the journey. Through subjective trial-and-error during each trip and extensive tweaking of the A.I. in between trips—the latter based on my own Telemetry recordings—I refined and personalized this mechanism to a point where I was soon achieving results nobody had achieved in the prior thirty-five years of project Trilobite. And that is the next part of my story...

Chapter 9

Meeting the Other

I found that the easiest way for me to rationally make sense of, and later remember, the transcendent insights attained during each trip was to frame the journey in the form of a dialogue. Naturally, this raises the question of *whom* I was dialoguing with. The most honest answer is: a deeply obfuscated but knowledgeable complex of my own mind that, at the same time, was also entirely alien to my ego. It became a habit for me and other Explorers—who later used similar Recipe setups—to refer to this psychic complex as 'the Other,' a designation inspired by our Continental Philosophy courses. Indeed, I spent substantial effort trying not only to tune my mental attitude to this dialogue format, but also to get the A.I. to optimize the Recipe for it. One's limited ego would play the part of the questioner, while the Other would answer the questions with deeper, broader knowledge of what's going on. The dialogue format—the dissociation it enabled between ego and Other—allowed one to retain one's analytical wits and memory access capacity in the ego complex, while bringing the deeper, broader aspects of consciousness out of obfuscation in the form of the Other. This simple dissociative trick allowed us to nail down the Club's original, apparently contradictory goals in a rather elegant manner. There was no complete ego dissolution, as in traditional psychedelic trances, but neither was the ego able to obfuscate the deeper aspects of mind any longer.

It took me a couple of journeys to adjust the Recipe and my own mental attitude to a point where the dialogue between ego and Other would routinely emerge. But once this was achieved, I had the ride of my life. What follows is an account of what I learned from these dialogues.

Notice that, although the reports below are necessarily restricted to words, the dialogues themselves weren't. The Other communicated in the form of images and the direct transmission of ineffable insights just as often as words. My attempt below has been to translate these other forms of communication into words as well as I could, though much has unavoidably been lost in translation.

Who the heck are you?

10, 9, 8, 7... I could feel the knot of my ordinary mental associations becoming untangled, different threads of thought and emotion being teased apart and allowed to starve in isolation. I didn't resist it, merely witnessing as huge mental spaces opened up in my mind. How incredibly spacious it was. Mundane questions, worries and concerns were gone. 6, 5... My awareness of my own body dissipated quickly, leading to mild anxiety. The body became distant, remote, even abstract. 4, 3, 2... It is impossible to describe one's state of consciousness at this stage. One drifts within an ocean of previously obfuscated mental contents, unspeakably huge vistas—comprised of images, affections and insights—opening up at each twist and turn. This unfathomable ocean felt as autonomous and tangible as the ordinary world, if not more.

1...

'This *feels* so concretely and palpably real!' I mentally remarked to myself.

'But it *is* concretely and palpably real,' a voice responded, seemingly out of the blue.

'What the heck?' I asked rather startled.

It is difficult to say whether the answer I then received was my own conclusion or something communicated by the voice:

'I am this "Other" you've been trying to find.'

A mental reality

I paused to gather my 'thoughts,' or whatever type of mental activity one manifests in that state of consciousness. I was surprised and excited, only reassured by the fact that I sensed great patience and serenity on the part of the Other. My struggle was in deciding which line of inquiry to pursue next. Part of me wanted confirmation of whether the Other was an aspect of myself or a separate, autonomous entity of some sort. Yet, I also felt irresistibly puzzled by his very first words: 'it *is* concretely and palpably real,' he'd said, referring to the unfathomable mental space where I now was. How could it be? I knew I was undergoing a glorified psychedelic trip enhanced by E.M. fields. I was lying in a scientific laboratory, monitored closely by over a half-dozen people. My eyes were shut and my ears plugged. Clearly, my experience was mental and, as such, not 'concretely and palpably real.'

'But isn't your ordinary waking reality ultimately *also* a mental experience?' the Other asked, in seeming awareness of what I was thinking. 'All you can know about it is experiential. Whatever else reality may be, apart from your *experience* of it, is just an abstraction of your intellect, forever beyond your life.'

This was disarmingly logical. Yet, habits of thought, when reinforced over a lifetime, are hard to break. So I insisted:

'Yes... But there is a clear difference between the world of my mind, inside my head, and the real world outside my head. For one, I need to have my eyes open to see the real world, while this experience right now, including you, can only be within my head. After all, my real eyes are closed right now.'

'Your confusion arises from a fundamental inversion: *it is your head that is in your mind, not your mind in your head.* This realm is indeed entirely within your mind. But so is your ordinary waking reality, your body included. Both realms are mental worlds unfolding within consciousness at all times. The act of focusing your attention on one particular realm obfuscates the others. That's why you cannot feel your body right now: your body is a *mental content* that belongs to another, now-obfuscated realm of mentation; another dream of mind, so to speak.'

I had never thought of things this way and the idea was strangely seductive. But if the Other was correct, the implications would be nearly unimaginable. The idea that the mind is inside the body—as opposed to the other way around—is behind everything we consider true about the world and ourselves. Not only are psychiatry, psychology and our understanding of death directly rooted in it, our economical, political, social, educational, scientific, philosophical and even religious systems are also indirectly based on it. We couldn't possibly have gotten it all so wrong for so long. We would have noticed problems and contradictions earlier. Yet, the edifice of our culture has survived for centuries standing on this very foundation. Picking up on my thoughts again, the Other continued:

'Nobody knows how the matter of the brain could possibly produce the qualities of experience. The edifice you speak of has only stood for so long because you've conveniently quarantined the most difficult and fundamental questions.'

I knew this was at least partly correct. The issue he was referring to is now known as 'the hard problem of consciousness.' We cannot even *conceive* coherently of a process by which arrangements of matter could produce subjective experience, let alone explain experience. It's a baffling mystery in neuroscience and philosophy of mind. But I wasn't ready to admit defeat:

'Perhaps, but neither can we ignore all the evidence for a world outside mind. For instance, if I close my eyes, I stop seeing because photons from a world outside my mind can no longer stimulate my brain via my retina. Moreover, there is overwhelming evidence that the brain has a lot to do with the mind. My very presence here is proof of it: right now, I am experiencing you because drugs are being pumped into my brain and electromagnetic fields are being beamed into my head.'

'The brain and the mind are surely not separate from each other. In saying that the brain is *in* the mind, I am saying precisely that they aren't separate. But that doesn't imply that there is anything outside mind. You're merely *assuming* that a world outside mind is the only possible explanation for sense perceptions, like your ability to see.'

'What other explanation can there possibly be?' I asked.

'Before we explore this question, remember how this conversation started: you experience this realm to be as real, as palpable, as concrete as your ordinary waking world. At the very least, this proves that mind is *capable* of producing fully convincing realities without the aid of anything external to it, correct?'

'Yes... Unless this realm actually isn't mental but material...' I retorted rather hesitantly. I knew I was directly contradicting my earlier stance, but I felt I needed to explore all alternatives. 'Perhaps this realm, too, is outside mind,' I continued, 'just like my ordinary waking reality. Perhaps the Recipe has just brought me to a parallel universe of some kind.'

'Oh, I see... And how would that work?' asked the Other with a slight overtone of mockery.

'I don't know. Maybe mind can tune into different material universes.'

'In that case,' he countered, 'mind would have to be fundamentally independent of your brain, not generated by it. Isn't that right?'

'True,' I admitted. 'This would indeed imply some form of dualism.'

'So how would you then explain the ordinary correlations between brain states and mental states?'

'It would still be conceivable that, after my mind chose to tune into my ordinary waking world, my experiences could be *modulated* — as opposed to *generated* — by my material brain in that world, just as empirically observed...' I was reaching and I knew it.

'Yes. However,' rebutted the Other, 'in that case the Recipe couldn't have caused your mind to tune into *another* realm, and then keep you here, simply by manipulating your brain from within your ordinary waking reality, could it?'

'Indeed not,' I conceded. 'My brain exists in the ordinary realm, so it couldn't have any influence on what happens here. Yet, I am here presumably thanks to the on-going interference of the Recipe with my material brain...'

'Precisely. So your hypothesis cannot be true.'

'OK. But then again,' I insisted, 'if the brain is in mind, how come the Recipe works? How come drugs and electromagnetic interference in my brain change my mental states?'

'Why wouldn't they? You are implicitly thinking in dualistic terms: you assume that your subjective experiences are one type of "stuff" while physical processes, like drug intake and exposure to electromagnetic fields, are another. But what I am suggesting is precisely that *both* are mental and, therefore, can affect each other just like your thoughts can affect your emotions. I am saying that *everything* is mental, including the drugs and electromagnetic fields, not only your brain.'

'And how does this answer my question?' I was genuinely confused.

'When you dream at night, the objects you see in your dreams do not correspond to a world outside your mind, do they? Yet, they can influence your subjective state within the dream: dreamed-up water can get you wet and make you experience cold within the dream; a dreamed-up lover can make you feel arousal within the dream; even dreamed-up drugs can make you trip within a dream. Moreover, you always have a dreamed-up avatar, whether implicit or explicit, since you always experience the dream from a localized, moving view-point *within* it.'

'I think I already see where you are going with this...'

'Your ordinary life is like a dream,' he continued anyway. 'Your physical body is inside your dreaming mind just like your avatar is inside your nightly dreams. The Recipe can change your state of consciousness for exactly the same reason that a dreamed-up lover can make you feel arousal, or that dreamed-up water can make you feel cold. The same goes for your earlier point about closing your eyes: if you close your avatar's eyes in a dream, you might also stop seeing within the dream. Whether this is the case or not depends merely on the particular *rules of cognitive association* that govern the dream by tying its unfolding experiences together. These rules are a kind of *belief system* in mind, encoding what mind *instinctively* believes must be the consequences of any given event or action. What then transpires in the dream is precisely what mind implicitly—in deep, highly obfuscated layers of cognition—believes must transpire. You stop seeing when you close your eyes in a dream if your dreaming mind expects that shutting your eyes should prevent you from seeing. In ordinary waking reality, you call the applicable rules of cognitive association the "laws of cause and effect" or "the laws of classical physics" or, even more deeply ingrained in your belief system, the "laws of classical logic." The only peculiar thing about the rules of cognitive association in ordinary waking reality is that they are rather stable and consistent, unlike those usually governing a nightly dream. Yet, this very stability and consistency are part of the belief system applicable to ordinary waking life. You implicitly, instinctively believe—and therefore expect—that nature must be rather stable and consistent.'

I don't know why but this resonated strongly with me. I intuitively knew that there was truth in this, even though I was extremely uncomfortable with the way it contradicted my worldview. In this state of cognitive dissonance, I offered:

'What you are saying is that this realm feels so real to me *not* because it is material, but because the ordinary waking world I consider real is, just like this realm, mental...'

'Precisely! *Both* realms are mental, this being the reason why you experience them in the same way. Reality is a *feeling*. Concreteness and palpability are qualities of *experience*, not of the abstraction you call the "material world." This realm is real not *despite* being in mind, but *because* it is in mind.'

I understood him perfectly, but the point raised many questions. If all reality was in my mind, did it mean that I was the only conscious being in the universe? Did it mean that all reality was my *personal* dream, other people being simply projections of my dreaming mind? And what about the Other? Was he, too, just a projection of myself? Now that I had finally interacted with him, he felt so autonomous and external to me that I began to question my original assumptions. I wanted to confront him with these questions but I felt exhausted. I needed time to process and integrate this experience and all the insights I'd had. The Other recognized this. Reassured, I then proceeded to mentally chant the mantra that would trigger the A.I. to stop the trip and bring me back. In the minutes during which my "re-entry" unfolded, I could sense the presence of the Other slowly fade away... I knew I'd miss him, but I also knew I'd be back soon.

The nature of self and others

Some of the drugs used in the Juice Mix caused the body to develop temporary resistance: if you used them again shortly after the previous trip, their effect would be markedly diminished. So I had to wait a full week before I could journey again, and even that amount of time was considered short by the attendant nurse. Luckily, she was sympathetic when I said I couldn't wait.

Indeed, there was more than just capricious eagerness behind my haste. I had to go back home to my day job in a little over a week, and I still hoped to squeeze in another journey during that time. Since my previous trip, I had tried to integrate and consolidate the insights I'd had. However, many more questions and doubts had arisen in my mind. I felt I needed to address them all before I could go back home in relative peace of mind.

It was a sunny Thursday afternoon when I returned to the lab for the next journey. I had already fine-tuned the Recipe based on the Telemetry recordings of my last trip and felt ready to encounter the Other once again. Sophie was there to see me off, as word of my earlier success had gotten around. There was general curiosity about what I'd bring back this time. The air was electrified with the reticent anticipation that Trilobite might— just *might*—have finally delivered.

The transcendent 'space' where the dialogues with the Other unfolded had the general feeling of being underground, like a cave or a subterranean installation. Many Explorers would describe it as a domed chamber, so we colloquially referred to it as 'the Dome.' Once in the Dome, in the presence of the Other, I wasted no time and went straight to the point:

'I am confused. You say that reality is the imagination of *my* mind, there being no external world. So does it mean that *I* am the only living being in the universe, everybody else being projections of *my* mind? Does it mean that you are just a projected aspect of myself? Neither possibility seems reasonable or plausible to me.'

I could sense the Other think something like 'OK, this will be delicate...' But he didn't quite 'say' it, whatever it means to 'say' something in that space. Instead, he offered this:

'The confusion rests in what you mean by the words "my" and "I." It's true that all reality is in *your* mind, but the "your" here does not refer to you as an individual person; instead, it refers to your true nature as impersonal mind. Your sense of personhood is an amalgamation of a particular experiential perspective—that is, a specific point of view within the dream— a particular set of memories and a particular model of self-identity. In other words, your personhood consists of *images* and *thoughts.* But images and thoughts are ephemeral, ever-changing. They come and go. As the constant witness of these changing images and thoughts, you can't *be* them, can you? Only your innermost subjectivity—the instinctive "I" feeling that precedes and couches all images and thoughts—is your true mind, wherein all realities unfold.'

Somehow this wasn't really satisfying to me.

'So reality doesn't *really* unfold in my mind, but in some kind of impersonal mind-at-large, *a la* Aldous Huxley...'

'This is where words become very delicate.' The Other seemed to be trying to be particularly precise at this point. 'I could answer "yes" to your question, but that would be misleading. It would lead you to think of mind-at-large as some kind of abstract entity that isn't really you. Yet, the instinctive and concrete sense of "I" that you feel right now, which precedes and couches all your perceptions, thoughts, emotions and memories, *is* mind-at-large. This way, mind-at-large really is the *felt* you; it just isn't your *concept* of you. If you stopped thinking and forgot everything you know, you would still have this same instinctive "I" feeling.'

'This is too subtle. I am not sure I really grasp this...' I protested.

'Then try the thought experiment I just hinted at: pretend right now that you forgot everything you know. Pretend that all your memories, theories, opinions, beliefs, everything, dissolved into oblivion without your losing consciousness. What's left?'

The mere invitation to try it instantly triggered the thought experiment in my mind. For what felt like several seconds, everything I knew about self and world vanished.

'Pure being,' I replied. 'I felt only a sense of pure being...'

'That's it! *Pure being*, unpopulated by thoughts, concepts, memories, etc. Every living creature feels this sense of pure being in exactly the same way. All organisms have the same instinctive "I" feeling that *is* mind-at-large.'

'But this is just a feeling, not an entity,' I pointed out. 'What does it mean to say that mind-at-large is a mere feeling? It would make more sense to me if you said that mind-at-large *has* the feeling you are talking about...'

'Stop looking for an object,' he rebuked me. 'Mind-at-large is the *subject*. All objects exist *in* mind-at-large as experiences, so mind-at-large itself can't be an object, can it? You must turn inward, to the innermost sense of pure being you've just felt. Only by *being* itself can mind-at-large know itself. Because it is all there is, including time and space, it cannot stand outside itself to observe itself as object.'

'This turns things inside out, but I am beginning to see what you mean,' I acknowledged. 'Mind-at-large is pure subjectivity. It can only pinpoint itself through its own most primordial inner sense of being...'

'Yes,' he confirmed. 'And its most primordial sense of being is *your* instinctive "I" feeling right now. Therefore, in the only way that matters, *you* are mind-at-large. The universe unfolds in *your* mind. It's just that *your* mind is not only yours; it is also *my* mind, the neighbor's mind, the co-worker's mind, the cat's mind, the ant's mind, etc., since we all share the same instinctive "I" feeling.'

'I think I got it...'

'I know you did, although you will need time to ponder about the implications and integrate them in your life.'

That was an understatement. Nonetheless, my original question hadn't been answered yet:

'OK, but then how come are there so many living creatures in the world? What is the nature of all these seemingly separate beings, given that mind-at-large is presumably one?'

'Your individual life is one among countless chains of associated mental contents in mind-at-large: it consists of specific sensations that lead to specific thoughts, which lead to specific feelings, which trigger other sensations, etc. Other chains—that is, other lives—consist of other sensations, leading to other thoughts, other feelings, etc. After all, what is a life but a distinctive series of experiences connected to each other through cognitive associations? The uniqueness of these associations is what characterizes your sense of personhood. To be a little more precise, each living being is in fact a distinctive *cluster*—not just a chain—of mostly *internally associated* thoughts, feelings and sensations imagined by mind-at-large. The biological body is what this cluster looks like from the perspective of other clusters. Each cluster becomes amnesic of the rest of mind-at-large because the dense cognitive associations within it lead to highly focused internal attention, which then obfuscates everything else outside the cluster.'

It wasn't lost on me that his last point about obfuscation confirmed Trilobite's hypothesis regarding how the Recipe worked: by inhibiting neural activity in targeted areas of the cluster—through drugs and electromagnetic fields—it reduced obfuscation, allowing the Dome and the Other to emerge out of a cognitive haze. At this stage of my work at Trilobite, however, I was already pretty much taking this for granted. So I decided to ask the Other about something else that had caught my attention:

'What did you mean by "internally associated" thoughts, feelings and sensations?'

'It means that experiences inside the cluster tend to repeatedly evoke other experiences *also inside* the cluster. Sensations may lead to habitual thoughts, which may evoke recurring emotions, which may trigger familiar memories, which in turn may lead to other similar sensations, etc., all mostly within the cluster. For instance, when you find an old painting long forgotten in your attic, you may think once more of your childhood home, which may make you feel like a kid again, which in turn may bring back memories of your parents, which may cause you to contemplate an old photograph of them, etc. This way, you end up with a set of mental contents that mostly reference each other, reinforcing their collective experiential footprint at the expense of every-thing else outside the cluster. It is this *internally associated* set that gives you a personal history and a sense of individual identity.'

So far so good, but I needed reassurance about a particular point that had been bothering me:

'So other people really *are* conscious, just like I am, right?'

'Yes, they are.' If the Other had a face, I'm sure he would be smiling at my insecurities. 'They are *other* amnesic clusters like yourself,' he continued.

Comfortable with this confirmation, I approached the more delicate point:

'And are *you* also an amnesic cluster of mind-at-large, just like other people?'

'No, I am not an amnesic cluster. I am the *rest* of mind-at-large, as partly actualized and perceived by your ego.'

'Now you've lost me... come again?'

'Amnesic clusters are like islands in an ocean of mentation,' he elaborated. 'The existence of the islands doesn't eliminate the ocean. I am what the ocean looks like from the vantage point of someone standing on your island; that is, your ego.'

'So any other Explorer who comes to the Dome can see you just as I do?' I asked, hardly disguising a little jealously.

'Anyone can potentially come here and talk to me, yes. But the view of the ocean is different from every island. And it isn't complete from any island, since from no one of them can the entire ocean be seen. The view from each island contributes a different but equally valid angle to humanity's understanding of the ocean. Thus, what you see of me is as much a function of your own individual peculiarities as it is of my nature. For instance, you have strong analytical tendencies, so you experience a rather analytical Other. Another Explorer with poetic or artistic tendencies would have a very different—though equally valid—experience of me.'

His metaphors were very helpful, even though I knew they

weren't complete or rigorous. What matters is that I understood what he was trying to say.

Finding the answers

'As the ocean, instead of a mere island,' I asked, 'do you know *everything*?' My interest in the Other was directly proportional to how much I thought he knew.

'Potentially yes, *but I only truly know what you or another living being asks me.*'

'How come?' I protested. 'Surely you either know something or you don't, regardless of being asked about it.'

'Whatever I have never been asked about by a self-reflective cluster of mind-at-large like yourself,' he continued, 'I know only *in potentiality*. Think of it as the light of a match: until you ignite the match, its light exists only in potentiality, in the form of energy chemically stored in its phosphorus head. But when you ignite the match, its light becomes *actualized*. Only then can it be *seen*. My knowledge is like the match: it exists complete, but only in potentiality, until you or someone else asks me about it. Your questions then partly ignite the match of my limitless insight, so its light can be seen. Only then does it illuminate existence.'

I couldn't help but be struck by the power of his metaphors. He was prepared, if so needed, to sacrifice rigor in order to ensure that I not only understood his point intellectually, but *groked* it with my whole being. If I didn't *feel* the insight he was attempting to convey, he wouldn't consider his job done.

'So before I or someone else asks you a question,' I insisted, 'even you don't know the answer?'

'I do know the answer always, but only *in potentiality*. In other words, I know it, but I don't know *that* I know it. The answer remains latent, like the light of a non-ignited match, and doesn't illuminate my experience; or yours.'

This was fertile ground and my thoughts were running wild:

'Why don't *you* ask yourself all relevant questions? You could then illuminate the whole of existence and eradicate ignorance!'

'*Because I am incapable of asking myself questions.*' What?! This was completely unexpected. But he continued before I could interject: 'Asking myself questions would require a particular cognitive configuration that arises exclusively within clusters like the human mind. Only the dense internal associations of a cluster enable one layer of cognition to become an object of inquiry of another layer of cognition. In other words, they enable you to think about your thoughts. And only by thinking about your thoughts can you formulate the probing questions required to make sense of existence. The reason is that all reality is in mind. Therefore, to understand reality one needs to inquire into the multiple subtle layers of hidden assumptions, expectations and beliefs in one's own mind. To do so, mind must turn in upon itself. It is this process of turning in upon itself that creates clusters, enables self-reflection and focuses the attention of egos at the cost of obfuscating everything else.'

While marveling at the cogency with which his elucidations came together, a critical insight suddenly struck me:

'This is the meaning of life! The human purpose is to light up the match of your latent knowledge!'

'That's a fair way to put it...' confirmed the Other, with slight hesitation.

The insight was incredibly powerful and rewarding to me, despite the rather cautious confirmation by the Other. A big part of me wanted to end the dialogue right then and there, to enjoy the afterglow. But there was still something nagging me...

Layers of cognition

'You alluded to "layers of cognition" a couple of times. I have a general intuition about what you meant, but could you perhaps explain it more specifically?'

'You perceive, feel and think in layers,' he answered. 'Each layer provides the beliefs and expectations that condition and facilitate the layer above. For example, when you see a bird, you uncritically project onto the perceived image everything you already believe about, and expect of, birds: their general body form, flight capabilities, likely behavior, place in the natural order of things, etc. Your perceptions, and all other cognitive associations that follow from them, are thus conditioned and facilitated by implicit, *underlying* beliefs and expectations. If they weren't, you would be discombobulated every time you saw a colorful feathered being darting around the sky.'

'Clear,' I interjected. But he hadn't finished his point yet:

'The thing is, you don't *question* your underlying beliefs and expectations while seeing the bird. You implicitly take them for granted. *Uncritically and implicitly taking something for granted is the effect of underlying, obfuscated layers of your cognition.* Here is another example: when you drive to work in the morning, your actions are conditioned and facilitated by your expectations regarding the way to work, the operation of the car, etc. While focusing on your driving, you take it for granted that, if you turn the wheel clockwise, the car will turn right; if you step on the break, the car will stop; if you turn left on the next intersection, you will arrive at work; etc. These implicit expectations reside in an underlying layer of your cognition that is obfuscated by the driving. *You act on these obfuscated expectations automatically, thoughtlessly.*'

'I see. I guess this applies to anything I do.'

'Indeed,' he confirmed. 'But notice that layered cognitive activity is not limited to the performance of tasks. It applies also to how you feel about life and self.'

'Could you give me a concrete example?'

'Whether you discern meaning in your life,' he obliged, 'is entirely conditioned by beliefs in underlying layers of your cognition. Deep within yourself, do you take it for granted that you are a material entity bound in space and destined to oblivion? If so, such belief will prevent you from experiencing your life's meaning.'

'I guess I just found out today that there *is* a transcendent meaning to life, after all!' I exclaimed enthusiastically.

'Then run with it,' he encouraged me, 'at least until you discover further nuances to your insight.'

He seemed to be hinting again at something he chose to leave unsaid. But by now I was mentally drained and had no energy to press him further. I knew that the Other could sense my exhaustion and wouldn't mind my aborting the journey. So the re-entry mantra was intoned and I left the Dome.

Upon coming round in the laboratory, I found Sophie starring me in the face. Her beautiful big eyes, full of anticipation, screamed out the question: 'So?! What has he told you this time?!' Behind her, several nurses and technicians pretended to busy themselves with their usual chores, secretly paying attention to what I had to say.

Manipulating beliefs

I had one more opportunity to visit the Dome and dialogue with the Other before I would have to return home. This would be my third journey after the Recipe had begun to reliably deliver me there. After it, months would pass before I would have another chance, so I had to get as much as possible out of it.

In both my previous experiences, I'd noticed that I only had enough mental stamina to engage in one general topic per session. The force of the insights was such that it left little room for a more eclectic discussion. So I carefully chose the topic I wanted to address in this final trip before my upcoming return home. It was a question that had been bugging me a lot since the last session and I was determined to confront the Other with it. To set my intention correctly, I kept on mentally repeating the question all the way through the final countdown, the Juice Mix already flowing through my veins.

'You seem to be in a fairly hardnosed mood today,' said the

Other rather sarcastically, but in good spirits.

'You are very eloquent,' I opened, 'but some of the things you say raise many questions.'

'Shoot,' he dared me. I was not sure I was comfortable with this lighthearted side of his.

'You said that ordinary reality is a kind of dream imagined according to a belief system; that the world behaves the way it does because, deep within, we *expect* it to behave like this. You compared it to the crazy causal associations of regular dreams—people changing shapes when we touch them, objects appearing out of nowhere when we think of them, etc.—which seem entirely plausible and natural during the dream, simply because they reflect our dreaming mind's implicit beliefs and expectations.'

'Right, go on,' he said. My interpretation of his earlier elucidations seemed to be correct.

'Well, then why can't I change the laws of nature just by wishing them to be different? After all, they merely reflect my own beliefs and expectations.' *Touché*, I naively thought.

'You're mixing up belief with volition,' the Other replied, instantly deflating my arrogance. 'Reality is a reflection of what you *believe* very deeply within your mind, not of what your ego *wishes for*. What people wish for is not necessarily what they truly believe in. As a matter of fact, most people wish for endless things they don't believe possible.'

'Right, I get that,' I conceded. But I still thought that there was something to my argument, so I persisted: 'Nonetheless, reality shatters people's beliefs all the time. Millions believed in the imminent second coming of Christ at several points in history, only to be disillusioned. Even today, many of my colleagues in science passionately believe their theories of nature only to watch experiments contradict and destroy their expectations. Reality doesn't seem to care at all about our beliefs.'

'When I said that reality reflects your beliefs,' he answered, 'I didn't mean the superficial beliefs of your *ego*, but those held in deeper, obfuscated layers of your cognition. As we discussed earlier, mind-at-large differentiates itself into clusters of mentation. This differentiation happens in layers. The cognitive processes in each layer condition those in layers above. The human ego spans but the top layers of differentiation. Underneath it there are many other layers, all the way down to the undifferentiated ocean of mind-at-large. The higher the layer of differentiation is, the denser the internal associations within a cluster and the more sparse the external associations between clusters. The beliefs that govern ordinary waking reality are not the beliefs formed in the superficial egoic layers, but in much deeper layers with comparatively many external associations.'

'Do you mean that the beliefs in question are unconscious beliefs?' I asked.

'They are *obfuscated* beliefs that completely escape the focus of your ordinary attention, yes. They aren't *literally* unconscious because there is nothing outside consciousness.'

'What about delusions?' I continued, without paying much attention to his last point. 'For instance, some people believe *very deeply* that they can fly. Then they jump off buildings and die...'

'These aren't deep beliefs, for they don't reside in deep layers of cognition. They are just *strong, sincere* beliefs *still in superficial layers*. The existence of very strong but relatively superficial beliefs in a cluster of mentation does not cancel out the effects — such as gravity — of beliefs concurrently held in much lower, less differentiated layers. There is no actual contradiction here, for these conflicting beliefs are all experienced in their own way, each within its own cognitive scope.'

I understood this but wasn't satisfied yet:

'You keep talking about a person's beliefs, but at the end of the day everyone shares the same world with everybody else. We all watch the sun set, have meals together, watch the same sports teams win or lose the same games, listen to music together, etc.

The same laws of nature apply to every human and even every living creature. For instance, high heat burns both a man and an amoeba. How come a man and an amoeba can share the same belief system?'

'Because the layers of differentiation in which this belief system resides are common to all biology,' he explained. 'The many external associations in those layers link clusters together.'

'Do you mean that the minds of all living creatures are interconnected at that level?'

'Yes, exactly. At that level, particular species haven't yet differentiated from one another. They remain interconnected. That's why you all share an underlying belief system: the mind of an amoeba, at that level, is one with the mind of a man. All amoebas and all men can thus share roughly the same dream you call ordinary waking reality, even though each individual has a different point of view within this common dream.'

His words were accompanied, in my mind, by astonishing visuals. I could see an endless three-dimensional structure of cosmic proportions, composed of countless layers. A homogeneous web of straight, long interconnect lines characterized the bottom layers. I knew that each interconnect line represented a chain of cognitive associations. Going up from bottom to top, broad but increasingly well-defined *tangles* of shorter, curled-up interconnect lines could be discerned, spanning many neighboring layers. Near the top, each tangle further differentiated into many small, dense *knots* of even shorter, even more curled-up interconnect lines, with vast empty spaces in between them. I knew that the knots were the clusters of cognitive associations the Other had described before. As such, each of them corresponded to a living creature emerging from the undifferentiated ocean of mind-at-large.

I could scan the layers from bottom to top and interpret this movement of my attention as the passage of time. This way, I could *see* the dynamic formation of the tangles and knots as progressively more advanced stages of a kind of chemical agglutination or cross-linking reaction.

Once again my mind was on fire. These ideas and images opened up huge new horizons and the potential implications were astounding.

'If, as you said earlier, mind-at-large is *my* own mind as much as it is anybody else's mind, it is presumably possible for me to gain awareness of deeper layers of universal mentation...'

'In principle it is,' he confirmed. 'By letting go of your ordinary attention in just the right way, you can indeed reduce the obfuscation of these deeper layers, which are always in your consciousness anyway.'

'But by accessing them just as I access the Dome right now, I could presumably change the belief system in these layers and thereby change ordinary reality. Yet, this doesn't seem at all possible.'

'If you were to reduce the obfuscation of the layers where the belief system behind ordinary reality resides, you would simply become cognizant *that* you have those beliefs. But you would still hold the same beliefs.'

'So there is no possibility to change the rules of cognitive association that govern ordinary reality?' I asked with a note of disappointment.

A silent pause ensued that seemed to last for several uncomfortable seconds. I wondered whether I'd said something wrong or whether the Other was simply hesitating. Finally, he continued slowly and emphatically:

'To change a belief system, you have to become lucid of the layers of cognition that *underlie* and *give rise* to it. In other words, you have to go at least one layer deeper than the layers where the belief system itself resides. And you have to do it in a critical, self-reflective manner.'

'So why doesn't anybody do it to make life easier? Why do the rules governing ordinary reality seem so implacable and immutable?' I probably sounded rather cynical here.

'Because self-reflective access to a layer of cognition requires back-and-forth associative interconnections between this layer and higher layers. Without them you can't think about your thoughts or inquire critically into your own hidden beliefs. However, such back-and-forth interlayer interconnections form only in the high-density associative environment of clusters. The belief system that governs ordinary reality, on the other hand, resides in layers much deeper than those where clusters develop, thereby escaping the reach of back-and-forth interlayer associations. The fisherman's line isn't long enough to reach those depths, so to speak. As such, people cannot change their ordinary reality because the corresponding belief system is too deeply ingrained, beyond the reach of self-reflection.'

'I think I understand this,' I commented, 'but could you try to explain it in simpler terms?'

'The belief system that governs ordinary reality is like a collective *instinct*: it's an automatism unreachable by lucid introspection and reasoning. Your sexual instincts, for instance, cannot be changed by mere rational judgment; otherwise celibate monks, ascetics and people with socially reviled sexual preferences would have easier lives. This is so because you cannot think about the mental processes that *underlie* and *give rise* to your instincts. You can only attain lucidity of the instincts' effects, not of their source. Likewise, humankind cannot change the rules of cognitive association whose reflection is the laws of nature.'

'But there are beliefs one can reflect critically upon and change,' I pointed out. 'For instance, any scientist who has ever changed his or her mind about the validity of a certain theory has done precisely that. And so has anyone who has ever changed his or her religious views.'

'Beliefs can form in any layer of cognition,' the Other clarified. 'Wherever they are in mind, they determine some aspect of your experience; that is, of your world. But some beliefs are superficial and accessible to self-reflective inquiry, while others are much more deeply ingrained, escaping the reach of back-and-forth interlayer associations. The belief system that underlies the laws of nature is of the latter kind.'

The complex unfolding of beliefs

'Yes, this is clear to me now,' I acknowledged, my skepticism somewhat soothed. 'I wonder about one thing, though. It seems to me that an exploding number of rules of cognitive association would be required to account for every aspect of ordinary reality. We would need a rule for what happens when I close my eyes, another for what happens when I sit under the sun, a different rule for the effect of each drug...'

'This is incorrect,' he interrupted me. 'The myriad effects that you are referring to arise as *compound implications* of basic, much more generic rules of association. Many of these generic rules simply correspond to what you know as the laws of classical physics, which aren't many. That the laws of classical physics are, in fact, rules of cognitive association doesn't change the fact that their effects can combine into higher-complexity implications. This way, there is no law of classical physics or rule of association dedicated to specifying what happens when you close your eyes; the effect of closing your eyes is the compound implication of much more generic regularities in nature.'

'So all rules of cognitive association are reflected in the laws of classical physics we know?'

'No, your knowledge of the patterns and regularities of nature is not complete,' he continued. 'Most significantly, while the classical laws you know apply all the way down to the level of molecules, there are organizing principles in nature—*wide-ranging* beliefs of mind-at-large—that only apply at the level of complex, macroscopic systems. Currently, you dismiss these purely macroscopic regularities as mere coincidences.'

'Are you referring to meaningful coincidences, or synchronicities, like getting a call from someone you happen to be thinking about, or getting an unsolicited job offer precisely when you are considering a change of career?'

'Yes, but not only synchronicities,' he answered. 'Certain aspects of physiology and metabolism, as well as other organizing principles that your science cannot study under controlled laboratory conditions, also reflect wide-ranging beliefs about how nature should behave.'

'Yet unknown laws of nature waiting to be discovered...' I commented with a sigh.

'Yes, undiscovered *mental patterns* reflecting *instinctive beliefs* and *charged with emotions,*' he clarified, 'which will remain unknown for as long as your science arbitrarily limits its own perspectives by unnecessarily inferring a world outside mind.'

The clarity, coherence and evocative power of his words were formidable. I just wasn't fully convinced yet because I suspected that, upon more careful examination, holes or gaps could still be found in his metaphysics. But I no longer had the mental energy to pursue the dialogue further. My most urgent questions had been addressed and I needed a break. Sensing all this, the Other offered:

'You have much to think about over the coming months. Integrating all you have learned takes time and shouldn't be rushed. There is a natural rhythm to everything. You are correct that the story is not yet complete and more elucidations are required, but we will have occasion to explore more when the time is right.'

Chapter 10

The origin of life, the universe and everything

Over a year would pass before I could return to Club premises and resume my journeys. The delay was entirely due to personal and professional circumstances of my own life, not to Trilobite. Indeed, despite the fact that advances in the Recipe since my earlier trips had been reliably delivering many other Explorers to the Dome—including Club leadership—project scientists were still eager for me to return. There was a somewhat unjustified expectation on their part that, like before, my own journeys could deliver even more advances to the Recipe. Moreover, my trip reports had turned into a kind of popular novel, the next chapter of which everybody wanted to read.

During this interlude of a year, I had continued to help refine the Recipe. Telemetry recordings and trip reports from many other Explorers were now flooding in, unveiling more specific correlations than ever before between neural activity (or rather lack thereof) and the most interesting elucidations of the Other. We zeroed in on these and developed a new setup to give the Other even more latitude and autonomy to convey his insights (or *her* insights, since many other Explorers experienced the Other as female). I had arranged to be the first Explorer to try this new setup and was very eager to see the results.

Space and time

The evening before my next journey, I had dinner with Sophie in a simple but delightful Italian restaurant very close to where I used to work when I first met her, a few years earlier. I used to be a regular there and the place brought back many good memories. It was a fantastic way to set the right mood for what was to come.

After catching up with developments in each other's lives, Sophie told me that another explorer she had originally brought into the project, and whom she had maintained regular contact with, wanted to suggest something to me. This woman was a well-respected, semi-retired clinical psychologist. She'd read my earlier trip reports and was amazed at the facility with which a straightforward dialogue with the Other emerged in my journeys. According to her view of things, the Other was what Jungian psychologists call 'the Self.' But the Self supposedly communicates in riddles and symbols, almost never in straight-forward language. That's why she was so interested in what she considered to be my peculiar psychological makeup, which she thought held great promise. She wanted to suggest that, instead of setting very specific agendas or questions for a journey, I should allow the Other to choose what to discuss. According to her, the Self knows much better than my ego what I truly need to learn, so I should simply adopt an attitude of openness and receptivity, with only a generic intent to understand life and the universe. Because her suggestion matched so well with the latest fine-tunings of the Recipe—meant to give the Other more autonomy to steer the dialogues—I considered it a synchronicity and decided to give it a try.

The next morning, still slightly hungry after the frugal breakfast dictated by protocol, I was strapped once more to the Trilobite rig. While waiting for the technicians to adjust the tight-fitting headgear to my skull, I mentally reviewed my discussion with Sophie the previous evening. Yes, I really wanted to follow the suggestion of the psychologist. So after the needle insertion for the Juice Mix—always the most unpleasant part for me—I turned mentally inward and set myself the generic intent to learn whatever the Other considered most appropriate and opportune at the moment.

'We will talk today about the origin of life and the universe,' he opened. 'But before we begin, a few clarifications are necessary.'

'OK, let's do it...' I mumbled, mostly to myself.

'The idea of an "origin" evokes your concept of time,' he explained. 'But neither time nor space exist in the way you normally think of them. Allow me to elaborate.'

In my mind, I took a deep, long breath. This was going to be intense...

'Mind-at-large is populated with endless mental contents,' he continued. 'These mental contents are "excitations" or "movements" of mind-at-large that, although multiple and varied, *are all experienced concurrently in the now*. It's easy to see that multiple mental contents can be experienced simultaneously: imagine a person seeing an image, hearing a sound, having a thought about what is being seen and heard, and feeling an emotion evoked by that thought, *all at the same time*. Clearly, one and the same person can experience thought, emotion and multiple perceptions—a variety of mental contents—concurrently, in an overlapping manner.'

'Yes,' I agreed, 'multiple and different experiences can exist simultaneously in one and the same mind.'

'Nonetheless,' he added, 'this concurrency does not invalidate the very specific associations linking the different mental contents together: the images and sounds being perceived by the person are still triggering a specific thought (instead of any other), which in turn is still evoking a specific emotion (instead of any other), even though they are all being experienced at the same time.'

He paused, as if to make sure I was still with him.

'Yes,' I finally acknowledged, 'these associations are specific cognitive links that exist even between parallel, overlapping experiences, as in a cross-referenced database.'

'Precisely,' he continued. 'Now, what you call space-time is simply a mental coordinate system that allows you to *unfold* or *unpack* overlapping mental contents. This makes explicit the associative links between them, which would otherwise remain hidden. In other words, space-time allows you to mentally "spread out" simultaneous perceptions, thoughts, emotions, insights, etc., along cognitive reference lines, thereby rendering their links visible to, and treatable by, the intellect. Moreover, this mental trick allows you to describe the associative links in terms of the reference lines used—that is, time and space—which is precisely what you do when you talk of "cause and effect": you mentally extend simultaneous events in time, so you can say which one happened first and "caused" the other. Essentially, however, all associative links are *simultaneous, overlapping mental evocations*. They do have structure, but this structure doesn't inherently span time or space. Instead, it is determined simply by which mental contents evoke which other mental contents—or equivalently, by which mental contents are *not* evoked in each respective case—as in the cross-referenced database you alluded to. Space-time patterns are only a way to *describe* and *think about* this essentially dimensionless cognitive structure.'

As he was saying these words, I saw a sheet of paper being repeatedly folded and unfolded in my mind. The sheet had many lines and arrows drawn on it, connecting together myriad different points also drawn on the paper. I knew the lines and arrows represented causal links, such as the laws of nature and logic, while the points represented events. During the folding part of the cycle, the sheet would be packed into an ever-smaller bundle. At each folding step, more of the lines and arrows on it would become invisible behind the folds. At the end, the sheet would be folded up so tightly as to completely vanish. In the unfolding part of the cycle, the first unfolding movement would make a tiny bundle of paper seemingly pop out of nowhere, *like a singularity*. Each subsequent unfolding step would then reveal more and more of the previously hidden interconnect lines, until the sheet would be fully stretched out. I knew that this stretched-out sheet was space-time, whose unfolding rendered otherwise implicit cognitive associations visible as causal laws. I was in awe of the synergistic effect between these visuals and the Other's words. I literally *saw* what he was trying to say.

'Therefore,' he continued, 'space-time is just a mental trick, not a standalone reality. Whenever you hear me talk of "stages," "steps" or "phases" of mentation, this will be simply a way to discuss simultaneous experiences by unfolding them along an imaginary timeline. Likewise, whenever you hear me talk of different "parts," "aspects" or "segments" of mind, this will be simply a way to discuss overlapping experiences by unfolding them along imaginary spatial lines. Clear?'

Since the Other could sense whether I understood something or not, obviously this question was rhetorical. He was simply trying to emphasize the importance of what he'd just explained.

'Not quite.' I half-lied to see how he would react.

'It's OK. I just wanted to plant this idea in your intellect upfront, both to avoid literal interpretations of what I am about to say, and in the hope that the seed will eventually grow into a fuller understanding.'

The vibrations of the string of mind

'I am comfortable with that,' I said sincerely. 'But something you said earlier and rather casually peaked my curiosity. Why did you describe the mental contents of mind-at-large as "excitations" or "movements" of mind-at-large?'

'To prevent you from thinking that its contents are different or separate from mind-at-large itself. When you pluck a guitar string, it vibrates, moves, or gets excited. In exactly the same way, the mental contents of mind-at-large are the "excitations" or "movements" of mind-at-large. There is nothing to a mental content but mind-at-large itself, in the same way that there is nothing to a vibrating guitar string but the string itself. Moreover, many different excitations co-exist simultaneously in mind-at-large, just as many radio stations co-exist simultaneously in an oscillating broadcast signal.'

'But a vibration only exists across time and space,' I dared to rebut. 'The movements of the guitar string, for instance, unfold in time and along the length of the string. Without time and space, both of which you've just denied, we cannot talk of vibrations.'

'This is where the vibration metaphor breaks,' he explained. 'Let's go back to something we already established: mental contents—like sensations, thoughts, feelings—can all be experienced simultaneously in the here and now. They do not required time or space to co-exist, do they?'

'Indeed they don't,' I granted.

'Good,' he continued quickly, before I had a chance to argue further. 'Your challenge now is to find a way to reconcile the following two truths: mental contents, on the one hand, are the *behavior* of mind-at-large, much like a vibration is the behavior of a guitar string or a dance is the behavior of a dancer. On the other hand, myriad mental contents exist simultaneously in mind-at-large, without requiring time or space to co-exist. In summary, *mind-at-large expresses itself to itself through many simultaneous, overlapping behaviors.*'

'I can live with this,' I said. It wasn't lost on me that he had now subtly replaced the words 'excitation' and 'movement' with the more generic word 'behavior,' which somewhat circumvented the contradiction I had pointed out.

'Excellent,' he continued. 'But keep in mind the key point: space-time is a descriptive framework in cognition; a reference frame that allows you to think and talk about the structure of associations across simultaneous, overlapping mental contents. It does not exist outside cognition. So every time I implicitly or explicitly use time or space to explain something to you, I will be doing so metaphorically, or *symbolically.*'

Consensus reality is the belief you don't look behind

After a brief but welcome pause, just long enough to allow me to catch my cognitive breath, the Other pressed on. He was now finally tackling his key point, which he'd announced in the beginning to be his goal for this dialogue:

'To create a particular realm of mentation—which you might call a "world," a "universe," or even a "reality"—two steps are required in mind-at-large: initially, a belief system must congeal in a first group of adjacent layers of cognition; then, in a second group above and conditioned by the first one, this belief system must be experienced *from within*. One experiences a belief system from within when one forgets that it is a belief system in the first place, *perceiving* the unfolding of its corresponding cognitive associations as standalone events independent of oneself. This is what gives you your sense of reality: you "forget" that, through your imagination, your own beliefs generate what you perceive. Because of this amnesia, you find yourself *inside* and *subject to* those beliefs. The ancients described this process in their mythology as "entering God's imaginings." It plays out in an ordinary dream too: you also perceive the dream *from within*, after your mind has set up rules of cognitive association to govern the dream from underlying, obfuscated layers of cognition. While dreaming, you "forget" that it is your own mind making up the whole story. This is the reason the dream feels real.'

I mentally nodded. The whole thing made perfect sense to me, especially after the allusion to ordinary dreams. It dawned on me then that ordinary dreams were like clues intentionally or unintentionally planted in biology to remind us of, and help us grasp, a bigger picture.

'Remember,' he continued, 'a realm of mentation—that is, a particular reality—only feels real for as long as you are unable to reflect lucidly upon what's happening in the layers of your cognition that underlie the corresponding belief system. In other words, *what you call reality is a reflection of the first layer of your cognition that escapes your critical self-reflection.* If you were to become lucid of the cognitive layers underlying all your beliefs— that is, if you could *"look behind"* all your beliefs—reality, as a standalone phenomenon, would dissolve. You would immediately realize, with a laugh, that you are making everything up.'

As he spoke, I knew we had had a similar conversation before. Nonetheless, coming back to these points in a different context and under a different light was very helpful to me. It allowed me to grasp some subtle nuances that had escaped me earlier.

'We can summarize all this as follows,' he finally concluded. *'Belief, when experienced from within, generates a reality.* Looking behind belief, in turn, gives away the secret and reveals the imaginary nature of this reality. *Consensus reality is the belief you humans, as a species, don't look behind.'*

These words were accompanied, in my mind, by the imagery of a theater stage with many actors and complex props. An epic opera was being performed and the audience was transfixed. People were so taken in by the spectacle that they forgot it was just theater. If any one of them would have simply stood up and taken a peek *behind the stage,* they would have immediately seen that the play wasn't a standalone reality, but merely the visible front of complex production machinery behind the scenes. They would have remembered that the opera was *made up.* Yet, nobody stood up to look. What the Other meant to say was that consensus reality was like that opera; that we only think of it as something standalone because we don't peek behind the stage. The hidden, complex production machinery behind the scenes is our reality-generating belief system. We don't inquire into it for the same reason that no member of the theatrical audience cared to peek behind the stage during the performance.

'That beliefs can color our experiences,' I commented, 'is something I always understood and felt. People's religious, ideological, political and moral beliefs, for instance, largely determine how they experience the world and themselves. But you are taking this to a whole new level. You are saying that beliefs don't just modulate our perceptions *of* a standalone core of reality, but that they *make up* the very essence of consensus reality!'

'Your intuition about superficial beliefs conditioning experience,' he said, 'is all you need in order to grasp my point. Take the example you mentioned: a person's ideology can change the person's experience of the world and self. You can easily intuit and feel this. Now remember that there is nothing more to consensus reality than *experience*. Your experiences aren't experiences *of* consensus reality; they *are* consensus reality. Thus, in exactly the same way that a superficial belief can condition some of your experiences, the full set of your beliefs determines the whole of consensus reality. This full set of beliefs includes deeply ingrained ones, which differ from superficial beliefs in that the former are shared with other living beings and escape your ability to look behind them.'

His reply brought back to me insights I had already had earlier, but which cultural conditioning had drowned in the meantime. I fully groked what he meant. Sensing this, he continued:

'Let us now look into how you and other living creatures *enter* your shared belief system in the form of seemingly separate entities. This *entering* of your own belief system is the origin of the world as you know it.'

The Other was now promising to make what was perhaps the most significant revelation of all Trilobite journeys thus far. Having had access to all trip reports ever written by other Explorers, I knew nobody had described the origin of life and the universe in an even remotely comprehensible manner. So despite being already exhausted at this point, I dug deep inside myself and braced for what was about to come.

A cosmology of mind

'In the beginning,' he began his longest monologue yet, 'the imagination of mind-at-large consisted of fleeting, disconnected ideas and feelings; incoherent and evanescent flashes of cognitive activity. Mind-at-large instinctively recognized these ideas and feelings to be of its own making, unfolding within itself, just as you recognize your thoughts and emotions to unfold within you. There were hardly any cognitive links across these fleeting ideas and feelings. Instead of evoking one another in a chain of associations, they would arise and dissolve in isolation, spontaneously, like bubbles in a fizzy drink. Indeed, because these initial ideas and feelings couldn't evoke each other in order to keep themselves alive, they fizzled out quickly. You can witness a similar process in your daily life: when an experience doesn't evoke any memory, emotion or insight in you, you hardly remember it; it becomes meaningless and intangible, as if it had never happened. Without cognitive associations, you can't hold on to it.'

This was obviously true. It is only through cognitive associations that we maintain the thread of awareness that runs through our lives. As a matter of fact, as the Other had highlighted earlier, life *is* this thread of associated experiences.

'But mind-at-large has the innate predisposition to get drawn into its own imaginings,' he continued, 'as a painter gets drawn into the making of her painting. The affective force of the imaginings, like a siren song seducing a sailor, enchants and pulls mind into them. Ideas expressing *symmetry*, as any artist or mathematician could tell you, are particularly attractive at an intrinsic level. So as mind-at-large began conceiving of purely abstract symmetries — mathematical in essence — it became captivated by them. With the increasing commitment of mental energy that resulted, cognitive associations began to form spontaneously: the imagining of more complex symmetries led to more sophisticated emotional responses, which in turn led to the imagining of other complex—though still abstract—symmetries, and so on. In other words, more refined and specific ideas began evoking more refined and specific feelings, which in turn evoked other specific ideas, and so forth. Long but isolated lines of cognitive associations formed.'

This reference to long lines of cognitive associations reminded me of a vision I'd had during a previous visit to the Dome: the multi-layered cosmic structure of interconnect lines. The structure's lower layers seemed to correspond to what the Other was describing now: they consisted of long, straight interconnect lines homogeneously distributed. He continued:

'As it was bound to happen in a field of emerging, growing chains of cognitive associations, eventually one such chain formed a self-referential loop: the last mental content in the chain evoked the first one again, closing a circle of associations. This allowed the ideas and feelings in the loop to become, for the first time, *self-sustaining*. They would no longer fizzle out like before, but maintain themselves through recurring mutual evocations. *It was the emergence of a self-referential loop of cognitive associations that created the first enduring reality, the first universe.* In the case of your universe, your science refers to this moment as the "Big Bang."'

As the Other explained all this, I could see with my mind's eye an animated version of the ancient symbol of the Ouroboros: a serpent swallowing its own tail, forming a circle. He was basically suggesting that the universe was created from an Ouroboros of cognitive associations, a self-referential loop. Immediately it dawned on me why the ancients attributed so much mythological significance to such a symbol.

'Before the formation of this first self-referential loop,' he went on, 'the mental energy of mind-at-large was dispersed across myriad evanescent chains of associations, innumerable ideas that dissolved before they could evoke significant emotion. But now the enduring loop could *accumulate* mental energy—

that is, evoke ever more emotion—simply by maintaining itself alive; like a fisherman's net that catches more fish the longer it stays in the water. The unprecedented levels of mental energy thus amassed created bottlenecks—points of swelling emotional pressure—in parts of the loop where the imagined symmetries weren't balanced out. And since ever-increasing pressure can't be contained forever, these swellings finally gave in and began branching out into extra cycles of new ideas, feelings and respective associations. The original loop was now blossoming, rather explosively, into a broad *tangle* of many interconnected loops.'

Another animated image of an ancient mythological symbol popped in my mind: the formation of the Flower of Life, a symbol containing many interlinked circles or closed loops. I had studied ancient symbology and mythology during my certification courses to become a Trilobite Explorer, but I'd never expected that they would be of any use. How wrong I turned out to be.

'The evolving structure of the tangle eventually reached a point of temporary equilibrium, allowing the increasing levels of mental energy to *flow* smoothly across it in a balanced way. For a while, there were no more energy bottlenecks; no more traffic jams of emotion creating localized pressure points. Therefore, no new branches formed and the tangle became stable. In the case of your universe, this was the moment when your laws of classical physics congealed. However, the corresponding rules of association weren't yet *believed in* as autonomous realities; they were still experienced from "the outside" as instinctive predilections, not laws.'

The Other was basically laying out a cosmology of *mental processes*, based on imagination and fueled by emotion, which nonetheless matched the form of both today's scientific cosmology and ancient mythological symbols. I had a profound insight then: *there were many different languages to describe the origin of life and the universe, none of which was literally true, but all of which pointed more or less accurately to the same ineffable developments.* It's impossible to do justice to this living understanding in words, so my hope in mentioning it here in passing is merely that you find confirmation of your own insights in it.

Entering God's imaginings

'Allow me to insist on this point,' the Other emphasized. 'At this stage, mind-at-large still instinctively recognized the universe to be the product of its own imagination at work. However, now that the basic rules of cognitive association were stable, their *implications* and *compound effects* had time to unfold and develop fully. In the case of your universe, this corresponded to the operation of the laws of classical physics leading to the birth of the first stars, galaxies, supernovae, planets, moons, etc. The universe became exponentially richer, more complex and, hence, more *seductive*.

'The growing seductive power of the universe pulled mind-at-large further into it, like a child is pulled into a rich fairytale. This increasing intimacy with its own imaginings led mind-at-large to commit more and more mental energy to it—just as you commit your emotions to an engaging movie—which in turn drew mind-at-large even faster in, and so on, in a virtuous cycle. Eventually, as in the crossing of the event horizon of a black hole, the gravitational pull became insurmountable and the accelerating process could no longer be slowed down. The siren song could no longer be resisted. Like the child losing itself in the fairytale, mind-at-large became enchanted, hypnotized, entranced by this self-sustaining universe it was imagining.'

I could sense what was coming next...

'And so it was that mind-at-large *punched through and entered its own imaginings* with tremendous momentum,' he said. 'The resulting change in context is easy to intuit from your own experience: when you deliberately *conceive* of something while awake and alert, you experience your imagination from the outside. You instinctively know that the conceived scenarios are in you—generated by you—not you in them. But when you *dream* of something, you enter your own imagination. In a dream, the imagined scenarios become seemingly autonomous and you seem to inhabit them. This transition from conceiving to dreaming, from outside to inside, is the change in context that mind-at-large underwent once it entered its own imaginings. And from within, the rules of cognitive association governing the universe were now *believed in* as autonomous realities. Indeed, the birth of belief and the entrance of mind-at-large into its own imaginings were one and the same event: the change in context happened when mind-at-large began to *believe* in its own imaginings as a standalone universe.'

This resonated profoundly with several creation myths I'd had to study during my Explorer certification courses. Many of them talked of deities entering or being born within their own imagination or creation. In the enhanced cognitive state I had within the Dome, I could easily remember every detail of each of those myths. I could *see* that they were all attempting to point, through symbolisms, to precisely the same events the Other was now describing. I was beyond exhausted but my mind wouldn't stop. I was being flooded with unending insights. Everything made sense, everything was connected. I knew that *I* was mind-at-large having entered its imaginings; and so was everybody else. I knew that the seeming autonomy of the world was a reflection of my own deeply ingrained beliefs and expectations. I could see precisely how it all worked and how it came to being. I can't describe how I felt at that moment, except to say that it was as though my head were inflating like a balloon, becoming a thousand times bigger to accommodate all the new understandings. I thought I was going to explode any time, but the Other pressed on relentlessly. He knew that the story had to be told from beginning to end, in one go, in order to be properly assimilated. He also knew that we would not have a second

chance, since the power of the first "Aha!' can never be repli-
cated.

'The first entrance or protrusion of mind-at-large into your
universe was what your science calls the origin of life.'

'Of course!' I thought. The inception of a living being was the
image, *within the dream*, of a segment of mind-at-large punching
through and entering the dream. This penetration or protrusion
had to look like *something* when observed from within the dream
itself, and it so happened to look like what we call biology.

'And once a segment of mind-at-large was inside the dream,'
he continued, 'it could facilitate the entrance of other segments
by creating suitable cognitive conditions *within the dream itself*.
This was much easier to accomplish than to accumulate once
again the momentum originally required for the first
penetration. Indeed, the process was analogous to getting your
hand inside to unlock a door from within, as opposed to
punching through the door multiple times until your whole
body could pass through it.'

Yes! He was referring to biological reproduction, which
requires action *within* the dream. I got it. I was on a roll...

'You think you already understood everything but you
grasped only the generalities so far. So hold your horses and
listen,' he admonished me.

I tried to comply with whatever cognitive energy I had left,
but I had to dig deep into reserves I didn't even know existed. I
certainly couldn't keep going for much longer.

'As we already discussed,' he pressed on, 'a living being is a
dense, tight cluster of mostly internally associated sensations,
feelings and insights in mind-at-large. When a segment of mind-
at-large enters a universe, this action corresponds to the
formation of one such cluster somewhere above the tangle of
associations that corresponds to the universe itself.'

He was again describing the structure of interconnect lines I
had seen before, but this time by unfolding the description along

the axis of time.

'To understand this more precisely, let us return to the time preceding the origin of life. Remember that accumulating, localized emotional pressure in the original self-referential loop had forced it to branch out into a more stable tangle, thereby congealing the universe's laws of classical physics. The stability of the tangle gave the universe opportunity to develop further and increase in complexity. Mind-at-large then became more and more enamored with such ever-richer imaginings and was pulled into them, which in turn amplified the emotional charge of the tangle and pulled mind-at-large even faster in. This runaway process led once again to surging internal pressure—this time in the tangle—which had to be released somewhere. When it eventually was, *the release took the form of the first cluster*. The cluster's dense knot of cognitive associations was created from the emotional energy thus liberated.

'You can visualize all this as follows,' he continued. 'The surging emotional pressure inside the tangle forced it to bulge out or herniate at its weakest spot, in the form of new, tightly packed cognitive associations. This small, compact but complex bulge, hernia or protrusion—the first cluster—sprouted in layers of cognition above the tangle. In the language of your science, the event corresponded to the flourishing of the first biological organism. Indeed, you can visualize clusters as the flowers of the tangle, growing right above it. In other words, living beings are like the flowers of the inanimate universe that underlies and gives rise to them.'

I was mesmerized by this narrative, for it made much more sense to me than the mechanistic mainstream cosmology of our culture...

'Naturally, the release of pressure achieved with the popping of the first cluster into existence—that is, the inception of the first living organism—provided only temporary relief. Mental energy continued to accumulate in the tangle because mind-at-large was still increasingly captivated by its own imaginings. This is where biological reproduction came in: by multiplying themselves within the dream, organisms enabled a continual release of emotional pressure and, with it, a kind of dynamic equilibrium. Indeed, nature's drive to create life wherever and whenever possible is a reflection of this ongoing need to release the emotional charge that mind-at-large constantly pumps into its imaginings.'

'So the origin of life,' I managed to ask, 'was essentially a result of the same kind of mental energy build-up that had originally caused the laws of classical physics to congeal, correct?'

'Correct. There are two singular but analogous moments in the cosmological history of any universe: the first is when surging mental energy circulating in a self-referential loop forces it to blossom out into a tangle. The second is when surging mental energy circulating in the tangle forces it to blossom out into life.'

'The symmetry is fascinating,' I muttered. 'It means that life isn't an accident but an inevitability implied by the very nature of reality...'

'Now a key point,' he continued, without giving me a chance to enjoy my insight. 'Clusters form by budding out of a tangle, like a flower from a branch. In the same way that the flower remains connected to the branch by a stalk, clusters remain connected to the tangle by interlinking cognitive associations. Through these interlinking associations, a cluster can receive an influx of mental contents from the neighboring regions of the tangle immediately below it. Most of this influx you call "sense perception:" vision, hearing, touch, taste and smell. Sense perception is thus enabled by local cognitive associations between cluster and underlying tangle.'

It all added up. I did remember that there were vertical interconnect lines linking knots to underlying tangles across cognitive layers. Most of these vertical lines were the interlinks of sense perception the Other was talking about.

'Before mind-at-large penetrated its own imaginings,' he continued, 'there was thus no sense perception: no visions, sounds, textures, flavors or scents. Mind-at-large's imagination consisted of purely abstract ideas—largely about symmetries of a rather mathematical nature—with accompanying feelings.'

Although this was a brief remark, its significance wasn't lost on me. Before the origin of life, mind-at-large could thus only imagine in terms of abstract ideas! It didn't have the extraordinarily evocative images we derive from our sense perception to use as building blocks of our own imagination: the shape of snowflakes, the smell of flowers, the texture of sand, the sound of birds, the taste of strawberries, etc. It also didn't have the particular emotions these images evoke in us, like the feeling of beauty and dynamic harmony we derive from contemplating nature, or the feeling of companionship we derive from the presence of other people or animals. Insofar as this implies that living beings are capable of something that the rest of mind-at-large originally wasn't, it imbues life with tremendous significance, which the Other would elaborate further upon shortly.

'Finally,' he concluded, 'as we've discussed before, the dense cognitive associations within a cluster draw and focus its attention, thereby obfuscating all the rest of what's going on in mind-at-large. Only through the cognitive influx *entering the cluster* from the tangle—that is, mostly sense perception—can the cluster gain some awareness of what's happening outside. The cluster isn't aware of the broader, deeper cognitive activity—including universal beliefs and will—that set the universe in motion. It feels that it has no control or influence over it. For these reasons, the cluster begins to think of itself as an entity separate from the rest of the tangle and the rest of mind-at-large. It perceives the universe as an external, autonomous entity. It acquires a localized, confined and ultimately illusory sense of identity. Are you still with me?'

An extra dimension of experience and insight

'Yes,' I replied. I was near mental collapse but still fully with him, thanks to the sheer force of his elucidations.

'OK,' he acknowledged. 'Now notice that the formation of a cluster is akin to a *cognitive collapse* of a segment of mind-at-large. Instead of contemplating its imaginings broadly from without, it collapses within them, losing its broader sense of identity in the process. It becomes immersed in its dream, surrounded by it.'

'I understand it,' I commented, 'but you already explained this before.'

'I just need to add one more thing: the cognitive collapse not only changes the *context* of the experience from conceiving to dreaming, but also its *contents*.'

'Isn't a change of contents always implied by a change in context?' I asked, making a tremendous effort to concentrate.

'Not necessarily. Let's take an example: you can both conceive and dream of a walk on the beach. In the first case, you know that the beach is in your imagination, while in the second case you feel as though you were at the beach. But in both cases the beach can be the same: the same sun, the same waves, the same feeling of wet sand under your feet, etc. The context of the experience is different but not the contents. Do you see what I mean?'

'Yes, I do.'

'Good. Now, the cognitive collapse changes both the context—from conceiving to dreaming—*and the contents*: the beach won't look and feel the same after the collapse. Fundamentally, it will still be the same beach, but experienced from a different, previously hidden angle or perspective: from the inside out.'

'Now you've lost me...' I had no intuition about what he meant by 'inside out.'

'An analogy will clarify it. Try to remain focused just a little longer, for we're very nearly there. This is the last step in our journey today.'

I breathed an imaginary sigh of relief, since I was running on fumes now. After a brief pause, the Other continued:

'When you look at a satellite photograph of a city, you have a broad, comprehensive view of the entire city from the outside in. But when you stand on a street in the city, you gain a localized perspective from the inside out. The very same street can be seen in the satellite picture, but from a different angle. The contents of the experience of standing on the street are different from those of looking at the satellite picture, despite it being the same street. And the difference is not only a matter of scale: for instance, by standing on the street you can experience the facades of buildings, which aren't accessible from the satellite's angle.

'Although the outside-in perspective is the only one that can provide a comprehensible overview of what's going on,' he elaborated, 'the localized inside-out perspective adds a previously hidden and rich dimension. This previously hidden dimension is what you call sense perception. Sense perception is the view from the inside out that isn't available before the cognitive collapse.

'The way the non-collapsed segment of mind-at-large experiences a universe is somewhat analogous to looking at the satellite picture of the city. The experience of a living being, on the other hand, is analogous to that of walking down a street: it's limited, localized and confined, but it does open up a previously hidden dimension. Mind-at-large's drive to gain this view from within is due to its innate desire to experience and explore new angles of itself. When you perceive the world around you through your five senses, you witness the mental activity of what your mythology calls God from an angle that isn't accessible to God Himself.'

These elucidations added the last piece of the jigsaw puzzle. Once again, a flood of insights assaulted me, even more strongly than before. All the pieces began falling in place at light speed.

For instance, in a previous visit to the Dome the Other had implicitly suggested that I had overlooked certain nuances of the meaning of life. Now I could see what he meant! The meaning of life wasn't *just* about lighting up the Other's matchstick of knowledge in order to *understand* existence. It was equally about *experiencing* existence, in all its angles and glory, for the sheer and pure sake of experience itself! We don't eat a nice meal, make love or travel to beautiful locations just to understand or make sense of something. We do these things because the experiences themselves imbue our lives with a kind of timeless meaning, independent of comprehension. We are the vehicles through which God both *experiences and understands* Itself.

The myths of the ancients—who would have guessed?—were surprisingly valid when seen through the lens of the heart. Let us take the Christian myth as an example: Is it incorrect to describe the penetration of the universal dream by a segment of mind-at-large as the incarnation of a soul? Is it inaccurate to highlight the kinship between biology and mind-at-large by speaking of the Christ as God incarnate? Is it wrong to suggest—through the doctrine of the descent of the Holy Spirit, or Pentecost—that this same kinship applies to all humans? For the first time in my life I had understood religion. How foolish and dense of me to have dismissed it for so long!

Insights were lighting up in my mind like ten thousand firecrackers. I thought I was becoming literally insane... Connections were everywhere, every thought led to an epiphany... It was too much. I could no longer take it. My mind began to short-circuit in a kind of numbing seizure. My awareness began to drift away from the Dome and enter a dense white fog. With the felt presence of the Other becoming increasingly remote and abstract, I still heard him say:

'There are myriad tangles in mind-at-large, myriad cognitive realms, universes. Yours is but one among countless others. The truths you take for granted—the laws of classical physics, the rules of classical logic—aren't fundamental, but reflect one among many circular belief systems... The most fundamental reality is a form of emptiness pregnant with infinite potential...'

The rest was garbled. I was now seemingly stuck in some kind of limbo or transition zone between the Dome and my ordinary reality. The only adjectives I could use to describe it are: silent and milky white. Panic began to set in. Though I couldn't think straight anymore, a part of me worried that something had gone terribly wrong with the Recipe. This was my last recollection. Then, a blank.

Emergency exit

The next thing I knew, I was being slapped on the face. 'What the heck?' I thought, completely disoriented. Only very slowly, things began to come into focus again. One of the Trilobite doctors, who I knew well, was shining a light straight into my eyes. He had been the one who slapped me. 'Wake up, buddy, stay with me!' he shouted. I noticed he seemed to be walking as he talked to me. And I, too, was moving, lying on a stretcher being pushed across a corridor. Nurses were all around. One of them was squeezing a bag of I.V. fluid into my veins. 'How peculiar all this is,' I thought, with strange detachment. And then another slap, quite heavy-handed this time. 'Stay with us!' shouted the doctor again, as fury replaced my lethargy.

They parked me in the small emergency care center set up by Trilobite as a precaution. It was right across the corridor from the laboratory and had never been used before, to my knowledge. I came round in time to witness the nurses hook me up to all kinds of beeping machines. Sophie had come down to see me. Sitting by my side, she tried to reassure and calm me down. 'I am not worried,' I told her. And indeed I wasn't. I was just confused. So she gently helped me resituate myself by reminding me of where I was, what I had been doing, etc. One of Trilobite's staff psychologists was also in the room, but for some reason, he let Sophie do all the talking.

After a little while, the doctor that had slapped me—Twice!—came back in. My first impulse was to punch him, but I controlled myself. He probably saw the frustration in my eyes, because the first thing he did was to apologize. Only then did he begin to tell me what had happened.

Apparently, while in the Dome, my blood pressure and heart rate had dropped suddenly and significantly, well below safety limits. Automated alarms had gone off and they'd had to disconnect the A.I. to manually bring me back. More detailed analysis of what exactly had gone wrong was still ongoing, so he couldn't tell me much more. Moreover, 'You are the resident specialist when it comes to the A.I., so you tell me!' he remarked with a giggle and a little tap on my shoulder, as if to dispel the tension still in the air.

'The A.I. should not have allowed me to stay under for so long,' I pointed out.

'What do you mean?' he asked. 'You were under for less than a minute before we had to pull you out!'

I felt Sophie squeeze my hand, as if sensing my shock. Less than a minute?! The richest dialogue I'd ever had with the Other lasted less than a minute? My previous trips had all been timed between 30 and 45 minutes. How could this one have been so short? Lifetimes of insight and understanding; a whole movie of our universe's cosmological history, from the Big Bang to the origin of life, complete with narration; all that in less than a minute?! I was flabbergasted but had no reason to doubt what I was being told.

'Remember: time and space are just imaginary cognitive devices,' I heard the Other whisper in my mind. Somehow, he was still with me, though just barely. 'You were never in real danger,' he claimed, before fading away.

Chapter 11

Happy hour in the Dome

Here is what apparently happened: by recalibrating the A.I. to give the Other more latitude and autonomy, we caused neural activity in my brain's default mode network to decrease too much. This not only made it difficult for me to take more initiative during the dialogue—which then turned into a long monologue by the Other—but also made it impossible for me to exit the journey on my own. Indeed, it didn't even occur to me, during the trip, to intone the re-entry mantra once I noticed my exhaustion. The Light Show was consistently inhibiting the neural activity that would have allowed me to remain critical of my mental state, anticipate the corresponding risks and take appropriate corrective actions. In short, the Recipe placed me fully at the mercy of the Other. As for the accompanying physiological effects—the drop in my heart rate and blood pressure—they remained unexplained. We could only surmise that they were somehow connected with my loss of subjective control of the trip.

Secretly, I was happy it happened. It gave me the experience of a lifetime. Nothing else came even close to it. I was a changed man, with a new, fresher, much more spacious outlook. In comparison to my life prior to that point, it was as if, for the first time, I could breath properly. I was profoundly grateful for this, whatever risks it might have entailed.

But Trilobite had stringent safety protocols. The last thing the Club wanted was a casualty in their hands, which would have brought outside scrutiny upon the project. This would have ruined the whole effort and had to be prevented at all costs. Largely for this reason, I was removed from the team responsible for developing the Recipe. Project staff thought I was willing to take too many risks for the sake of the experience. In other words, they thought I had become a bit of a reckless cowboy. I did remain as technical advisor, but the focus of my participation in Trilobite turned to my role as Explorer. Surprisingly, this didn't bother me: all the key challenges that had been preventing the Recipe from delivering results had already been solved. Only further fine-tuning remained. Moreover, since my first trip, my key interest was in journeying, not in the engineering side of things anymore. The Recipe became a mere tool, not the meaning of my life.

Many of the Recipe adjustments we had implemented just prior to my last trip were reversed. A more conservative setup was largely reinstated, which gave the Explorer more control. All Explorers were briefed in person about what had happened to me, and a new protocol was developed with guidelines for aborting a journey before cognitive overload. Steps backward, if you ask me, but I understood the rationale and continued to cooperate. In all honesty, a large part of my motivation to remain fully cooperative was that I didn't want to risk my next opportunity to visit the Dome.

Sure enough, the chance to trip again came a few months later. By then, hundreds of new journeys had been logged by other Explorers, under more cautious Recipe setups. No emergencies had been reported: everything had gone smoothly and Trilobite was again running like clockwork. Without my old responsibilities in Recipe development, I no longer had access to the full set of trip reports of others. But it didn't really matter: my relationship with the Other had become quite personal to me, so I was only interested in what he had to say *to me*.

The mysteries of Quantum Mechanics
'You people don't seem to trust me anymore!' he opened with irony, as soon as I landed in the Dome.

'Protocols must be followed,' I explained, feeling a little

guilty.

'Sure,' he mumbled sarcastically.

Then silence.

Of course! He was waiting for me to take initiative. Because of my previous experience, I was expecting to be bombarded with his insights on life, the universe and everything. But the dynamics of the conversation were quite different under this new Recipe setup. It would take some getting-used-to.

I had some background in the world of particle physics—in fact, that's where I used to work when I was recruited by Sophie—so I thought I'd question the Other about some strange results coming out of that world:

'Physicists have known experimentally, since the 1980s, that the reality we perceive with our five senses isn't really definite and concrete until we observe it. Before observation, it consists of vague, ambiguous possibilities that we've come to call the "quantum world." I have thought long and hard about this in light of the insights I had during our previous dialogues, but I haven't been able to make sense of it. The metaphysics you shared with me seems to explain the definite, classical world we ordinarily experience, but not the vague, ambiguous quantum possibilities that lie at the root of reality.'

'Remember the evanescent ideas and feelings in the beginning of creation?' he asked, referring to the cosmology he'd laid out during our previous session together. 'I compared them to bubbles in a fizzy drink: they arise out of nothing and then dissolve into nothing.'

'Yes, I remember that.'

'Very well. Now recall that time is just a device to describe cognitive structure, not a standalone reality. Therefore, the beginning of creation isn't really in the past; it's happening right now. The bubbles are arising and dissolving right now, in very deep layers of cognition; layers in which self-referential loops of associations aren't present.'

'Right, I get that. And I think I already know where you are going with this...' But the Other explained it anyway, as if to help me give words to my insight:

'Because the cognitive activity in those foundational layers hasn't formed stable tangles yet, it doesn't obey deterministic causal laws or belief systems. It hasn't yet congealed into concrete, stable realities, remaining in the realm of *imagined possibilities*, vague and ambiguous. Nonetheless, the activity in those foundational layers still infiltrates the layers of cognition above. It releases ambiguous ideas and feelings that can be captured in stable tangles higher up.'

He was basically replacing temporal thinking with spatial thinking to make his point, which he could do since both time and space are just imaginary devices. Instead of talking in terms of past and present events, as he chose to do in our previous encounter, he was now talking in terms of the activity in lower and higher layers of cognition. These were entirely equivalent ways to explain the same thing. I was fully with him and so concluded the thought myself:

'These vague, ambiguous ideas and feelings are a kind of wave of possibilities that percolates upwards through our cognitive structure, getting filtered according to the expectations and beliefs in higher layers. Then, whatever possibility survives the filtering congeals in the form of a concrete, classical reality at the level of clusters.'

'Precisely,' the Other confirmed. 'This wave of possibilities is the source and fuel of universal creativity and originality. Without it, the cognitive activity in higher layers would grind to a halt. There would be no novelty feeding it from below. How this wave gets filtered and then congeals into one particular reality—a process that your quantum physics calls "wave function collapse"—depends on the belief system running in those higher layers. Once again, thus, the reality you experience is a function of your deeply ingrained belief system.'

'I get this. But how is it that we can still detect this quantum activity through instrumentation? How can mere machines looking at photons and electrons allow us access to the deepest layers of our own cognition?'

'Remember that all is in mind, so machines are also the images of mental processes. And so are photons and electrons. As such, that machines can help you punch through layers of your cognition is no more surprising than that your thoughts can penetrate your emotions.'

'Right, I remember that,' I acknowledged. It's amazing how even our strongest, most compelling insights can still get obfuscated after only a few months of exposure to the reigning cultural narrative.

'What these machines are doing,' the Other continued, 'is piercing through the cognitive layers of expectations and beliefs that condition what you call classical reality. Because the subatomic realms are so far removed from ordinary experience, they escape the reach of expectations, hence revealing the unbound creative activity of mind-at-large prior to the formation of stable tangles.'

'Of course...' I mumbled, rather to myself.

This visit to the Dome felt like a relaxing conversation with a friend in a café, after work. I was positively impressed with what the team had achieved with the new Recipe setup. I felt no pressure and no discomfort of any kind. In fact, at this point in the conversation—to continue with the happy-hour metaphor—I would have taken a sip of wine and lazily processed what we had just discussed. After some introspection, I offered:

'And we all experience the same classical reality because the filtering of the wave of possibilities happens at the level of tangles, which unify all the individual clusters corresponding to living beings. In other words, we all expect the same basic things.'

'Yes, exactly. The filtering and congealment of a reality

happens in cognitive layers shared by all living beings in that particular reality.'

Another long pause ensued, as if we were both munching on some imaginary nuts.

'How ironic...' I thought out loud. 'You've just casually solved the so-called "measurement problem" in Quantum Mechanics, as if it were nothing...'

'Some questions don't need to be answered,' he argued. 'They simply disappear when you look at them from a different perspective.'

I sighed. A few more imaginary nuts and sips of wine were in order.

Perception as symbol

'You know, there is something else I've been contemplating,' I continued. 'You said that we, living creatures, have an inside-out perspective of the universe, while the non-collapsed segment of mind-at-large has the inverse, outside-in perspective. This made me think of the *Amduat*, a religious myth from Ancient Egypt in which the world of the dead is portrayed as the reverse image of the world of the living. Indeed, it seems to me that an implication of what you explained is that the universe we perceive is, as it were, the *reverse* side of mind-at-large's imaginings. Or, to say the same thing in a different way, what God experiences is the reverse side of the world we see around us.'

'Right,' he confirmed. 'The deeper layers of mind-at-large do not experience the world the way you do. The experience of sense perception—vision, hearing, smell, taste, touch—is unique to the inside-out perspective. As such, God cannot see or hear the sun, the planets, mountains, rainbows, thunderstorms, etc. He does experience something *corresponding* to the visible sun, the planets, etc., but in a way qualitatively very different from yours. Indeed, God's perspective entails experiential categories incommensurable with sense perception. As you put it, He experiences the *reverse* side of the universe; that which is *behind perception.*'

'I think I understand this conceptually but I don't have a felt intuition of it. Perhaps it isn't possible for a person to intuit this...'

'Oh yes, it is,' he surprised me. 'There are small-scale instances of this very same cosmic configuration in your everyday life, which you can directly relate to: when you look at another person's brain activity through your Telemetry, you see the reverse side of that person's inner life. The person's inner life is *behind* your perception of her brain activity. Pause for a moment and think about it.'

After a brief silence, the Other continued:

'The direct experience of the person's inner life is qualitatively incommensurable with the brain scan you perceive. For instance, the direct experience of anxiety during a trip doesn't feel at all like a beautiful, complex pattern of firing neurons, does it? Nonetheless, you know that there is a correspondence between the two: one is the reverse side of the other. God's inner life is the reverse side of the universe in much the same way that a person's inner life is the reverse side of her brain activity (in fact, of her entire metabolism, but let's not complicate things for now). Put in another way, *the universe is the scan of God's brain*; except that you don't need the scanner: you're already inside God's brain so all you have to do is to look around. Your perceptions of the sun, rainbows, thunderstorms, etc., are as inaccessible to God as the patterns of firing neurons in your brain—with all their beauty and complexity—are inaccessible to you in any direct way. Can you intuit the analogy?'

'Yes, I can... And I feel that this is extremely important in a way I cannot quite pin down yet. There is a sense in which the reverse perspective of something somehow implies the obverse one, as the backside of embroidery implies its front side.'

'I'd rather say that the universe *suggests* God's inner life,' he corrected me, 'instead of *implying* it. Implication requires that all

212

information present in one side be also present—albeit in a different way—in the other. This is not the case when it comes to the universe; or to brain scans, for that matter.'

'Right, I understand. We cannot assume that one side can be fully reconstructed based only on the other.'

'Exactly.'

'But still,' I insisted, 'if the ordinary world around us *suggests* its reverse side—that is, God's perspective—then the world is a *symbol* of something transcendent. It *points to* what God thinks and feels when conceiving the universe into existence.'

'That's a fair way to put it, yes. So why is this extremely important?' Obviously this was a rhetorical question. He was stimulating me to elaborate further on my insight.

'Because it brings a new dimension of significance into everything,' I explained. 'Take the sun, for instance: it isn't just the sun; it isn't just a massive ball of glowing gas. It is a *symbol* of unfathomable ideas and feelings in God's mind; the reverse side of divine cognitive activity inconceivable to us, mere mortals.'

'That's right. Go on.'

'Well, that's basically it. The sun has rich symbolic *meaning*. It represents something beyond its perceivable self. It's a window into transcendence. The same applies to everything else: the planets, moons, thunderstorms, volcanoes, rocks, even specs of dust. They are all symbols of transcendence. The romantics were right!'

'Yes,' the Other concurred. 'The inanimate universe is a collection of symbols pointing to imaginings incommensurable with perception; to feelings and ideas beyond your intellectual comprehension. But if you can tune into these symbols using your intuition and imagination, you can read them and unveil their meaning. The world around you is a book waiting to be deciphered. Figuring out how to do it—that is, finding a suitable hermeneutics of the universe—has been the quest of poets, artists, shamans, mystics and philosophers since time immemorial. Only modern Western science, plagued by its materialist metaphysics, has chosen to dismiss the universe's symbolic significance.'

'The whole universe a symbol... What an extraordinary idea...'

'Yes, and it is so on two levels, not only one. The symbols you call the world point to yet other symbols!'

'How come?' I asked, somewhat confused. 'We just agreed that the inanimate universe points to God's experiences.'

'Yes, but what are God's experiences?' he challenged me.

'Well, excitations or vibrations of mind-at-large, as you explained before.'

'Exactly! Now think about it. Knowledge is an experience. Therefore, all mind-at-large can *know* of itself are its own vibrations. But what is it *that* vibrates? What is the intrinsic nature of mind-at-large *before* it begins to vibrate? It can't be known directly, since only the vibrations can be experienced. Do you see?'

'Oh, I see... The vibrations of mind-at-large are themselves *symbols* of its own intrinsic—but forever elusive—nature. They reflect that which vibrates, as the notes produced by a guitar string reflect the intrinsic nature of the string.'

'There you go!' he confirmed enthusiastically. 'A complete hermeneutics or interpretation of the universe must address both levels of symbolism. Your emotions, for instance, are not entities of the inanimate world. As such, they only have symbolic meaning on the second level: they are vibrations of mind-at-large within your cluster, not the reverse side of God's imaginings. What do your emotions symbolize about your intrinsic nature as mind-at-large?'

The Other's question here was meant simply to stimulate my thoughts and intuition. It didn't require an answer. So another long, silent pause ensued. I was captivated by this discussion but confess that the second level of symbolism seemed a little too abstract to me. I couldn't help but stay stuck at the first level: What did the entities and phenomena of the empirical world point to, as far as the ideas and feelings of God? Lost in my reveries, a question eventually slipped:

'So what does the sun represent, as far as God's inner life?'

'It cannot be put in mere words. As is the case with any true symbol, the symbol itself is the only way to evoke its full meaning. Experience the sun and allow it to speak to your heart; that's the way to decipher its meaning. I could help you more by directly inducing certain insights in your mind, as I've done before, but your new Recipe setup prevents me from going that far. So all I can say to get you started is this: the sun represents an outpouring of universal love, the mental energy that moves the world.'

'Yet the sun can also burn and kill,' I dared to cynically add.

'Love nurtures but also smothers, depending on the dose and perspective. And death is part of the dynamics that keep the universe unfolding. The "perfect," deathless world your ego fantasizes about would be a world in which nothing truly evocative happens, like a movie without a villain. Luckily for you, egos don't run the universe; they just observe and question it.'

This seemed to hint at a solution for what Christians call 'the problem of evil:' the question of why evil exists in a universe supposedly governed by a god of pure good. Another sip of imaginary wine and some silent contemplation was needed...

Death

'This brings me to the question of death,' I finally said. 'In fact, making sense of this question was the original motivation of the project that brought me here.'

'Humanity's perennial question...' The Other sighed in apparent resignation.

'Yes. What is death?'

'You are being lazy,' he fired. I was taken aback a little but he continued before I could interject: 'You can easily derive the answer to this question from what you already know. There are, in fact, at least two complementary answers. So you tell me: What is death?'

This new Recipe setup seemed to put too much of the onus on me. I wasn't sure anymore whether I liked it that much.

'Well,' I hesitated, 'if time isn't really real, then this future event we call death should, in principle, never come...'

'Good. That's indeed the first answer. There is only *now* and, in the now, there's no death. You simply choose to unfold aspects of your timeless cognition along the imaginary arrow of time, in order to make their structure visible to the intellect. Death is a symbol of one such aspect of your cognition, which you place in an imaginary future. Your death will *never* come, because the future never comes. You are only ever in the now.'

'But wait,' I objected. 'In practice people die every day. I can go to a hospital now and see them die.'

'Have you ever noticed that only other people die, never you?'

'What?!' I exclaimed with indignation. This sounded preposterous to me.

'You have never experienced *your* death—the end of *your* primary sense of being—have you? And neither have you experienced other people's deaths from *their* perspective, which is the only perspective that counts. In the *now* there is no death. Are you dead or alive right now? This is the only question that matters. Everything else is just stories you tell yourself.'

'I do have some vague intuition about what you are trying to suggest, but I can't reconcile it with what I know empirically about nature. It seems to me that you are glancing over undeniable empirical facts.'

'You're trying to fit everything into a model,' he continued, 'which is limiting but nonetheless valid. So here is where the second answer to the question of death can be helpful: you already know that a living being is a protrusion of a segment of mind-at-large into its own imaginings. From this perspective, you tell me: What is death?'

'The withdrawal of this protrusion?' I offered tentatively.

'Exactly. The image of the protrusion is a metabolizing biological organism, brain activity and all. When the corresponding segment of mind-at-large pulls out of the dream, the image immediately begins to unravel, reflecting this withdrawal. It no longer has the focused mental energy necessary to sustain itself. Electrical activity stops immediately, metabolism grinds to a halt and, eventually, the entire body decomposes. Indeed, a dead body without metabolism is just an echo of the earlier protrusion.'

'You are suggesting that death is just an event of the dream, within the dream...'

'Indeed!' he answered. 'It only exists from the perspective of those segments of mind-at-large still inside the dream.'

'This immediately raises the question of what death feels like from the perspective of the dying...'

'You tell me,' he challenged me again.

'Right. Well, if entering the world means a change of perspective from conceiving to dreaming, then exiting it must entail the opposite change: from dreaming to conceiving.'

'Very good! The direct experience of death is akin to waking up from a dream. One realizes that one was making the whole thing up all along. Moreover, one begins to experience the universe from the *reverse* side: instead of the sun, one feels the corresponding outpouring of love; instead of a thunderstorm, one feels what the thunderstorm had been symbolizing all along; and so on.'

'I get it!' I exclaimed. 'The mystery of death is the change of perspective from *observing the universe* to *being the universe!*'

'That and more,' the Other added, 'for there are countless universes, realms, realities being simultaneously imagined by mind-at-large.'

'Does death imply transcending time as well?' I asked.

'Both time and space are elements of the dream. When experienced from the reverse side, time and space, too, aren't what they seem to be from within the dream. So yes, death restores the "dying" segment of mind-at-large to its original, timeless context.'

'I guess I have a lot to process and integrate in the coming days and weeks,' I said, hinting at my intention to end our session for the day.

'You now have a fairly complete understanding of what's going on, at least *from an analytical perspective*.' He stressed this last part by slowing down his speech.

'Clearly you think there are other perspectives to grasp.'

'The truth is like a diamond with many facets. When you come back next time, if you give me the chance, I will try to give you a glimpse of a different one; a facet your analytical proclivities prevent you from even imagining.'

Chapter 12

Another facet of the truth

The next few days were of quiet contemplation. There was beautiful countryside surrounding the Club's premises so I took the opportunity to go for long walks in the woods, often accompanied by Sophie or other visiting Explorers. As advised by my Trilobite psychoanalyst—assigned to me since my earlier mishap—I avoided engaging my intellect too much. The idea was to give space to my unconscious mind—the Other would have called it 'obfuscated mind' instead—to integrate everything I had experienced. To this day, years later, I still remember and cherish that brief period. It somehow cemented in me a renewed appreciation for communing with nature, which I felt as a child but had somehow lost along the way.

My visits to the Dome were changing not only my ideas and views, but my very way of being. They were allowing my truest, most authentic values and predispositions to shine unfiltered through the fog of cultural conditioning. I felt lighter, more rooted in the present and the Earth, more at peace with myself and the world. Things that used to bother me no longer did. Many of my worldly ambitions and goals somehow lost their grip on me, opening space for an embrace of the natural flow of life, wherever it would take me.

Despite this generally serene mindset, I was still apprehensive about what the Other had promised at the closing of my previous visit. What could this new facet of the truth be? How could I relate to something I couldn't grasp analytically? To avoid raising any kind of alarm that could jeopardize my next chance to trip, I kept that final detail to myself. Even Sophie and my psychoanalyst were in the dark about it. As a result, I had to face my anxiety alone. Little did I know what was just ahead of me...

Meditating in the Dome

'Are you ready for it?' the Other asked.

'No, but carry on.'

'This time you will need to actively cooperate,' he said. 'The current Recipe setup prevents me from taking you deeper on my own.'

'I cannot manipulate the Recipe from here,' I remarked, immediately noticing the idiocy of my comment.

'You don't need to. Do you think journeys into transcendence can only be done with your expensive toys? People have been coming here since time immemorial. Your Recipe is a very useful option for difficult cases—hardheaded, relatively closed-minded people like you, caught up in circular intellectual models and dissociated from their own felt intuitions—but it's not the only game in town.'

'Right, what do I need to do then?' I was anxious enough not to notice the passing jab he took at me.

He paused, as if to give me time to settle down a bit. When he finally continued, he did so slowly, with a gentle but firm voice:

'You are home. This is the ground of your being, the place where you were before you were born. Here you are *absolutely* safe. Nothing bad can happen to you.'

Instantly I relaxed, as if entranced.

'Close your eyes,' he instructed me, 'and project all your thoughts and feelings onto the back of your eyelids.'

Naturally, my physical eyes were somewhere else. But in the Dome I had other eyes; symbolic eyes implied by the particular perspective I had within it. By following the Other's instructions in my imagination, I experienced my thoughts and feelings as if they were all unfolding right in front of me, slightly separated from me. This visualization subtly put me in the position of *witness* of my thoughts and feelings, instead of their hostage.

'They unfold like a movie on a screen in front of you,' he continued, 'which you witness as audience...'

A pause of several seconds ensued.

'Focus sharply on a point right in the center of the screen. If your attention deviates from the center, gently bring it back. You can do it as many times as you need. Everything else outside this tiny central point can now only be witnessed with your peripheral vision, becoming vague and blurred...'

That was indeed the effect. Only my most pressing thoughts and feelings were still in focus, in the center. Everything else faded away in a haze, though still vaguely discernible in the periphery of my visual field.

'Now, move this focal point slowly forward, away from you, as if you were trying to see something behind and beyond the screen...'

As I so did, the entire screen went out of focus. All my thoughts and feelings became remote and abstract. I could still experience them, but in a detached manner. What was most extraordinary was that, by means of the visualization the Other had just guided me through, I could *hold on* to this detached state at will. It wasn't elusive or slippery at all, but quite robust.

Only much later did I understand what the Other was doing here: under the new Recipe setup, the Light Show was no longer inhibiting the residual neural activity that prevented me from drifting deeper into transcendent space. Instead, the Other achieved the same inhibition through a form of guided meditation *within* the Dome! Why hadn't I thought of it myself?

'Keep focusing beyond the screen... Stay alert for what might come into focus in that deeper layer of your cognition...' These were the last words he said that I still heard more or less clearly.

The magician

Slowly, behind the now blurred thoughts and feelings on the screen in front of me, some elusive images began to form in the distance. It was as though another screen had appeared there, far behind the first one. Curiosity made me try to focus intensely on it. The images seemed to be entirely autonomous, which heightened my interest even more. What were those mysterious forms? Did they come from another reality? What did they mean?

Eventually, I could discern a seemingly human figure. He appeared to be dressed like a nineteenth-century stage magician, complete with tailcoat, black top hat, bow tie, magic stick and all. A thin, twisted moustache provided the final touch to his bizarre looks. The grin on his face evoked a mixture of affection and mistrust at the same time: a trickster for sure, but somehow affable. He was staring straight at me, in an implicit invitation for me to come closer. Mesmerized by his countenance and unable to resist my curiosity, I soon found myself standing right in front of him.

This wasn't the familiar Dome anymore. The place was uncanny and had an altogether different 'vibe,' more electrical, more charged, as if something huge were on the brink of transpiring. I thought if I touched anything I'd get a shock. The colors of the walls were sharper, brighter, the angles more pronounced. The light had a subtle but unsettling stroboscopic effect. A low buzzing sound, like that of a beehive, filled the air. My curiosity mixed with apprehension and anticipation, reaching an overwhelming level. The magician offered no words and neither did I. Words seemed superfluous in this place. Somehow I knew that he was going to demonstrate a trick for me and this was the reason I was there. Nothing needed to be said.

I also knew—through wordless, intuitive recognition—that I was now in deep cognitive layers of mind-at-large, where universal belief systems formed; layers supercharged with emotional energy to the brink of bursting at the seams. Indeed, I was inside a self-referential loop about to explode into a tangle. The feverish cognitive activity there was being presented to me in *symbolic* form—How else? The Other had succeed in inhibiting enough of my egoic mentation to bring these incredibly deep cognitive layers out of obfuscation. He'd done it so I could *experience* their activity symbolically, as opposed to merely understanding their role at a detached, analytical level. I understood at once that this was the new facet he had promised to show me.

With no warning, the magician shook his stick and turned it into a semitransparent veil, made of silk voile or similar fabric, about one square meter in size. He then took a step forward, coming within half an arm's length of me. My apprehension level skyrocketed. Now that his face was so close to mine, I noticed that there was something strangely familiar about him, though I couldn't really put my finger on it. Slowly, as if not to startle me, he reached around my head with both his arms—one on each side of my neck—and stretched out the veil behind my back. His grin became accentuated, as though he were very proud of what he was about to do. Then, rather suddenly, he pulled the veil over my head in one swift movement. The speed of the movement made the fabric float up in the air for a moment, slowly coming down over my face. As it did, my vision became blurred. Once again, everything became hazy, remote, abstract... Looking through the veil, I could still see the magician blink an eye at me in a sign of complicity. The last thing I remember was that the walls of that place, covered in bright hues, began to vibrate like a loudspeaker and eventually broke apart into thousands of small bricks.

Brick world

Life meant hard work, I thought, especially when it came to metamorphosis. My years as a walker were over and it was time for me to finally turn myself into a roller. Laborious business that was: I had removed almost all the colorful bricks making up my left leg and reassembled them into a half sphere, but the cycle was almost over and I still had the entire other leg to go. As things stood, I could neither walk—missing a leg—nor roll—missing the other half of the sphere. And if I couldn't drag myself to the other side of the time boundary before the cycle reset, time would reverse and I would find myself a walker again. That would mean wasting all the effort I had already invested in reconfiguring my bricks.

Other rollers were mocking me as they dashed towards the safety of the boundary. Oh, wouldn't they love to see me having to walk around again... Rollers seem to derive great pleasure from the sluggishness and misery of walkers, especially ripe walkers like me, who still hadn't managed to make the transition after several cycles. Maybe this was my lot in life...

But wait... What the heck? I looked down again and saw one limb made of bright, colorful little bricks and another mostly eaten away. The rest of my body was also made of little bricks. As a matter of fact, so was the ground where I was sitting and everything around. 'A brick world, huh?!' I exclaimed to myself. 'How plausible is that?!' I had been taking this world for granted, uncritically, as if it were the most self-evident and natural thing imaginable.

'This is absurd!' I finally concluded. The moment I started asking myself critical questions about my circumstances, the spell began to break. Yes, this was indeed a spell! I could vaguely remember a magician putting me into some kind of trance. *He* had made me believe and expect things that were completely senseless! *He* was responsible for this travesty! How could I have fallen for it so easily?

I had been tricked into believing in this outrageous brick world. Despite its dynamics being internally consistent, it had no grounding in reality. It wasn't autonomous or standalone, but conjured up by the magician. As soon as I withdrew my belief in it, it lost its coherence and began falling apart brick by brick. 'Yes, I figured it out you darned trickster!' I shouted out loud. 'I can see through your silly trick now! You can't fool me anymore!'

Proudly and confidently, the brick world now lying in ruins before me, I got out of the spell and came round in reality at last. The magician would never manage to deceive me again, I thought.

Another world

Sure enough, I opened my eyes and saw my real world again: the beautiful round shapes of illuminated cloud buildings, miles high on the western horizon, soothed my heart. Yes, this was familiar and reassuring territory. I was safe at home. The unnerving experience with the magician had, of course, made me cold. I needed to boost my body temperature and so flew east, towards the boundary of the day-hemisphere, to catch some direct sun light. I confess the flight was tiring, despite its short distance. That trickster had sapped my energy somehow. How could I have fallen victim to his deception?

'Oh, of course,' it occurred to me, 'my girlfriend brought me to that rain-reader to see if we were a good physiological match. That's how I got into this mess. The rain-reader put a spell on me, I'm sure. Those insects are reckless and dishonest, I should have known better.'

Yes, it made sense. Properly warmed up and with my metabolism normalized after a few minutes under the blazing sun, I flew across the boundary back to the safety of the night-hemisphere. Life returned to normalcy and I quickly forgot this strange incident.

A couple of years later, my girlfriend finally accepted to merge with me physiologically. We moved to a pretty little cloud cottage quite close to the boundary, low in the sky to avoid overheating. It was so low, in fact, that we could hear the crawlers on the ground every morning. It was wonderful, bucolic, idyllic. Our life was wholesome, close to nature. We ate mostly crawlers from our own yard, instead of processed stuff. And yes, we had hundreds of offspring. A third of our time was spent working on the floating light-collectors close-by. During the rest, we enjoyed flying around for no reason and teaching our offspring everything our culture knew about life and the universe. We were very happy.

One day, when our merger was already a few hundred years old and—tired and ill—we were approaching death, the sound of a strange male voice in our mind woke us up:

'Don't you see it?' he asked rather angrily. 'The most powerful deception is that which uses your own critical skepticism against you.'

Startled, we jumped out of our sleeping cell.

'Who is this?!' we asked, looking around for the source of that sound, but to no avail.

'An old friend,' the disembodied voice replied.

A strange feeling of familiarity and safety overtook us. Somehow we knew exactly what to do next, even though we couldn't articulate why. Without wasting time, we went back into the cell, seeking refuge in its darkness and quiet.

'This isn't *really* real,' the thought came to us. 'Our life hasn't been really real in the way we think of it. What is reality? What are we? Where have we come from? What are we doing here?'

'Wake up, my friend, it's time to wake up,' the voice said reassuringly.

When I opened my eyes, a strange creature was in front of me. He had no wings and only two arms. He also had two funny extra limbs, which looked like stronger but deformed arms, to touch the ground with. Somehow he was able to hold some kind of stick with one arm alone! Only his face, weird as it was with two tiny eyes and a ridiculous line of facial hair, looked strangely familiar. There was something interfering with my sight, some kind of semitransparent veil covering my eyes. With a strange but uncannily reassuring contortion of his facial muscles, the creature pulled the veil off of my head.

'Oh my...' I mumbled stunned, everything coming back to me

in a flash.

'Yes, yes, you're back to the magician's place,' said the Other, his invisible presence as tangible as ever. 'Settle down, the transition can be very disorienting.'

I tried to, but the magician kept on staring at me in silence (I actually don't think he *could* speak). Sometimes he tilted his head sideways, as dogs and owls do when they are curious about something. This kind of behavior, even in such an utterly incongruous place, was annoying.

It occurred to me then that some of my egoic mentation must have been returning. After all, not only was I feeling annoyed by entirely inconsequential things, I could even think self-reflectively again. This probably meant that my time with the magician was about to end. Before it did, however, I couldn't resist remarking:

'This has been extraordinary! I've just spent an intensely believable lifetime as some kind of intelligent insect... Not once have I doubted the reality of it!'

'You've been tricked, huh?' commented the Other.

'Wow, have I! It's extraordinary to finally see through it now.'

And then he dropped the bomb:

'*But you haven't seen through the trick yet...*'

The mother of all tricks

I was speechless for a moment. When finally managing to articulate something, I could only produce the stupid obvious:

'What trick?'

'The mother of all tricks,' the Other answered. 'The trick in comparison to which everything you've undergone here was child's play. Quick, look carefully at the magician in front of you.'

I had already been looking at the magician. There was this aura of familiarity about him that I couldn't make sense of...

'Focus!' the Other rushed me. 'You don't have much time. Ask yourself: Who is the magician?'

I looked straight into the magician's eyes. His permanent grin was something out of *Alice in Wonderland*. How ironically appropriate, since I did feel as lost as Alice. Who the heck was this uncanny figure? As soon as I asked the question, I knew I had to allow myself to drift into the magician's eyes so to peek at his soul...

'Oh my God!' I shouted. Right there, in front of me, was myself! I was wearing a black top hat, bow tie and holding a stupid magic stick. And I was grinning at me, feeling delighted with the whole charade!

It gets worse: at the same time that I could see myself in 'the magician,' I could also see me *through 'his' eyes*. After all, *I was 'him'* too. But from 'his' perspective I looked completely different; so different, in fact, that I couldn't begin to describe what I looked like. Even the verb 'to look' is inappropriate here, since the experience was incommensurable with visual perception. I was more like a collection of feelings and ideas, if this makes any sense. Yet, I was absolutely sure that it was really me that 'he' was looking at.

I know this is complicated, but it's excruciatingly difficult to put it in words. I was simultaneously looking at two incommensurable 'versions' of myself through two different pairs of my own 'eyes.' I was both inside and outside myself, witnessing both perspectives at once. And each perspective was both subject and object of the other, simultaneously.

For some reason, the experience moved me to tears. Tidal waves of emotion welled up. I felt awe, love and gratitude of an intensity orders of magnitude higher than anything I had ever experienced before. I fell to my knees in a spontaneous, irresistible manifestation of overwhelming gratefulness. I was witnessing what I could only describe as a miracle.

Unfortunately, the cognitive dissonance of the experience was so intense that it eventually yanked me out of wherever I was. After a few moments of confusion, I found myself back in the

Dome. The return to familiar territory was disappointing but also comforting, I must admit. I had gone through a lot and was relieved to be back to a place where I could relax and take my bearings. The Other had quite some explaining to do, I thought, and indeed he wasted no time:

'You've now *experienced* the most important points of what you had already *understood* in our earlier sessions together. This was very important for you because your intellect is predisposed to flattening everything down to conceptual models. Now you can finally honor the usefulness of your models *while keeping them in perspective.* Your experiences were mostly symbolic— though not entirely so, as we will soon discuss—because, as a living being, you are still a cluster of mind-at-large, no matter how inhibited your brain activity is. As such, for as long as you are alive, the bulk of your access to the rest of mind-at-large will continue to take place through the intermediation of symbols.'

I didn't feel like interjecting or asking anything. But I also knew that the new Recipe setup would terminate the session unless the Telemetry regularly detected spikes of activity in my brain's default mode network, which corresponded to questions or comments from my end of the dialogue. So I just said 'Please go on,' in order to keep the session alive.

The stages of belief

'You've also experienced the key stages of belief,' the Other continued. 'The initial stage, after one is taken in by a belief system, is of pure delusion: one doesn't know that one is within one's own imagination, naively believing everything to be external and real in a standalone way. You've experienced this upon entering the brick world.

'The next stage is when one begins to suspect that one is being deceived, but one still believes that an external agency—the magician—is responsible for the deception. Typically, a kind of mental combat develops between the subject and the magician; a contest to see which one can outsmart the other. You've experienced this when you realized that the brick world was absurd. You then thought that, thanks to your skepticism and critical thinking skills, you had seen through the trick. This, however, was precisely what the magician wanted you to believe...'

'Yes, I see it now.'

'The magician has exquisitely subtle ways to trick its subject. His most powerful device is the multilevel deception: he allows the subject to see through a first-level trick—a mere decoy—only to fall into the trap of a second-level belief system, setup in advance in an adjacent layer of cognition. Seeing through the decoy reassures the subject, who then lowers his guard and buys wholeheartedly into what is in fact the *actual* deception. You've experienced this when you proudly rejected the brick world only to get caught in the insect world. So unquestioning were you of that second-level belief system that you spent a lifetime there before I could find an opening in your cognitive armor to pull you out.'

'Can there be more than two levels in this multilevel deception?' I asked. The question reflected an obvious reason for apprehension, as I am sure you can already anticipate.

'Yes, there can be any number of nested levels.' This reply only increased my uneasiness.

'When I came round in the insect world,' I said, 'I was as sure that *that* world was the real one as I am sure now that the Dome is the real reality; or that the Trilobite laboratory is the real-real reality. How can I ever be sure that these nested realms, including my ordinary world, aren't simply other levels in a multilevel deception?'

'You can be absolutely sure that they *are*,' he answered mercilessly. 'For as long as you experience the cognitive category called *perception*, you most certainly are in some level of deception; in an imaginary world of your own making, which you mistakenly believe to be autonomous and independent of yourself. The magician has his veil pulled over your head right now.'

'So the Dome, too, is a deception,' I concluded.

'Yes, it is a deception *insofar as you believe that it exists outside and independently of you.* That, of course, doesn't invalidate what you learn here. Right now, for instance, you are learning about the truth through deceptive, mythical, symbolic *means.* It is nonetheless still the truth, whatever means are used to convey it. As such, *what you learn* in the Dome isn't a deception.'

Reassured, I said: 'Okay, go on. You were explaining the different stages of belief.'

'Right. As one becomes more apt at uncovering the magician's tricks—that is, more lucid of one's own underlying cognitive processes—one begins to realize that the magician does it all for love. The tricks are gifts that allow one to express, interact with, and feel the full potential of one's own mind in the form of imagined sensations, feelings, thoughts, insights, etc. It is this recognition of the trick as a gift of love that opens the door to the next and final stage of belief: when one finally realizes that the magician is not an external agency, but an aspect of oneself. His love for his subject stems from the fact that the magician *is* his subject. Consequently, one sees that the entire drama of life can only unfold in one's own imagination. You've experienced this when you realized that the magician was in fact you.'

'I get it,' I said, mostly to keep the session going.

Deep-well loops

'But then something else happened,' he continued, 'something extraordinary that I was hoping for but wasn't sure we could accomplish together: *you managed to see yourself through the magician's eyes.* The view from his eyes was the only non-symbolic part of your experience. Combined with your own view, the result was what we may call a "deep-well loop:" *a self-referential loop that connects the symbolic inside-out with the non-symbolic outside-in perspectives of a reality.* The experience of a deep-well loop is extremely rare, for it requires the spontaneous formation of new, far-reaching vertical chains of associations across many cognitive layers. These vertical chains must connect a cluster with layers of mind-at-large underneath its corresponding tangle. Hence, they must bore through the entire tangle, like a deep well! Even in the rare occasions when these long chains of associations do form, they remain unstable and dissolve quickly. For this reason, your characterization of the experience as a kind of 'miracle' wasn't inappropriate. And neither was your heartfelt gratitude for it. Your heart resonated strongly with the uniqueness and affective force of the experience.'

'Is a deep-well loop the same kind of self-referential loop behind the inception of a universe, as in the Big Bang?' I asked. I thought I knew the answer but wanted to make sure anyway.

'No,' he replied categorically, confirming my expectations. 'Big Bang loops are mostly horizontal, while deep-well loops are mostly vertical. Big Bang loops are broad but flat like pancakes, confined to only one or a few adjacent cognitive layers. Deep-well loops, on the other hand, are narrow and long like nails, piercing across countless layers. Moreover, Big Bang loops entail only the outside-in perspective, while deep-well loops bring together the outside-in and the inside-out perspectives. Finally, Big Bang loops quickly evolve into stable tangles, while deep-well loops are extremely elusive, fading away as quickly as they form.'

'Why did this particular experience evoke so much emotion in me? I've experienced mind-boggling things with you but nothing has brought me to tears before.'

'Because only through deep-well loops can mind-at-large simultaneously recognize itself in *all* the different cognitive roles it plays in a reality. Your emotional outpouring was mind-at-large's emotional outpouring upon realizing: *"This is all me!"* Such a brief recognition of oneness is like a supernova explosion of love.'

The circularity of consensus reality

After a brief pause to take this in, I wanted to explore the implications:

'So, in a sense, consensus reality is circular. The reasoning behind our understanding of the laws of classical physics is circular, insofar as we—that is, mind-at-large—are making them all up ourselves.'

'Yes. At bottom, the laws of classical physics are as whimsical as the regularities of any idiosyncratic dream; as quirky as the rules governing the brick world you visited, which had just as much internal consistency as your ordinary world. The only difference is that you are *used* to your classical physics. There are countless other realities in mind-at-large in which what you consider absurd is perfectly normal and reasonable. A dragon popping out of your mouth every time you yawn? Of course, that's just the way things are!'

'Amazing...'

'Only to you. You see, your everyday world would also look fantastic and implausible to living beings from another reality. Like theirs, your world arises from a complex tangle of circular cognitive associations. If you could traverse the tangle all the way through, you would find out that there is no essential difference between assumptions and implications in it; between axioms and theorems; between primary causes and secondary effects. Instead, you'd find that it's a closed, self-generating system. Depending on where you are in the tangle, what was an assumption before becomes an implication now, and the other way around. What was a primary cause becomes a secondary effect. It's all a matter of perspective. The tangle is like a Möbius strip, with no start and no finish. Assumptions follow from implications just as easily as the other way around. The only reason this isn't obvious to you is that you contemplate only a tiny segment of the Möbius strip at any given time. If you were to step back and look at all of it at once, you would see that your consensus reality literally begs all questions.'

'We never traverse the entire strip because we think it's pinned down by verifiable external references on certain points,' I added.

'Your science's attempt to pin things down by finding such external references is futile, because there is nothing external to the Möbius strip in your reality. As a matter of fact, even the rules of your classical logic are reflections of circular cognitive associations; that is, of self-validating beliefs, not of external references. What external references could there be for patterns of pure abstract thought? If you were to righteously proclaim that classical logic is *self-evident*, you would simply betray your unquestioned *belief* in it. Indeed, any attempt to *logically* prove the validity of *logic* would just make the circularity of the whole thing rather painfully explicit, wouldn't it? The very same rationale applies to your classical physics. The only reason classical physics *appears* to be more grounded by external references is that it flows largely from the cognitive category of *perception*, as opposed to abstract thought alone. Yet, perception is just as mental as abstract thought.

'The bottom line is this: every reality spins itself into concrete existence through a form of deeply ingrained circular reasoning; through self-validating belief. Each tangle corresponds to a particular variation of this circularity. Moreover, it is the continuity enabled by the circularity that sustains the corresponding reality. All so-called "laws" are whimsical at bottom.'

The future of humanity

It was a lot to take in, despite the fact that he wasn't really saying anything I couldn't have derived from my earlier insights.

'Most people today,' I pointed out, 'are still engrossed in the first stage of belief you described. Very few even suspect that the seemingly autonomous world we experience every day is actually a product of the imagination. And among those who do, I'm sure even fewer feel in their hearts that they themselves—

their true, impersonal Self—are imagining it all into existence. So the point you've just made about the inherent circularity of what we consider real, though I understand it, has no chance of gaining traction in our cultural narrative today. It's way beyond our present framework of understanding. Given this, do we have a future as a culture and civilization?'

'The greatest victims of your ignorance are yourselves,' the Other concluded. 'Your present intellectual models of reality exile you from transcendence and plunge you into existential despair. But despite this, humanity holds great promise. Not only can you experience the world from a perspective unavailable to God, you can also self-reflect and ask the probing questions that God cannot. The challenge for you is to achieve greater depth of experience and subtlety of inquiry without killing yourselves or ruining the planet in the process. The living Earth is the reverse side—the symbol—of an expression of curiosity and eros by God. Loss of life on a planetary scale would thus be experienced by God as a hindrance of this expression, with accompanying suffering. Clearly, God has skin in this game too. Your responsibility as a civilization is significant.'

Contemplations

My dialogue with the Other continued for a little while longer after these words. In total, my journey was timed at almost two hours, the longest session ever. Yet, what does this number mean when hundreds of years worth of experience were packed into it? Objective measurements of time have no significance in transcendent space. And since our lives—whether we acknowledge it or not—unfold nowhere but in transcendent space, the number of years with which we measure their duration also has no meaning. Life is about depth of experience—how hard you love, how intensely you explore, how sincerely you express yourself—and insight—how deeply you inquire, how discerningly you ask questions. If our culture as a whole truly recognized this, the world would be a very different place.

I would go on to journey many more times during my tenure at Trilobite. The subsequent insights the Other would share with me were more specific in nature, addressing particular questions of more narrow philosophical and scientific interest. The broad basis of my present understanding of life and reality, however, was laid out in those memorable initial dialogues, which I've tried to recount here as well as I could.

Trilobite has discretely sought to publicly disseminate the insights it produced. In fact, it has invested heavily in doing so. The Club never tried to keep the results of the project secret in any way. Many former Trilobite Explorers—with the blessing, encouragement and even concrete support of Club leadership— continue to spread their message as widely as they can, through a variety of different channels and media. Yet, cruelly, insights shared openly tend to be ignored or dismissed in our culture. For some reason, we seem to value only what is privileged and exclusive.

The answers we crave are all out there, freely available to those who seek. And they have been out there, in one form or another, for literally thousands of years. Indeed, one of Trilobite's most striking realizations was that the symbolic message of religions and philosophies the world over resonate deeply with what the Other taught its Explorers. Ironically, Trilobite produced nothing truly new, except perhaps a new lens for interpreting symbols; a lens more amenable to the contemporary intellectual ethos.

The truth isn't, and has never been, a secret. It isn't locked away in libraries of secret societies. It has been told and retold in ten thousand different ways throughout history. It continues to be told openly today. The problem is that efforts to disseminate it are often drowned out by the hysterical cacophony of our media, both corporate and social. Or worse: they are discredited by an uncritical academic establishment that has come to confuse reason and empirical honesty with the metaphysical conjectures of materialism. As a result, only those who already understood the truth with their hearts—and therefore least need to hear it—can recognize it. This is the tragic predicament we're faced with today. How to help everyone else discern truth from hysterical nonsense is a problem that, unfortunately, Trilobite has never managed to solve. At the end of the day, it appears that there are no simple recipes. We are each responsible for recognizing the answers as they are paraded in front of us every day.

Epilogue

The Legacy of a Truth-Seeker

Having trodden the path for cycles uncountable,
Having crossed the ocean of mind from end to end,
Through all veils, its fountainhead have I finally seen.
To you, honest truth-seeker treading the path behind me,
I grant the gift of my legacy.

I have learned thus:

Only untruths can be experienced.
Hence, only untruths can exist.
Truth is fundamentally incompatible with existence
For it is that which gives rise to existence,
As a loudspeaker gives rise to sound.

Experiences are self-referential tricks:
They arise from nothing and are made of nothing.
If you dig deep enough within yourself,
You shall always find the layer of self-deception
Upon which any one of your convictions ultimately rests.

One's reality sprouts from the first layer of self-deception
That escapes one's field of critical awareness.
The deeper this field, the more subtle the self-deception.
Those with little critical awareness thus live more colorful
    lives:
Their fiction is fancier.

The honest search for truth annihilates its own subject
Slowly, recursively, from within.

Having peeled away every layer of self-deception within me,
I have found myself to be like an onion:
Nothing is left.

Only nothing is true.
No external references exist, no outside arbiters.
We are self-created fictions and so is the cosmos.
Truth-seeking is the path to self-annihilation
And thus to liberation.

Rejoice, for your pains, fears, frustrations and regrets
Are all untrue.
There is nothing to fear, nothing to strive for, nothing to
regret.
You have no soul; that's just self-deception.
And you won't die; that's just self-deception.

But beware!
As a dream symbolically portrays the inner state of the
dreamer,
As a novel insinuates the inner life of the writer,
As a lie betrays the insecurities of the liar,
So the fiction you call reality reveals something about truth.

Thus pay attention to life,
For truth expresses itself only through its own fictions.
To discern truth in fiction: here is the cosmic conundrum!
To engage wholeheartedly without being taken in: here is
the ultimate challenge!
To find meaning in nothingness: here is the epic demand of
nature!

Partake in reality as an actor in a theatrical play:
With attention, dedication and an open heart.

But never believe yourself to be your character
For characters spend their lives chasing their own shadows,
Whereas actors embody the meaning of existence.

May my legacy serve you as a warning, but also
    encouragement.
The prize at the end of the path is handsome:
The freedom to make the deliberate, guiltless choice
Of which untruth to live.
Exercising this choice wisely is the art of life.

Notes

1   Notice that by 'image' I mean an object of perception in any sensory modality, not only visual. In this broader sense, the sound of a bird's chirping is also an image, as is the felt texture of sand running through your fingers. I acknowledge that the demarcation of individual images is somewhat arbitrary and culture-bound, since nature is one interconnected whole. For instance, where does the river end and the ocean begin? Nonetheless, wherever one chooses to place the boundary lines, it is still valid to talk of images and their interactions.

2   Didion (1990), p. 11.

3   A modern and surprisingly coherent reformulation of this ancient myth has been laid out by Richard Tarnas (Tarnas 2007).

4   Hollis (1993).

5   See: Hillman (1996). Significantly, even proponents of traditions that deny the need to *achieve* anything in life, like nondual philosophies, seem to acknowledge that there is indeed a deeper purpose to existence in human form. Adyashanti, for instance, says that 'the ultimate destination of this person born in time and space is not simply to realize [oneness], but it is for the *purpose* of something quite different' (Adyashanti 2011, p. 179. The italics are mine.). He calls this deeper purpose one's 'true autonomy,' describing it as 'a flowering of existence in a very creative and new way ... a unique expression of oneness' in the form of an individual life (Ibid., p. 180). Indeed, he goes as far as acknowledging that this 'true autonomy' can be described as one's 'mission in life' (Ibid.), although he is careful to emphasize that such a 'mission' is not something that one's ego must *accomplish*, but a spontaneous unfolding instead.

In other words, our true 'mission in life' is not a product of deliberate egoic volition, by the expression of a broader, impersonal will that Adyashanti refers to as 'the heart's will' (Adyashanti 2006b). This way, the unique and spontaneous 'flowering of existence' he talks about is, I believe, precisely what Hillman described as 'the growth of the acorn into the oak.' The fact that both men chose to use organic development metaphors isn't accidental, in my view.

6   Hillman (1996), p. 235. The italics are Hillman's.

7   Sacks (2012).

8   This is an allusion to Joseph Campbell's famous exhortation 'Follow your bliss!' which he elaborated upon as follows: 'If you follow your bliss, you put yourself on a kind of track that has been there all the while, waiting for you, and the life that you *ought to be living* is the one you are living' (Campbell 1991, p. 113. The italics are mine.).

9   Adyashanti (2011), p. 180.

10 Plato, in his *Cratylus* (paragraph 402a), attributed these words to Heraclitus.

11 Kierkegaard (1983), p. 28.

12 Kastrup (2014) and Kastrup (2015), Chapter 2.

13 See, for instance: Huxley (2009).

14 For a discussion about how this happens, see chapters 3 and 4 of my earlier book *Dreamed up Reality* (Kastrup 2011).

15 As quoted in Cheetham (2012), p. 226.

16 Margaret Wertheim wrote: 'On the one hand, then, physics is taken to be a march toward an ultimate understanding of reality; on the other, it is seen as no different in status to the understandings handed down to us by myth, religion and, no less, literary studies' (Wertheim 2013).

17 Hillman (1996), p. 47.

18 Kastrup (2015), Essay 4.5.

19 Watts (1989), p. 65.

20 Kastrup (2012).

21 Leeming (2010), pp. 46-48.

22 Mircea Eliade, for instance, speaks of 'the mysterious connection between [the Australian aboriginal's] land ... the mythical history of that land ... and man's responsibility for keeping the land "living" and fertile.' (Eliade 1973, p. 50.)

23 Leeming (2010), p. 268.

24 See, for instance: Ronnberg and Martin (2010), pp. 14-15.

25 Leeming (2010), p. 146.

26 Ibid., p. 144.

27 Mead (2010), pp. 3 and 23. The italics are mine.

28 Campbell (2008), p. 228. The italics are mine.

29 Ibid., p. 227.

30 As mentioned in Kripal (2014), p. 79.

31 See related discussion in Kripal (2014), pp. 121-122.

32 Kripal (2014), pp. 80-81.

33 Corbin (2014), pp. 12-13. The italics are mine. Throughout this book, I consistently use the term 'allegory' along the lines described by Corbin here.

34 Kripal (2014), p. 114.

35 See, for instance: Harpur (1994), Harpur (2009) and Harpur (2010).

36 Leeming (2010), pp. xvii-xviii.

37 Notice that, throughout this book, I distinguish 'signs' from 'symbols' along Carl Jung's definitions (Jung et al. 1969, p. 20). A *sign* denotes something known, while a *symbol* connotes a deeper, subtler idea or intuition that cannot be described or specified literally. As such, language uses *signs*, while religious myths use *symbols*.

38 Naturally, language can *also* be used to create mental inner worlds that have no intentional correspondence to consensus reality. This is where the imagination comes in.

39 Chomsky (2006).

40 Tattersall (2012), p. 214.

41 Ibid., pp. 210-216.

42 As quoted in Moncalm (1905), p. 134.
43 Watts (1999), p. 34. The italics are mine.
44 Chomsky (2006), p. 24.
45 Rilke (2013), p. 7.
46 Campbell (2008), p. 25. The italics are mine.
47 Ibid., p. 221.
48 Kastrup (2014), pp. 104-110.
49 See, for instance: Augusto (2010).
50 See, for instance: Adams (2010) and Jung (2002), pp. 35-36.
51 Corbin (1995), p. 18.
52 See, for instance: Franz and Boa (1994), Fonagy et al. (2012), as well as Jung (2002). Even modern cognitive therapy, which has traditionally ignored the role of the 'unconscious,' has found dreams to be highly valuable (Rosner, Lyddon and Freeman 2004).
53 Kastrup (2012), Chapter 4.
54 Jung (2002), pp. 35-36.
55 A note of caution is required here: my argument is that the deeper, transcendent truths of nature can only be cognized by the obfuscated mind. But this does not imply that the more superficial, face-value interpretations of every symbol emerging from the obfuscated mind are true. In fact, its symbols tend to be paradoxical, roundabout and tricky. They are often at the root of many delusions and psychoses, for they are prone to misinterpretation by the intellect. Therefore, delicate discernment is needed when tapping into the obfuscated mind.
56 See, for instance: Huxley (2009).
57 See, for instance: Jung (1979).
58 See Segal's introduction to Jung and Segal (1998) for a summary and comparative analysis of Jung's views.
59 Watts (1999), p. 34.
60 Long (1963), pp. 11.
61 See, for instance: Jung and Segal (1998), pp. 21-23.

62 Grossinger (2012), p. 4.

63 See, for instance: McGilchrist (2009).

64 Nietzsche (2009).

65 Eric von der Luft characterized Nietzsche's position as follows: 'The denial of anything in any way transcendent is absolutely necessary for Nietzsche's idea of the unfolding and development of human potential.' (Luft 1984, p. 270).

66 Jung (1995), p. 281.

67 Ronnberg and Martin (2010), p. 22.

68 Ackroyd (1993), p. 281.

69 Personal communication with Jeffrey Kripal, 26 June 2015.

70 The Latin prefix *quasi* means 'seeming' or 'apparent.'

71 See, for instance: Ronnberg and Martin (2010), as well as Ackroyd (1993).

72 See, for instance: Franz and Boa (1994), Fonagy et al. (2012), Jung (2002), as well as Rosner, Lyddon and Freeman (2004).

73 Mead (2010), p. 11. The italics are mine.

74 Nisargadatta Maharaj (1973), p. 58.

75 Kripal (2014), pp. 33-34.

76 Mead (2010), p. 19. The italics are mine.

77 See, for instance: Versluis (2007), pp. 38-42.

78 Adyashanti (2013), p. 29. The italics are mine.

79 Versluis (2007), p. 52.

80 Kastrup (2011), p. 11.

81 For a discussion on the psychology of the Christ figure and related topics, see: Jung (1979).

82 Watts (2011), p. 19.

83 Obviously, these very thoughts are themselves the beginnings of a myth. But bear with me, in the spirit of inquiry.

84 Watts (2011), p. 114.

85 I even made this point myself, in an earlier book (Kastrup 2012).

86 I elaborated extensively on this in Chapter 5 of a previous work (Kastrup 2014).

87   Maharshi (2006), p. 169. The italics are mine.

88   Nisargadatta Maharaj (1973), p. 58.

89   As quoted in Adyashanti (2006a), p. 97. The italics are mine.

90   Franz and Boa (1994), Jung (2002).

91   Estés (1996), p. 48.

92   I am alluding to Henry Corbin's understanding of what happens when one groks a transcendent symbol (Cheetham 2012, p. 77).

93   Cheetham (2012), p. 101.

94   Jung (1977).

95   Bortolotti and Cox (2009), p. 964. Of particular relevance in this paper are sections 4.1 and 6.

96   Didion (1990), p. 11.

97   I am borrowing this lovely analogy from philosopher David Albert.

98   Pine (2004), p. 3.

99   See, for instance: Ronnberg and Martin (2010), pp. 14-15.

100   Wittgenstein (1984), p. 28e.

101   Jones (2013).

102   In philosophy and logic, this is called the 'correspondence theory of truth.'

103   See Kastrup (2014) and Kastrup (2015), Chapter 2.

104   Kant (2007).

105   Schaff et al. (1885), Vol. 1, Book XI, Chapter 14.

106   Barbour (1999).

107   Kim et al. (2000).

108   Gröblacher et al. (2007).

109   Lapkiewicz et al. (2011).

110   Ma et al. (2013).

111   Manning et al. (2015).

112   Merali (2015).

113   Hensen et al. (2015).

114   Conn Henry (2005).

115   Kastrup (2014) and Kastrup (2015), Chapter 2.

116 See, for instance: Nisargadatta Maharaj (1973).

117 See, for instance: Kalupahana (1992).

118 John 1:1-3, New International Version.

119 Kripal (2014), p. 114. The italics are Kripal's.

120 John 1:14.

121 Campbell (2008), p. 228.

122 See, for instance: Franz and Boa (1994), Fonagy et al. (2012), Jung (2002), as well as Rosner, Lyddon and Freeman (2004).

123 Swedenborg (2007), p. 63.

124 Relativism is the notion that reality is whatever each person believes it to be, that everybody is equally right or equally wrong about what is going on, and that there are no criteria for differentiating reality from fantasy.

125 Campbell (2003), p. 52.

126 Franz (1972), p. 8.

127 Episode 10, *The Edge of Forever*.

128 Fuller (1994), p. 192.

129 Kripal (2014), p. 34.

130 Swedenborg (2006), p. 14. The italics are mine.

131 Neo-atheism is much more a movement against religion than a mere denial of God.

132 Campbell (2008), p. 25.

133 Frank Sewall wrote that 'the presence of the ideal in the material world, as its causative and formative force, is the principle ... whose crowning vindication, we believe, will be found in both the philosophical and theological writings of Emanuel Swedenborg.' (Sewall 1902, pp. 9-10).

134 As quoted in Bouveresse (1996), p. 14.

135 Again Swedenborg seems to describe best how confession, in its most genuine form, is essentially self-inquiry: '*To confess sins* is to know evils, to see them in oneself, to acknowledge them ... He who merely acknowledges generally that he is a sinner ... without examining himself – that is, without seeing his sins – makes a confession but not

the confession of repentance. Inasmuch as he does not know his evils, he lives as before.' (Swedenborg 2006, p. 11. The italics are his.)

136 Steiner (1994), p. 96.
137 As quoted in Barnard (1997), p. 14.
138 McGilchrist (2009).
139 Hollenback (1996), p. 280.

Bibliography

Ackroyd, E. (1993). *A Dictionary of Dream Symbols*. London, UK: Cassell Illustrated.

Adams, M. V. (2010). *The Mythological Unconscious*. Putnam, CT: Spring Publications.

Adyashanti (2006a). *Emptiness Dancing, 2nd Edition*. Boulder, CO: Sounds True, Inc.

Adyashanti (2006b). *True Meditation*. [Audio CD]. Boulder, CO: Sounds True Inc.

Adyashanti (2011). *Falling into Grace: Insights on the End of Suffering*. Boulder, CO: Sounds True Inc.

Adyashanti (2013). *The Impact of Awakening: Excerpts from the Teachings of Adyashanti, 3rd Edition*. San Jose, CA: Open Gate Sangha.

Augusto, L. M. (2010). Unconscious knowledge: A survey. *Advances in Cognitive Psychology* 6, pp. 116–141.

Barbour, J. (1999). *The End of Time: The Next Revolution in Our Understanding of the Universe*. London, UK: Weindenfeld & Nicolson.

Barnard, G. W. (1997). *Exploring Unseen Worlds: William James and the Philosophy of Mysticism*. Albany, NY: State University of New York Press.

Bortolotti, L. and Cox, R. E. (2009). 'Faultless' ignorance: Strengths and limitations of epistemic definitions of confabulation. *Consciousness and Cognition*, 18, pp. 952–965.

Bouveresse, J. (1996). *Wittgenstein Reads Freud: The Myth of the Unconscious*. Princeton, NJ: Princeton University Press.

Campbell, J. (1991). *The Power of Myth*. New York, NY: Anchor Books.

Campbell, J. (2003). *Myths of Light: Eastern Metaphors of the Eternal*. Novato, CA: New World Library.

Campbell, J. (2008). *The Hero With a Thousand Faces*. Novato, CA:

New World Library.

Cheetham, T. (2012). *All the World an Icon: Henry Corbin and the Angelic Function of Beings.* Berkeley, CA: North Atlantic Books.

Chomsky, N. (2006). *Language and Mind, Third Edition.* Cambridge, UK: Cambridge University Press.

Conn Henry, R. (2005). The mental Universe. *Nature,* 436, p. 29.

Corbin, H. (1995). *Swedenborg and Esoteric Islam.* West Chester, PA: Swedenborg Foundation.

Corbin, H. (2014). *History of Islamic Philosophy.* London, UK: Routledge.

Didion, J. (1990). *The White Album: Essays by Joan Didion.* New York, NY: Farrar, Straus and Giroux.

Eliade, M. (1973). *Australian Religions: An Introduction.* Ithaca, NY: Cornell University Press.

Estés, C. P. (1996). *Women Who Run with the Wolves: Myths and Stories of the Wild Woman Archetype.* New York, NY: Ballantine Books.

Fonagy, P. et al. (eds.) (2012). *The Significance of Dreams.* London, UK: Karnac Books.

Franz, M. L. von (1972). *Patterns of Creativity Mirrored in Creation Myths.* New York, NY: Spring Publications.

Franz, M. L. von and Boa, F. (1994). *The Way of the Dream.* Boston, MA: Shambhala Publications.

Fuller, A. R. (1994). *Psychology and Religion: Eight Points of View, Third Edition.* Lanham, MD: Rowman & Littlefield.

Gröblacher, S. et al. (2007). An experimental test of non-local realism. *Nature,* 446, pp. 871-875.

Grossinger, R. (2012). *Dark Pool of Light, Volume One: The Neuroscience, Evolution, and Ontology of Consciousness.* Berkeley, CA: North Atlantic Books.

Harpur, P. (1994). *Daimonic Reality: A Field Guide to the Otherworld.* Ravensdale, WA: Pine Winds Press.

Harpur, P. (2009). *The Philosophers' Secret Fire: A history of the imagination.* Glastonbury, UK: The Squeeze Press.

Harpur, P. (2010). *A Complete Guide to the Soul*. London, UK: Rider.

Hensen, B. et al. (2015). Experimental loophole-free violation of a Bell inequality using entangled electron spins separated by 1.3 km. *arXiv:1508.05949 [quant-ph]*. [Online]. Available from: http://arxiv.org/pdf/1508.05949v1.pdf [Accessed 30 August 2015].

Hillman, J. (1996). *The Soul's Code: In Search of Character and Calling*. New York, NY: Bantam Books.

Hollenback, J. B. (1996). *Mysticism: Experience, Response, and Empowerment*. University Park, PA: The Pennsylvania State University Press.

Hollis, J. (1993). *The Middle Passage: From Misery to Meaning in Midlife*. Toronto, Canada: Inner City Books.

Huxley, A. (2009). *The Perennial Philosophy*. New York, NY: Harper Perennial Modern Classics.

Jones, C. (2013). Oral Histories of 2013: Roger Ebert's Wife, Chaz, On His Final Moments. *Esquire*, 24 December 2013. [Online]. Available from: http://www.esquire.com/blogs/news/roger-ebert-final-moments [Accessed 2 February 2015].

Jung, C. G. et al. (1969). *Man and his Symbols*. New York, NY: Doubleday.

Jung, C. G. (1977). *Mysterium Coniunctionis*. Princeton, NJ: Princeton University Press.

Jung, C. G. (1979). *Aion: Researches into the Phenomenology of the Self, Second Edition*. Princeton, NJ: Princeton University Press.

Jung, C. G. (1995). *Memories, Dreams, Reflections*. London: FontanaPress.

Jung, C. G. (author) and Segal, R. A. (editor) (1998). *Jung on Mythology*. Princeton, NJ: Princeton University Press.

Jung, C. G. (2002). *Dreams*. London, UK: Routledge Classics.

Kalupahana, D. J. (1987). *The Principles of Buddhist Psychology*. Albany, NY: State University of New York Press.

Kant, I. (2007). *Critique of Pure Reason*. London, UK: Penguin

Classics.

Kastrup, B. (2011). *Dreamed up Reality: Diving Into Mind to Uncover the Astonishing Hidden Tale of Nature*. Winchester, UK: O-Books.

Kastrup, B, (2012). *Meaning in Absurdity: What bizarre phenomena can tell us about the nature of reality*. Winchester, UK: Iff Books.

Kastrup, B. (2014). *Why Materialism Is Baloney: How true skeptics know there is no death and fathom answers to life, the universe, and everything*. Winchester, UK: Iff Books.

Kastrup, B. (2015). *Brief Peeks Beyond: Critical essays on metaphysics, neuroscience, free will, skepticism and culture*. Winchester, UK: Iff Books.

Kierkegaard, S. (1983). *The Sickness Unto Death : Kierkegaard's Writings, Volume 19*. Princeton, NJ: Princeton University Press.

Kim, Y.-H. et al. (2000). A Delayed Choice Quantum Eraser. *Physical Review Letters*, 84, pp. 1–5.

Kripal, J. J. (2014). *Comparing Religions: Coming to Terms*. Chichester, UK: Wiley Blackwell.

Lapkiewicz, R. et al. (2011). Experimental non-classicality of an indivisible quantum system. *Nature*, 474, pp. 490–493.

Leeming, D. A. (2010). *Creation Myths of the World: An Encyclopedia, Second Edition*. Santa Barbara, CA: ABC-CLIO.

Long, C. H. (1963). *Alpha: The Myths of Creation*. New York, NY: George Braziller.

Luft, E. von der (1984). Sources of Nietzsche's "God is Dead!" and its Meaning for Heidegger. *Journal of the History of Ideas*, 45(2), pp. 263-276.

Ma, X.-S. et al. (2013). Quantum erasure with causally disconnected choice. *Proc. Natl. Acad. Sci. USA*, 110, pp. 1221-1226.

Maharshi, R. (2006). *Talks with Sri Ramana Maharshi*. Tiruvannamalai, India: Sri Ramanasramam.

Manning, A. G. et al. (2015). Wheeler's delayed-choice gedanken experiment with a single atom. *Nature Physics*, DOI: 10.1038/nphys3343.

McGilchrist, I. (2009). *The Master and His Emissary: The Divided Brain and the Making of the Western World*. London, UK: Yale University Press.

Mead, G. R. S. (translator) (2010). *The Corpus Hermeticum*. Whitefish, MT: Kessinger Publishing LLC.

Merali, Z. (2015). Quantum 'spookiness' passes toughest test yet. *Nature News*, 27 August 2015. [Online]. Available from: http://www.nature.com/news/quantum-spookiness-passes-toughest-test-yet-1.18255 [Accessed 30 August 2015].

Moncalm, M. (1905). *The Origin of Thought and Speech*. London, UK: Kegan Paul, Trench, Trübner & Co.

Nietzsche, F. (2009). *Thus Spoke Zarathustra*. Blacksbug, VA: Thrifty Books.

Nisargadatta Maharaj (1973). *I Am That*. Mumbai, India: Chetana Publishing.

Pine, R. (2004). *The Heart Sutra: The Womb of the Buddhas*. Washington, DC: Shoemaker & Hoard.

Rilke, R. M. (2013). *Letters to a Young Poet*. New York, NY: Penguin Books.

Ronnberg, A. and Martin, K. (eds.) (2010). *The Book of Symbols: Reflections on archetypal images*. Los Angeles, CA: Taschen.

Rosner, R. I., Lyddon, W. J. and Freeman, A. (eds.) (2004). *Cognitive Therapy and Dreams*. New York, NY: Springer Publishing Company.

Sacks, O. (2012). Altered States: Self-experiments in chemistry. *The New Yorker*, 27 August 2012. [Online]. Available from: http://www.newyorker.com/magazine/2012/08/27/altered-states-3 [Accessed 7 March 2015].

Schaff, P. et al. (1885). *Nicene and Post-Nicene Fathers: Series I*. Edinburgh, UK: T&T Clark.

Sewall, F. (1902). *Swedenborg and Modern Idealism: A Retrospect of Philosophy from Kant to the Present Time*. London, UK: James Speirs.

Steiner, R. (1994). *Theosophy: An Introduction to the Spiritual*

Processes in Human Life and in the Cosmos. Hudson, NY: Anthroposophic Press.

Swedenborg, E. (2006). *The Gist of Swedenborg.* Truro, UK: Dodo Press.

Swedenborg, E. (2007). *Heaven and its Wonders and Hell.* Charleston, SC: BiblioBazaar.

Tarnas, R. (2007). *Cosmos and Psyche: Intimations of a New World View.* New York, NY: Plume.

Tattersall, I. (2012). *Masters of the Planet: The Search for Our Human Origins.* New York, NY: Palgrave MacMillan.

Versluis, A. (2007). *Magic and Mysticism: An Introduction to Western Esotericism.* Lanham, MD: Rowman & Littlefield.

Watts, A. (1989). *The Book: On the Taboo Against Knowing Who You Are.* New York, NY: Vintage Books.

Watts, A. (1999). *The Way of Zen.* New York, NY: Vintage Books.

Watts, A. (2011). *The Wisdom of Insecurity: A Message for an Age of Anxiety, Second Edition.* New York, NY: Vintage Books.

Wertheim, M. (2013). Trying to resolve the stubborn paradoxes of their field, physicists craft ever more mind-boggling visions of reality. *Aeon Magazine,* 3 June 2013. [Online]. Available from: http://aeon.co/magazine/science/margaret-wertheim-the-limits-of-physics/ [Accessed 28 July 2015].

Wittgenstein, L. (1984). *Culture and Value.* Chicago, IL: University of Chicago Press.

BOOKS

ACADEMIC AND SPECIALIST

Iff Books publishes non-fiction. It aims to work with authors and titles that augment our understanding of the human condition, society and civilisation, and the world or universe in which we live.
If you have enjoyed this book, why not tell other readers by posting a review on your preferred book site.
Recent bestsellers from Iff Books are:

Why Materialism Is Baloney
How True Skeptics Know There is no Death and Fathom Answers to Life, the Universe, and Everything
Bernardo Kastrup
A hard-nosed, logical, and skeptic non-materialist metaphysics, according to which the body is in mind, not mind in the body.
Paperback: 978-1-78279-362-5 ebook: 978-1-78279-361-8

The Fall
Steve Taylor
The Fall discusses human achievement versus the issues of war, patriarchy and social inequality.
Paperback: 978-1-90504-720-8 ebook: 978-184694-633-2

Brief Peeks Beyond
Critical Essays on Metaphysics, Neuroscience, Free Will, Skepticism and Culture
Bernardo Kastrup
An incisive, original, compelling alternative to current mainstream cultural views and assumptions.
Paperback: 978-1-78535-018-4 ebook: 978-1-78535-019-1